Understanding Chinese Society

As China gains power – economically, politically, and militarily – and interaction between the Chinese and people outside China increases, it becomes more and more important that we understand the social factors that influence the daily lives of China's population.

This new introductory textbook is suitable for all students taking a course on Chinese society. It presents both historical and contemporary contexts and the latest available research findings. With chapters covering many key aspects of life in China, including religion, social policy, and welfare, the history and impact of the Chinese Communist Party, familial relationships, ethnicity, gender, the media, and the education system, this textbook gives the reader a user-friendly and comprehensive introduction to the most important issues affecting Chinese society today. It also includes handy pedagogical features such as a chronology of the People's Republic of China, further reading suggestions, and related novels, films, and autobiographies. Armed with such a book, readers will not only gain a deeper understanding of Chinese society, but a rewarding appreciation for the people, cultures, and social organizations of the world's most populous country.

Written by a team of internationally renowned contributors from the UK, China, Australia, Singapore, and Hong Kong, *Understanding Chinese Society* is suitable for anyone studying Chinese society, Chinese studies, and Asian sociology.

Xiaowei Zang is Professor of Chinese Studies and Head of the School of East Asian Studies at the University of Sheffield, UK.

Understanding
Chinese Society

Edited by
Xiaowei Zang

Routledge
Taylor & Francis Group

LONDON AND NEW YORK

First published 2011
by Routledge
2 Park Square, Milton Park, Abingdon, Oxon OX14 4RN

Simultaneously published in the USA and Canada
by Routledge
711 Third Avenue, New York, NY 10017

Routledge is an imprint of the Taylor & Francis Group, an informa business

The right of Xiaowei Zang to be identified as editor of this work has been asserted by him in accordance with the Copyright, Designs and Patents Act 1988.

Typeset in Times New Roman by
Florence Production Ltd, Stoodleigh, Devon

British Library Cataloguing in Publication Data
A catalogue record for this book is available from the British Library

Library of Congress Cataloging in Publication Data
    Understanding Chinese society/edited by Xiaowei Zang.
        p. cm.
    Includes bibliographical references and index.
    1. China–Social conditions–2000–   I. Zang, Xiaowei.
    HN733.5.U53 2011
    306.0951'09045–dc22   2011012252

ISBN 978-0-415-61988-2 (hbk)
ISBN 978-0-415-61989-9 (pbk)
ISBN 978-0-203-80328-8 (ebk)

Contents

Illustrations

Figures

Tables

Contributors

Marjorie Dryburgh is Lecturer in Chinese Studies in the School of East Asian Studies at the University of Sheffield, UK.

Yi-min Lin is Associate Professor in the Division of Social Sciences at the Hong Kong University of Science and Technology, China.

Chunrong Liu is an Associate Professor of Political Science in the School of International Relations and Public Affairs, Fudan University, China.

Jieyu Liu is an Academic Fellow in Chinese Studies at the White Rose East Asia Centre, University of Leeds, UK.

Yunfeng Lu is an Associate Professor of Sociology at Beijing University, China.

Colin Mackerras is an Emeritus Professor at Griffith University, Australia.

Gerard A. Postiglione is a Professor in the Faculty of Education, University of Hong Kong, China.

Xiaowei Zang is Professor of Chinese Studies and Head of the School of East Asian Studies at the University of Sheffield, UK.

Qian Forrest Zhang is an Assistant Professor in the School of Social Sciences at Singapore Management University.

Xiaoling Zhang is an Associate Professor in the School of Contemporary Chinese Studies at the University of Nottingham, UK.

Lucy Xia Zhao is Lecturer in Chinese Studies in the School of East Asian Studies at the University of Sheffield, UK.

1 Introduction

Xiaowei Zang

When I was working on my PhD in sociology at the University of California at Berkeley from the mid-1980s to the early 1990s, the majority of the students of East Asia were preoccupied with Japan and the Four East Asian Tigers. The few students who ventured into Chinese studies chose to major in Chinese language, Chinese history, or Chinese politics. The study of Chinese society did not appeal to students because at that time, the People's Republic of China (PRC) was weak economically and had limited influence on international affairs. It was ruled by the Chinese Communist Party (CCP) and struggled with an inefficient planned economic system and a large, growing population. The 1989 Tiananmen Square tragedy discouraged hopes for political liberalization and democratization in the PRC. China seemed stagnant and hopeless.

Surprisingly, significant changes have taken place in China since then. The Chinese economy has expanded at an explosive rate for the past three decades. China surpassed Japan as the world's second-largest economy in the first half of 2010. Its economy is more than 90 times bigger than when Chinese market reforms were launched in 1978. According to experts at Goldman Sachs and PricewaterhouseCoopers, China is on course to overtake the United States as the world's largest economy around 2020. There are significant talks about how G-2 (i.e. Chinamerica) is replacing G-8 and G-20. Today, no major global issues can be satisfactorily addressed without China's effective involvement.

As the PRC has become powerful economically and politically, interaction between Chinese people and people outside China has also become more frequent and important. It is no longer sufficient for students to study Chinese language, history, and politics. They must also equip themselves with knowledge of various aspects of Chinese society. Studying Chinese society is itself intellectually rewarding as one can appreciate the people, cultures, and social organizations in the world's most populous country. Pragmatically, it is impossible to learn the causes of Chinese economic growth without a good understanding of Chinese society. While economic governance relies very much on government policy and market activities, it is also partly dependent on societal organizations including the family, kinship, etc. How social fabrics in China function and how Chinese people live their everyday lives have a direct impact on economic behaviours and market transactions in the PRC.

However, the vast majority of books on China focus on Chinese history and politics. Students and professors are unable to find a suitable book for a course on Chinese society. *Understanding Chinese Society* is written specifically to address this issue. It offers students exposure to a readable, well-grounded exploration of some major issues affecting Chinese society today, and familiarizes them with available resources for learning about Chinese society. The key issues *Understanding Chinese Society* addresses include: What are the key features of the family and marriage institutions in China? How are women and men faring differently in Chinese society today? How are ethnic minorities faring in China? How are religion and cultural inspirations expressed? Other questions on state-society relations, education, the mass media, the neighbourhood, etc. are also examined in this textbook. *Understanding Chinese Society* explores and answers these and other important questions with the best foundational and cutting-edge scholarship and addresses the increasing fascination about Chinese society among students outside China.

Understanding Chinese Society is written by an international team of experts on Chinese society drawing on their teaching and research experience at major universities in Australia, China, Hong Kong, Singapore, and the UK. Each chapter is written by a contributor with expertise in the subject, who provides both a historical and a contemporary context and reference to the latest available scholarship. *Understanding Chinese Society* places the collected material in its historical and intellectual context. It is an essential textbook for a course on Chinese society and work of reference for courses such as Chinese politics and comparative sociology. It is destined to be valued by scholars and students as a vital one-stop pedagogic resource.

In Chapter 2, Marjorie Dryburgh reviews changing understandings of what it means to be Chinese and the ways in which place, culture, and history have been reinterpreted across time as building blocks of Chinese identity. In examining the concept of place, she recognizes the tensions between the idea of 'one China', and the substantial regional variations in topography within the territories now identified as Chinese, as well as the ways in which these have produced variations in local cultures and practices and, at times, profound divisions within the all-China community. In exploring 'Chinese culture', she highlights both the mechanisms through which Confucian traditions were propagated through Chinese elites, and the limitations of Confucian cultural authority in the face of challenges from Daoist and Buddhist traditions. In discussing Chinese histories, she argues that the understanding of the present and the future has been drawn in different ways at different times. In addressing the identity crises of the early twentieth century, she points to the external and internal pressures that shaped emerging Chinese nationalisms, and the ways in which national and social identity were negotiated through the mass media. In considering the post-1949 era, she highlights the intensive state engagement in the public processes of identity building, in the reshaping of opportunities for individuals, and the assertive provision of new models of personal, social, and national identity. Finally she suggests that the reinvention of Chinese traditions, and the reinterpretation of place and history, continue in reform-era China, in an increasingly complex debate as identity is mediated between competing social, official, and commercial interests.

Lucy Zhao discusses ritual and the life cycle in Chapter 3. Different societies have developed distinctive rituals to demarcate, regulate, and commemorate the different stages of life. In this chapter, Zhao introduces readers to some milestones in the life cycle among Han Chinese: birth and childhood, entry into adulthood, marriage, retirement and old age, and death and memorial celebrations. Zhao discusses the rites in China at a general level. She points out that there can be different rites for the same life event in China during different historical periods. Also, some rites have been passed down for generations, others have been given different meanings, and others have faded away from daily life. Equally important, Zhao argues that not everyone in China practises popular rites, some people practise some rites but not other rites, and certain rites are commonly practised in some places but not in other places. There are also differences in adherence to rites in terms of age, gender, class, etc. Ethnic minority groups in China perform different rituals. Zhao's chapter facilitates readers' understanding of other aspects of Chinese society examined in various chapters in this book.

Xiaowei Zang provides readers with an introduction to the family and marriage in China in Chapter 4. Zang first discusses a popular belief that in traditional China many people lived in large, multi-generation families. However, recent studies have challenged this view. Next, Zang shows that households in traditional China are thought to have been large partly because of high fertility rates. There has been a gradual movement towards small family size and low fertility. The major change apparently took place after the 1970s. Because of the post-1970 demographic transition, China's fertility has reached a level well below replacement. Some scholars have attributed the fertility decline to China's birth control policy, others however have argued that the main determinant of the demographic transition is socioeconomic factors. China's below-replacement fertility has attracted attention from scholars given its social costs and the long-term demographic effects such as accelerated population aging, elderly care, sex-selective abortion, distorted sex ratios, and changes to the Chinese family and kinship system.

Zang also examines the changes in the marriage system and shows the increases in late marriage and free choices. However, love and romance are a necessary but not a sufficient precondition for a lasting relationship in China. Other considerations include status similarity, health, chastity, and domestic skills. Zang then shows significant changes in sexual norms in China. Sex is no longer a taboo topic as it was before the 1980s. There have also been changes in the official attitude towards homosexuality in the post-1978 era.

Finally, Zang examines the historical trends in divorce, three major forms of marriage dissolutions, and possible causes of marital breakdowns in China.

In Chapter 5, Jieyu Liu discusses gender and sexuality in China. She first outlines the ways that gender and sexuality affect the organization of Chinese society in both public and private domains. In pre-modern China, Confucianism acted as the core principle for regulating society and prescribed a patriarchal, patrilineal, and patrilocal family system where men dominated women. As continuing a family line through male primogeniture was the priority task in the family, sexuality was mainly harnessed to serve the needs of procreation of future generations. In the past century, various national projects have challenged Confucian ideologies and practices and re-arranged relations between men and women. However, due to an insufficient understanding of gender in the socialist modernization project, inequalities between men and women persisted. Despite the fact that women were officially mobilized into the workplace, the gendered division between domestic sphere and social production was maintained. In recent years, opening up the economy and the availability of new communication technologies have led to the emergence of new sexual cultures and made sexual alternatives possible. However, sexuality is enmeshed with gender relations. The abundance of sexual discourses has re-sexualized women. While men are happily engaged in sexual consumption, women's sexuality is still highly moralized. The chapter concludes that a widely held biological determinist belief of gender not only normalizes heterosexuality and makes other sexual alternatives deviant but also limits the liberating effects of such social transformations for women.

Chunrong Liu examines community and neighbourhood in China in Chapter 6. He scrutinizes changes and continuities in the rural community and urban neighbourhood, with a focus on grassroots-level social solidarity and its impact on the post-1978 context. He shows the explosive growth of new social organizations such as rural solidarity groups, urban property-based organizations and spontaneous bottom-up activisms in the post-1978 era, and argues that the grassroots-level social transformation is deeply rooted in market reforms, which have undermined the socialist social control system and collective good regime, opened up new horizons for community interactions, and contributed to the growth of community autonomy. There have developed community-based governance and welfare programmes including villager committee election, 'new socialist countryside building' and 'urban community building'. These initiatives have shaped the opportunities and resources as well as boundaries for the making of grassroots social solidarity and the creation of conditions for the emergence of civil society in China.

Gerard A. Postiglione discusses the challenges, policies, and practices of education in China's rapidly changing society in Chapter 7. He first discusses the imperial legacy and provides detailed information about the modern education system in China. He then examines the educational system in Mao's China of 1949–76. Next, he argues that education in the post-1978 era is increasingly responsive to and shaped by market demands. These include the demand of individuals and employers for relevant knowledge and skills to boost their career prospects, and the demand of the urban middle class for higher cultural status though social competition for educational credentials. He discusses the development of private schools in China and identifies the problems of school access and equity as they affect rural girls, children of rural migrants, and ethnic minorities.

In Chapter 8, Qian Forrest Zhang discusses status and hierarchies in China. Social hierarchies and inequality in a society are shaped by the modes of production that extract and transfer surplus among social groups through economic activities. In Mao's China, the centrally planned economy established a powerful tributary mode of production (TMP) that extracted surplus from rural areas to cities and from commoner producers to cadre-officials. This TMP created two fundamental hierarchies in socialist China: the urban-rural divide and the official-commoner divide, both of which were based on politically defined statuses. China's post-1978 transition has led to both a resurgence of the traditional petty-commodity mode of production (PCMP) and the rise of a capitalist mode of production (CMP). The PCMP and CMP have created new social hierarchies that are based on people's economic positions in the market and are making today's Chinese society increasingly stratified by a hierarchy of economically determined classes, rather than a hierarchy of politically determined status groups. For example, in both rural and urban areas, a new economic elite has emerged, who accumulated their wealth from entrepreneurial activities under the CMP. The rank of petty-commodity producers has also increased sharply through urban self-employment and household-based commercial productions in rural areas. The nature of the urban–rural divide is also changing. Although the politically defined urban and rural statuses are still in effect, economic positions in the labour and housing markets are becoming more important in determining rural migrants' life chances in cities and in shaping inequality between urban and rural areas. The TMP, however, has remained powerful and the divide between officials and commoners has persisted. Despite the decline of surplus extraction from rural areas, dismantling of the central-planned system, and privatization of many state-owned firms, the state has maintained its extractive power through the monopoly positions of large-scale state-owned firms and its own monopoly of urban land.

Colin Mackerras examines ethnic minorities in China in Chapter 9. The Chinese state officially recognizes 56 ethnic groups: the Han and 55 ethnic minorities. Some of the ethnic minorities are quite similar culturally to the Han, but others are very different indeed. Although there are many commonalities among ethnic minority groups, they illustrate great diversity in terms of language, religion, the arts, architecture, diet and family practices. Mackerras shows that the ethnic populations have been rising consistently in the PRC and the proportion of the minorities within the total Chinese population has increased greatly since 1953. Although the population of ethnic minority groups is less than one-tenth of China's total, they represent a wide range of cultures and live in the strategically important geographic areas of China. Mackerras then examines official policy towards the ethnic minorities and how it relates to reality, including the governance of ethnic minority autonomous regions. The government's economic priorities in the ethnic areas are to promote development, in the hope that raising the standard of living will persuade the ethnic minorities to wish to remain part of the PRC and promote their loyalty towards the state, as well as improve ethnic harmony and good relations among the various ethnic groups. There are preferential policies for minorities in a range of areas, such as employment in government positions, enrolment in higher education, and in matters of population control. Minorities are entitled to preserve the positive aspects of their own cultures and are entitled to use their own languages not only at home but in the public sphere, such as in government, law, and education. However, the government bans the use of religion to try to destabilize the state; and in politically sensitive regions authorities are frequently so cautious in interpreting religious observation as political opposition as to contravene freedom of religion. Mackerras also discusses occasions when factors such as political dissatisfaction, the fear of being culturally submerged, ethnic inequalities, and the fanning of discontent from outside or inside China have led to ethnic violence and animosities, including movements that have tried to separate particular ethnic areas from China. To show this point Mackerras analyses the major disturbances that occurred in the Tibetan areas in 2008 and in the Xinjiang capital Ürümqi in 2009. However, he argues that the Chinese state has handled its minority problems quite well, considering how serious these are, and that the overall trend since the middle of the twentieth century has been towards a better-integrated Chinese state.

In Chapter 10 Yunfeng Lu provides readers with basic information about religion in China. He first outlines religions in traditional China and describes the transition of religions and state regulations since 1949. The Chinese government has recognized five religions: Buddhism, Daoism, Islam, Protestantism, and Catholicism. Confucianism, sects, and other traditional religions were not recognized. During the period of the Cultural Revolution, Mao worship, a kind of political religion, was in its heyday. The collapse of political religion witnessed the rise of religion and quasi-religion in the 1980s, especially the expansion of Protestantism in rural areas and the growth of qigong organizations in cities. When qigong organizations were prohibited in the late 1990s, Buddhism and Protestantism occupied the market niche, developing quickly in urban areas. While state regulation can exert much influence on the fate of a specific religion, it cannot reduce the religious demand. Where there is religious demand, there are religious suppliers, which accounts for the religious revival in contemporary China.

In Chapter 11, Yi-min Lin describes the transformation of work in post-1978 China. China has the world's largest workforce, which totalled 780 million in 2009. Lin first highlights the basic features of the Maoist system of employment and behavioural control in the workplace. He shows that the CCP's capital-intensive economic development strategy and the desideratum of social and political control combined to shape the patterns of authority relations in the workplace. Lin traces the main threads of economic institutional change since 1978, focusing on the decline and weakening of state-socialism and the rise of capitalism as the basic mode of economic organization. This transformation has occurred thanks to three mutually reinforcing developments: internationalization, market-oriented reforms among state-owned enterprises, and privatization. It has also been accompanied by the accelerating processes of industrialization, urbanization, and demographic transition, as well as profound technological advancements, breakthroughs, and diffusion. Lin also examines migration, urban social security reforms, and the rise of the private sector. The authority structure imposed before the reform has broken down. Yet tension and conflict in the workplace have increased as a result of the growth and exacerbation of old and new problems, such as growing economic insecurity, inhumane treatment of workers, and persistent and new forms of social injustice. Related to this is a widely noted phenomenon – the 'sweatshop' practice of organization and management. Over time, such proto-capitalist practice has faced growing constraints posed by changes in state labour policy and legislation, fuller development of the labour market, structural and technological changes, rising social pressure, and more effective organization of collective action by workers.

Xiaoling Zhang provides a detailed study of the mass media in China in Chapter 12. She argues that as a party that came to power as much through the power of the pen as through the barrel of the gun, the Chinese Communist Party leaders know all too well the importance of ideological domination and the use of mass media as part of the Party's ideological apparatus for social mobilization and control. Media and communication are an ideological state apparatus, and their first and foremost function is to reflect the regime's point of view on ideological issues.

The economic reform in China since 1978 has brought a radically changed communication landscape shaped by an unprecedented growth in the number of newspapers, TV stations, satellite channels, and Internet expansion. It has become more pluralized, commercialized, and liberalized. Changes in China's media sphere during this period are not the result of a single event, but the consequence of a number of overlapping and interrelated factors and forces, including commercialization, the new global and regional structure and environment, pluralization which partly (but not exclusively) results from commercialization, China's multifaceted interactions with the outside world, and the advancement of new information and communication technologies. More importantly, all these changes are happening in the context of the Chinese Communist Party wanting to manage the whole process and to stay ahead of the unwanted consequences of the reform. These overlapping and interrelated factors and forces constitute the backdrop to the transformation of mass media, although the backdrop itself is in continuous flux. Chapter 12 starts with a brief review of the history of China's communist communication, which serves to provide the context within which the country's media reform and the fast-moving social transitions in the reform era have been occurring. It then introduces the transformation of mass media as a result of accelerated commodification, globalization, rapid advancement of media technologies, and intensified ideological and social struggles. This chapter serves to improve our understanding of the continuities and changes in China's mass media after the economic reform. It finishes with challenges both the Party-state and the media industry face in furthering the development of mass media in China.

In Chapter 13 Xiaowei Zang outlines a brief history of the Chinese Communist Party before 1949, the socialist transformation in the Mao era of 1949–76, and the post-1978 market reforms. Next, Zang examines the system of government, describing its institutional components, the principles by which they operate, and the ways in which the CCP controls the government. Zang also discusses the changing state-society relations in the PRC since 1949. While there has been continuity in the major government institutions and the persistence of one party rule in China, there have been significant political changes in the post-1978 era due to the receding role of the state in society, the demands of market reforms, and the open door policy. Some scholars have complained bitterly about the slow process of political liberalization since 1978. Zang shows the considerable extent of democratization in China. This chapter provides important contextual material for readers to reflect their understanding of various aspects of contemporary Chinese society discussed in Chapters 2–12.

Understanding Chinese Society is fully indexed and is equipped with a basic chronology of the People's Republic of China. Further reading, novels, and some films/documentaries are recommended at the ends of many chapters for readers who want to know more about the relevant subjects of Chinese society. When the contributors wrote their chapters they made no assumptions about the reader's knowledge of China. Each chapter was written in such a way that it would be easily accessible to everyone interested in China. The book is not intended to be a Chinese Society ABC nor an encyclopaedia of China, but an effort to open a door to provide the reader with some details about social organizations and daily life in China. The book can help some-one currently studying Mandarin to appreciate the language in China's social context. It can be a useful companion to someone planning to visit or spend time as an exchange student or expatriate in China. It can also provide the reader with the answers or the means to think of the answers to questions which may arise when he or she meets and interacts with people in China. Once the reader is armed with background information like this he or she would be in a good position to achieve a deeper understanding of Chinese society or become more socially functional in China.

2 Foundations of Chinese identity

Place, past and culture

Marjorie Dryburgh

What does it mean to be 'Chinese' today? Identity provides the frameworks within which individuals locate themselves within a community: as individuals, we see ourselves as members of many overlapping communities – of nation or hometown, of gender and generation, of class or of profession, of recreation or consumption, of social or historical experience – and *personal* identities are therefore made up of changing combinations of these various collective identities. While a community may declare its collective identity to be fixed, essential, and timeless, scholarly understandings of identity have focused on the ways in which identities are socially constructed and subject to repeated negotiation, and on the interplay or tensions between multiple identities – between gender and class, between region, ethnicity and nation, and the variations in any of these adopted by different groups (Calhoun 1994).

Given the dramatic changes that China has undergone, in the past century since the collapse of the imperial order in 1911 and within living memory, we should expect those discussions of identity to be intensive, complex, and shifting, as different understandings of China's past and future, and of 'Chinese traditions' are reinterpreted to meet the needs of China today. We should consider also *whose* rendering of Chinese identity we have before us: we should not assume that the understandings of identity present in state-sponsored, media-borne, public discourse are the same as those revealed in everyday behaviour at local level. Finally, we should be conscious of the images of China that come to us from our own local media or popular histories, or from film and fiction. Representations of China in Europe and north America were until relatively recently dominated by a handful of central images of a China that valued the community over the individual; that was generally internally homogeneous and governed by rigid 'Confucian' principles and a strict social hierarchy headed by scholar officials over farmers, artisans and, finally, merchants; that was resistant to change and distrustful of external influence. Recent scholarship has done much to highlight the complexities behind these quite simple images, and an examination of the building blocks of identity in China – in place, culture and history – reveals significant diversity, in the vitality of regional identities, in reinterpretations and assertive challenges to core values, and in changing understandings of China's past and its meanings.

Geography: placing 'China'

The People's Republic of China today covers a territory that stretches from Korea in the north-east across the southern borders of Siberia to Tajikistan, Kazakhstan and Pakistan in the west, and through Tibet to Vietnam and Burma in the south-west. It is important to note first that China in this current form is a relatively recent creation, and second that this territory – covering an area comparable in size to the United States – contains enormous internal variation.

While images of China overseas are often dominated by the rice terraces and karst limestone landscapes of the south, much of what is marked as China's earliest history and most ancient culture unfolded in a handful of provinces in the Yellow River basin, where landscape and climate are very different. Archaeologists have located the capitals of the early dynasties, Shang, Zhou, and Qin, in modern Henan and Shaanxi provinces; the philosophers Confucius and Mencius, who articulated the core values of the imperial era, were both natives of modern Shandong. The expansion of the empire to incorporate all of modern China proper, as well as Manchuria in the north-east, Mongolia, Xinjiang in the north-west, Tibet in the south-west, and Taiwan, entered its final stages only in the eighteenth century. Each expansion drew in variations of land, custom, and language, and accompanying potential challenges to the idea of a unitary China. For centuries, therefore, China has been marked by regional variations rooted in climate and topography and manifested in dialect, the arts, culinary traditions, and commercial development; and regional identity was thus an important complicating factor in the negotiation of all-China identity.

G. William Skinner (1977: 212–16) proposed that China should be understood as a collection of nine 'macro-regions': bounded by geographical features such as mountain ranges, and centred on major river systems, the primary transport and commercial arteries of pre-twentieth century China, these macro-regions developed close internal trading relations and a relatively high degree of social and cultural coherence. Despite the emergence of national markets, first in luxury goods and then in staples such as grain, between the ninth and fourteenth centuries, there was much less contact between macro-regions. These remained distinct in many ways into the twentieth century, and robust local cultures therefore competed for attention and allegiance with awareness of a wider China.[1]

Topographical and environmental differences influenced local cultures and societies. For example, as noted earlier, the earliest traces of civilization now identified as Chinese are tied to the relatively cold, arid north China plain, where the climate favoured crops such as wheat, millet, and sorghum but did not make farming particularly fruitful, and therefore did not encourage an early emergence of commerce or of a powerful commercial class that could challenge the state or provide an alternative space in which social interests could be negotiated. By the fourteenth century, however, the economic centre of gravity of the empire was shifting southwards to the Lower Yangtze region ('Jiangnan', south of the river), where the wetter, milder climate allowed a more productive agriculture that consequently fuelled rapid growth in commerce. Rising status for traders destabilized traditional social hierarchies, and Jiangnan and its cities – Yangzhou, Suzhou, and Nanjing among others – became the heartland of a newly commercialized culture that owed significantly less to formal official or imperial patronage than that of earlier centuries (Chow 2004; Marmé 2005). By the late eighteenth century, with the incorporation of Manchuria, Mongolia, Xinjiang, Tibet, and Taiwan into the empire, China was possibly better understood as a multi-ethnic empire than as a unitary state. Although that empire was at this time ruled by a Manchu 'conquest' dynasty, and although the new territories and their people were understood as exotic and alien, influence in these outlying regions was an assertive statement of imperial power and prestige (Teng 2004).

Different regions of China also varied in their apparent level of interest and engagement with the world beyond China's shifting borders. Early western scholarship suggested that China's relations with its neighbours were governed by a 'tribute system' that interpreted all contact as a form of homage by lesser, 'barbarian' powers to a culturally superior China, and this understanding did much to feed the stereotype of a 'closed' and inward-looking China (Fairbank and Reischauer 1989).[2] It is arguable of course that the magnitude of the task of governing the empire drew official attention inwards until external forces presented a threat, and that this has skewed the treatment of external contact in official sources. But it is also clear that, where external contact was a matter of routine – for example, in the Southeast Coast and Lingnan regions, and on the inland frontiers of the north and west, there was much more intensive and pragmatic interaction through trade and traffic of persons than the 'tribute system' framework would encourage us to expect. We should not ignore the significant periods of disunion in China's history, between the third and sixth centuries, the early tenth century, and most recently in the 'warlord' era of the 1920s: when the centre declined, the pull of regional loyalties, and the power of regional organization and identification rose correspondingly. Despite these regional shifts and variations, the idea that there was nonetheless 'one China', has remained a powerful one.

Chinese traditions: Confucianism and beyond

Chinese identity is also rooted in shared traditions though, here again, we see shifts in principles and interpretations. For much of the imperial era, social and political beliefs among the elite were most visibly shaped by the ideas of Confucius (*c.* 551–479 BCE), a philosopher and adviser to rulers, as recorded after his death and elaborated by his followers. But this was by no means the only source of important values, particularly among the common people; and the meanings of Confucianism even among the ruling elite changed significantly over time.

Why, then, did Confucianism appear so important? Again, the explanation lies partly in the governing classes' control of the written records: the people who had the education to record their understanding of Chinese society and its workings, and the prestige to ensure that efforts were made to preserve those records were educated from childhood in Confucian texts and traditions. A Confucian education was an important marker of social status, and the route towards prestigious government service lay in a Confucianized examination system. Like the Greek or Roman classics or the Christian canon in Europe, the Confucian canon in China did much to shape the mental landscape of the ruling classes. It provided instruction in proper values, stories that demonstrated proper and improper behaviour, and offered an assurance that the rulers of the empire were united by clearly articulated common culture (Elman 2000).[3] The durability of Confucianism was enhanced by periodic reinventions, most significantly in the second century BCE, when it was established as a philosophy of government; after the eighth century, when it extended its attention from statecraft to cosmological enquiry to meet the challenges posed by Buddhism; and in the eighteenth century, when a new school of 'evidential research' emerged to question the canon itself and its relevance for China centuries after its production.

The core values associated with Confucianism – an insistence on the importance of the family, of education, of public service – appealed to the relatively powerful, while the inclusion of benevolence among Confucianism's cardinal virtues offered a promise of justice and security that could be used to pacify the weak and disaffected. These values were also broad enough to be adapted and re-imagined as society developed, offering an appearance of continuity even in times of dramatic change. So central has Confucian culture been to understandings of Chinese elite identity that culture and values have been taken at times as more important defining elements of Chineseness than, for example, descent or ethnicity, and this centrality of Confucianism has been invoked to suggest that incomers – even conquest dynasties – might be effectively 'sinicized', or made Chinese, through the adoption of core values and behaviour. Better understandings of Chinese historical concepts of ethnicity (Dikotter 1992), and of the relations between alien rulers and Chinese elites, have challenged this argument (Ho 1998; Rawski 1996), but its durability nonetheless highlights the importance attached to values as a means of binding communities together in China.

Despite its influence in public life, however, Confucianism was by no means the only important source of shared values, and other schools of thought also shaped personal identities and served as a focus for local community activity. Confucian principles and the Confucian pre-occupation with social activism were challenged both by Daoism, an indigenous Chinese school that emerged in the same period as Confucianism, and by Buddhism, which reached China from India in the second century and was well established across the empire by the middle ages. Both attracted the philosophical interest of the educated elite, were highly influential in the arts, and became the source of much popular religious practice (Schwartz 1985). At a popular level, therefore, 'Chinese values' were an eclectic mix of principles culled from different and competing traditions that might vary according to locality and social class.

Histories of China

The past matters to Chinese identity. Discussions of the past connect China today with its ancient civilization, and while many aspects of China's history are still understood in stereotypical terms as 'feudal', the material heritage of the imperial era is celebrated; and the past is a source of stock tales and characters, positive and negative, that one could call on to frame later experience. China conventionally claims a 5,000 year history: written histories purportedly record events that date back to around 2600 BCE, and there is a rich archaeological record.[4] While it is not possible to tie some of the earliest archaeological finds specifically to the written sources, it is nonetheless clear that organized and materially sophisticated societies flourished in central China from a very early period (Liu and Xu 2007). Chinese history was intensively, though selectively, documented by China's governing elites. The earliest systematic history, Sima Qian's *Records of the Historian*, was compiled in the first century BCE, and comprised chronologies of historical events, biographies of emperors, nobles, and other notable individuals, and treatises on topics such as rites, astronomy, river management, and other areas of state interest (Hardy 1999). Later histories of the empire borrowed heavily from this template, and the writing of histories became a core official project, each new dynasty compiling a history of its predecessor while routinely documenting its own activities. The cumulative effect of this activity was to create a body of work that tied the foundation of each dynasty to principles of legitimacy that appeared consistent across recorded history, and that heavily emphasized continuity rather than change.

This image of an 'unchanging China' has had a powerful hold over foreign imaginings of China. While some early visitors, such as Jesuit missionaries, enthusiastically recorded Chinese prowess in technical fields including mathematics and astronomy, later visitors, particularly those thwarted in their dealings with the Chinese state, were far more likely to interpret their own failures as evidence of Chinese intransigence and cultural stasis, and the judgement had profound and long-standing effects on official attitudes to China and academic work alike.[5]

However, that appearance of continuity dissolves if we shift our attention from the empire-wide, official record to the local and personal histories that more recent academic work on China is using so effectively. Regional histories of China offer rich data on the local unfolding of empire-wide developments, and personal writings such as private biographies and epitaphs, family histories and genealogies, letters, poems and essays on diverse subjects that China's educated elite were expected to produce show us how personal identities were articulated and how some relatively affluent Chinese understood their society and their own place within it.

While official histories might reflect the shift from aristocratic to bureaucratic rule in the middle ages, or the changes in taxation practice that followed the growth of commerce in the early modern era, local and personal histories show far more clearly the deeper impact of those changes. These histories show how the 'gentry' families who supplied the imperial state with its officials built and manipulated social networks to make powerful friends and arrange advantageous marriages. They show how rising volumes of trade created a powerful class of merchants who were able to compete with the gentry through charitable works and displays of wealth and taste (Lufrano 1997; Clunas 1991). They show the powerful economic and social constraints on many Chinese women beside the growing expectation that the daughters of the gentry would themselves be educated (Bernhard 2002; Mann 1997). These histories therefore highlight the negotiations of power, interest, and allegiance that were central to identity construction in late imperial China.

By the eighteenth century, attitudes towards the past itself were the subject of debate in official circles. Ambivalence towards the past became more acute in the nineteenth century, as Chinese faced first economic, then political and military pressure from imperialist powers, primarily Britain and France. Defeated in foreign wars – from the Opium wars of the 1840s, through the first Sino-Japanese War of the 1890s – China was forced to conclude a series of 'unequal treaties' that conceded trading and residence rights, and control over territory and local affairs in treaty ports to foreign powers. These defeats overstretched the material resources of the state, leaving China vulnerable to further external challenges and internal disruption, and eroded the legitimacy of the Qing dynasty and eventually of the imperial order itself. The governments of the new republic had little more success than their predecessors in resisting external pressure, and the first decades of republican rule were marked first by further economic and political losses and then by the traumas of all-out war with Japan in the 1930s and 1940s. This period is now most commonly remembered in China as a century of 'national humiliation' (Cohen 2003), and the insistence that the past was to be remembered above all as a series of mistakes that must not be repeated was a common element in reformist and revolutionary thinking in the twentieth century.

Self, community, and nation in the early twentieth century

The traumatic encounter with foreign imperialism in the nineteenth and twentieth centuries forced China to re-evaluate its place in the world. While the revolution of 1911 replaced the dynastic order with a new republic, it did not resolve either the practical problems or the wider anxieties that had emerged in the previous century. Through the 'May Fourth' era of the 1910s and 1920s, this continuing failure fuelled an energetic questioning of the core principles that governed Chinese society and its future. Many prominent debates revolved around political philosophies: did anarchism or Marxism offer practical answers to China's problems? Could democracy be made to work in Chinese conditions? At the same time, though, questions of identity ran through the discussions: could 'Chinese traditions' be adapted to the modern world? What would be gained or lost by the adoption of foreign ideas or foreign technologies? How should individual Chinese understand their own place within communities such as family, workplace, or native place? How did these smaller, face-to-face communities relate to China as a whole? What were citizens of the new republic expected to do, or know, or be (Chow 1967)?

This also marked a new interest in nationalism. The foreign powers that had defeated China in the wars of the past decades were understood to be driven and directed by a sense of nation that defined a collective project and set out the responsibilities of individuals to the national community. Reformers, such as Liang Qichao and revolutionaries, such as Sun Yat-sen, argued that one of China's great failings was the absence of any shared sense of national interest, and the obscuring of a sense of national community by loyalties to native place, family and status group, and that this had left China vulnerable in the face of foreign pressure, and allowed its relegation to inferior status in its dealings with foreign powers (Bergere 1998). Discussions of nationalism therefore drew in both outward-facing questions of international status, and inward-facing questions of cohesion and community. While the outward-facing questions have historically attracted more attention, their impact on the ground – like foreign pressure in China – was extremely uneven, and they have rarely formed the basis of a persuasive and durable nationalism. The inward-facing questions, of how the national community was to be understood and taken to heart by its members, have been less visible, but equally intractable.

We see these questions through the writings of Chinese intellectuals, but they touched on problems that other Chinese faced every day. Economic development in the cities and pressure on farmers in the countryside created new opportunities and new insecurities, forced many to seek new sources of income, and encouraged migration to cities. This produced changes that went far beyond intellectual life. By the 1920s, for example, women were far more likely to work outside the home, not only in traditional occupations such as domestic service, but in factories, department stores, offices or schools; and this, as much as the early debates on feminism and the traditional status of Chinese women, presented them with new challenges and new choices (Goodman and Larson 2005).

Both abstract and practical questions were discussed in the expanding Chinese press (Reed 2004). Newspapers had circulated in China in the nineteenth century, and had been influential in supplementing informal, personal communication among officials and the educated classes of current events and the state of the empire. Now, however, the very rapid expansion and diversification of the print media in the 1910s and 1920s changed the whole game. Scholars have pointed to the role that the print media have had in shaping nationalism in other societies (Anderson 1983); while the readership for newspapers in China was still limited by low literacy levels and constraints on distribution, many more people now had direct, personal access to a far greater variety of content and opinion on both national and social matters. Highbrow journals such as Chen Duxiu's *New Youth* and the fiction of writers such as Lu Xun have been extensively examined for their discussions on the new literature, science and democracy and high-level reform; but Shanghai's flourishing tabloid press, with its coverage of celebrities, scandals, and social anxieties, attracted a wider audience, who had not only some appetite for sensationalism but possibly also first-hand experience of the economic uncertainties, the pressures on working women, and the compromises and detours required to survive in a new China that underpinned the tabloid dramas (Goodman 2005).

New revolutionary communities after 1949

The establishment of the People's Republic of China in 1949 was hailed as the creation of a 'new China', as the point at which the Chinese people had 'stood up' after centuries of oppression by landlords, bureaucrats and foreign invaders. New China required that a new Chinese people come forward as citizens of the new order; while much of the rhetoric of the early People's Republic focused on building socialism, nation-building, and identity formation, assertively championed by the CCP and state, were also important parts of the project.

Many key reforms of the 1950s and 1960s therefore served both practical and nation-building ends. Land Reform was presented as a step towards securing the welfare of China's farmers, and making agriculture more productive in order to feed a new population of industrial workers. At the same time, it overturned traditional rural socio-economic hierarchies, and gave every family a class label – poor, middle, rich peasant, or landlord – that defined their place in the new order. The expansion of primary education was designed to eradicate illiteracy and build the basic skills needed for national economic development and modernization; it also instilled revolutionary and national values, as a counter-weight to local and traditional cultures. The policies of the Great Leap Forward were championed as a means to catapult China into international economic pre-eminence, but their application also became a test of loyalty and dedication.

These efforts to transform the present and future were accompanied by a radical reinterpretation of China's past, and the reshaping of understandings of national histories was central to the CCP's training of its own members, to its rehabilitation of outsiders, and to its socialization of the citizens of new China. Workplace and community meetings, the media, and art forms such as cinema drew mass audiences into emotional engagement with stories of China's recent history and people were encouraged to consider their experiences and past actions within that national context (Apter and Saich 1994). The revolutionary epic *The East is Red* (1965) echoes these strategies. This 'play-within-a-film' charted the humiliations suffered by China at the hands of foreign imperialists and traditional Chinese elites, and the rise of the Communist Party as China's saviour, connecting that national journey from oppression to liberation with common experience. An opening framing sequence tracks across central Beijing and follows an audience into the auditorium where the drama is ostensibly staged: wherever, and in whatever company, we see the film, we begin watching over the shoulders of another audience in which families, the elderly, blue- and white-collar workers, and members of China's minority nationalities, were all represented.

Broadcasting and the print media – now owned by the state – were also important in instilling a sense of the nature and mission of the national community (Chapter 12). The competing voices of the pre-war media had gone, and were replaced by a striking uniformity in tone and content. Consumption of the media message was also a communal activity, and many would read a newspaper publicly displayed on a glass-fronted notice board rather than buying a personal copy, or hear the radio broadcast over loudspeakers in a workplace canteen. The mass media thus became a central element in the CCP's thought work, constructing the 'imagined community' (Anderson 1983) of socialist China, and displaying and embedding it in the everyday lives of the people. While newspapers typically emphasized explanation and directive, other forms such as *reportage*[6] offered vivid and emotionally engaging stories of revolutionary lives and models (Laughlin 2002).

The drive to reshape identity pervaded visual as well as written media. Images of the new China were ever present in propaganda posters displayed in homes and workplaces, rallying support and raising awareness of specific campaigns, and setting out the benefits of belonging to the new national community. While it is easy to read these as instructions as to what the people of new China must do, they also suggested who they might be, displaying models of the new citizen at work, study, and (occasionally) at leisure, showing newly-liberated women as workers at the forefront of China's industrial modernization, farmers as teachers of urban youth, and the young as both heirs and pioneers of the revolution (IISH and Landsberger, n.d.). The meanings of these nameless models were explored in greater depth through revolutionary martyrs and exemplars whose life stories became patterns for the new ideal Chinese. The most famous of these was Lei Feng (雷锋, 1940–62), the orphaned son of a poor family who lived only to serve the revolution and his army comrades through modest acts of selflessness and first came to prominence only in 1963 after an untimely, accidental death. Other models too, such as peasant organizer Fang Zhimin (方志敏, 1899–1935) and cadre Jiao Yulu (焦裕禄, 1922–64) formed part of a cult of 'red martyrdom' that was reflected in public monuments and commemorations (Hung 2008) as well as in exhortations to learn from Lei Feng and others.

This intensive, top-down work of moulding new identities left little visible space for negotiation, leading us to question how fully this identity discourse was accepted by most Chinese: how many recognized enough of their own lives and experiences in revolutionary propaganda to accept the models of identity that accompanied it; how many presented an appearance of compliance in pursuit of a quiet life. Here again, new scholarship is beginning to tease out some of the personal and local experiences behind the official stories, suggesting that official identity discourse was adapted and complicated by place, gender, and status (Lee and Yang 2007).

Modernization, globalization and the re-imagining of China

As we examine China today, we find the forces shaping identity shifting ever more rapidly. Attitudes to the past, to traditional culture, and to the regions within all China are changing; dramatic economic development is allowing the more fortunate to define themselves in terms of their new choices in work and leisure, while at the same time creating a growing gap between rich and poor, urban and rural. The work of community-building, both in the immediate communities of place and profession (Chapter 6), and in virtual communities online, is becoming more complex. The voice of the state, which was at one time almost the only voice audible in discussions over the nature and future of 'China', is now only one of a babble of competing voices; at the same time, the authorities as aspiring identity-builders are becoming more sophisticated, and more instrumental, in their presentations of China as they understand it to a range of audiences.

Efforts to create reformed citizens for a reforming China continue, both in official discourses of 'civility' (*wenming*) and 'quality' (*suzhi*) in public communication, and in the search for new models of identity. While the cult of Lei Feng was briefly revived in the 1990s, the focus has shifted somewhat to emphasize different qualities and achievements. Thus, on the one hand, shifts in official media content, notably in the rising use of human interest stories to illuminate social issues, allow community and model qualities to be identified without the creation of icons on the scale of Lei Feng; on the other hand, the public appetite for contemporary biography (Chua 2009), celebrity lives and fictional treatments of real-life dilemmas has engaged commercial interests in the negotiation of identity; and rising access to the Internet, blogs and microblogs is creating new spaces for self-representation and community-building. In that context of pluralism and contention, the building blocks of identity in place, culture, and history are being reshaped to meet new needs.

The meanings of place in China have shifted dramatically with rapid, but uneven, economic development, and with rising personal mobility. Major cities such as Shanghai – and to a lesser extent many others on the eastern seaboard

– are bound into global networks of trade and consumerism. They present a self-consciously cosmopolitan face to the world and are developed as magnets for financial and human capital and as the motors of China's future. The speed of this development is in stark contrast to conditions in poorer inland regions, despite government efforts to reduce the disparity; this rising inequality has a potentially corrosive effect on national community as it calls into question the extent to which coastal and inland regions can be seen to be partners and beneficiaries in a shared project. While coastal development has been heavily dependent on labour migration and the displacement of growing numbers of Chinese from poorer regions, legal and social discrimination against migrant workers in the cities has underlined the fissures within the China-wide community. Discussions of local cultures by some inland provincial leaderships have aimed to address this problem on two levels, working to enhance provincial economic status by promoting the province as a destination for inward investment, but constructing local cultures as more authentically Chinese than those of coastal provinces, and as untainted by the problems that have come with rapid development (Oakes 2000).

As economic development provides new opportunities – for some, at least – and the state becomes less assertive in promoting explicitly socialist values, social identity is defined increasingly in terms of wealth, occupation, and consumption of goods or services, from restaurants to electronic media. In this context of greater pluralism, traditional cultures, too, are becoming more visible; but the apparently familiar figures of Confucianism and religious Buddhism are made to serve contemporary uses. After a century in disrepute, Confucius is becoming respectable again, and 'Confucian' private schools in Chinese cities are attracting media attention (BBC News 2008), and this may suggest a hankering in some quarters for traditional values; but the figure of Confucius is also deployed in the global branding of China, in the expanding programme of cultural outreach and soft power run through the new network of 'Confucius Institutes'.[7] Traditional religion, too, is adapting to new social landscapes. In some areas, local temples are as central to the building of identity and community and to practical public works projects as they are to worship; in others, they are tied into transnational networks of patronage and nostalgia (Chau 2006).

Finally, China's recent and distant pasts are still under reinterpretation. Some aspects of the past have become assets to be displayed and commodified, as tourist destinations for domestic and foreign travellers, or as World Heritage sites, such as the tomb of the first emperor near Xi'an, or the imperial Summer Palace in Beijing; and archaeological finds are a prominent topic in the official press (People's Daily 2010), emphasizing that to be Chinese is to inherit one of the world's great cultures. Other histories are more contentious, as even a cursory glance at Chinese cinema demonstrates. Chinese films set in the past – from art-house fare such as *Farewell My Concubine* (Chen Kaige 1993), to blockbusters such as *Hero* (Zhang Yimou 2002) are familiar to Western audiences as exotic, visually sumptuous experiences; but Chinese audiences appear to examine historical content more critically. While *Hero* attracted massive audiences in China, it was criticized for masking the darker aspects of the career of the first emperor Qin Shi Huangdi with a glossy, Hollywood-style wrapper (Wang 2009). Although it is often films that attract official criticism – Tian Zhuangzhuang's *The Blue Kite* (1993), which covers the Cultural Revolution, and Jiang Wen's bitter war story *Devils on the Doorstep* (2000) – that receive most attention overseas, the case of *Hero* suggests that histories old and new matter to Chinese mass audiences as well. This may be particularly acute when recent history is discussed. Whereas experiences and memories of the Cultural Revolution and its aftermath are divided and often contentious, Chinese suffering during the war with Japan (1937–45) is a common point of reference both for survivors of the war and for younger Chinese, and this collective understanding of Chinese victimization can be mobilized in support of anti-Japanese commentary in the press and in public demonstrations. As the war passes from personal, living memory, its place in collective memory and its value in identity-building depend on the retelling of the wartime story in schools, in the media and in public monuments.

The foundations of Chinese identity therefore are not fixed. Place, past and culture offer a range of ideas and precedents that can be adopted and adapted to meet the needs of the time, though understandings of those needs may be the subject of debate or dispute between different groups and the processes of identity formation depend on constant negotiation. While it is still the voice of the relatively powerful that is most audible in these debates and negotiations, we can now hear other voices, and see with far greater clarity than was once the case the work involved in securing a common understanding of the nature of the Chinese community and the bonds that draw it together.

Notes

1   Skinner's macro-regions, and the modern provinces to which each roughly corresponds were: Northeast China (Liaoning, Jilin and Heilongjiang), North China (Hebei, Shandong, Henan), Northwest China, (Shanxi, Shaanxi, Gansu), Upper Yangtze (Sichuan), Middle Yangtze (Hubei, Hunan, Jiangxi), Lower Yangtze (Jiangsu, Zhejiang, Anhui), Southeast Coast (Zhejiang, Fujian), Lingnan (Guangdong and Guangxi autonomous region), Yungui (Yunnan and Guizhou); Skinner 1977, 212–16.

2   The work of John King Fairbank was tremendously influential in early twentieth-century English-language scholarship on China; for a detailed critical discussion of his legacy, see Cohen 1984.

3   Benjamin Elman's homepage at http://www.princeton.edu/~elman/ gives electronic access to much of his work on Confucianism.

4   There are numerous historical surveys of China; the best concise recent work is probably Ropp 2010.

5   This is most visible in the mid-twentieth-century scholarship on China – again, see Cohen 1984 for a fuller discussion – but the assumptions underlying the 'unchanging China' construct survived for longer in 'world histories' such as Braudel 1995.

6 Laughlin defines *reportage* as 'any deliberately literary non-fiction text that narrates or describes a current event, person or social phenomenon' (2002: 2).
7 See the online presence of the Confucius Institutes at http://about.chinese.cn/en/.

Bibliography

Anderson, Benedict (1983) *Imagined Communities: Reflections on the Origin and Spread of Nationalism*, London: Verso.

Apter, David and Saich, Tony (1994) *Revolutionary Discourse in Mao's Republic*, Cambridge, MA: Harvard University Press.

BBC News (2008) 'China's thriving Confucian schools', available at http://news.bbc.co.uk/1/hi/world/asia-pacific/7169814.stm, accessed on January 9, 2011.

Bergere, Marie-Claire (1998) *Sun Yat-sen*, Stanford, CA: Stanford University Press.

Bernhardt, Kathryn (2002) *Women and Property in China, 960–1949*, Stanford, CA: Stanford University Press.

Braudel, Fernand, tr. Richard Mayne (1995) *A History of Civilisations*, London: Penguin.

Brook, Timothy (1998) *The Confusions of Pleasure: Commerce and Culture in Ming China*, Berkeley, CA: University of California Press.

Calhoun, Craig (1994) 'Social theory and the politics of identity', pp. 9–36 in Craig Calhoun (ed.), *Social Theory and the Politics of Identity*, Oxford: Blackwell.

Chau, Adam Yuet (2006) *Miraculous Response: Doing Popular Religion in Contemporary China*, Stanford, CA: Stanford University Press.

Chow Kai-wing (2004) *Publishing, Culture and Power in Early Modern China*, Stanford, CA: Stanford University Press.

Chow Tse-tsung (1967) *The May Fourth Movement: Intellectual Revolution in Modern China*, Stanford, CA: Stanford University Press.

Chua, Emily Huiching (2009) 'The good book and the good life: bestselling biographies in China's economic reform', *China Quarterly*, 198: 364–80.

Clunas, Craig (1991) *Superfluous Things: Material Culture and Social Status in Early Modern China*, Cambridge: Polity.

Cohen, Paul (1984) *Discovering History in China: American Historical Writing on the Recent Chinese Past*, New York: Columbia University Press.

—— (2003) 'Remembering and forgetting national humiliation in twentieth-century China', pp. 148–84 in Paul Cohen, *China Unbound*, London: Routledge.

Dikotter, Frank (1992) *The Discourse of Race in Modern China*, London: Hurst.

Elman, Benjamin (2000) *A Cultural History of Civil Examinations in Late Imperial China*, Berkeley, CA: University of California Press.

Fairbank, John King and Edwin Reischauer (1989) *China: Tradition and Transformation*, Boston: Houghton and Mifflin.

Goodman, Bryna (2005) 'The new woman commits suicide: the press, cultural memory, and the new republic', *Journal of Asian Studies*, 64(1): 67–102.

Goodman, Bryna and Wendy Larson (2005) *Gender in Motion: Divisions of Labor and Cultural Change in Late Imperial and Modern China*, Lanham, MD: Rowman and Littlefield.

Hardy, Grant (1999) *Worlds of Bronze and Bamboo: Sima Qian's Conquest of History*, New York: Columbia University Press.

Ho, Ping-ti (1998) 'In defense of sinicization: a rebuttal of Evelyn Rawski's "Reenvisioning the Qing"', *Journal of Asian Studies*, 57(1): 123–55.

Hung, Chang-tai (2008) 'The cult of the red martyr: politics of commemoration in China', *Journal of Contemporary History*, 43(2): 279–304.

IISH (International Institute of Social History) and Stefan Landsberger (n.d.), *Chinese Posters: Propaganda, Politics, History, Art*, available at http://www.chineseposters. net.

Laughlin, Charles A. (2002) *Chinese Reportage: the Aesthetics of Historical Experience*, Durham, NC: Duke University Press.

Lee Ching-kwan and Guobin Yang (2007) *Re-envisioning the Chinese Revolution*, Washington, DC: Woodrow Wilson Center Press.

Liu Li and Xu Hong (2007) 'Rethinking erlitou: legend, history and Chinese archaeology', *Antiquity*, 81(314): 886–901.

Lufrano, Richard John (1997) *Honorable Merchants: Commerce and Self-cultivation in Late Imperial China*, Honolulu, HI: University of Hawai'i Press.

Mann, Susan (1997) *Precious Records: Women in China's Long Eighteenth Century*, Stanford, CA: Stanford University Press.

Marmé, Michael (2005) *Suzhou: Where the Goods of all the Provinces Converge*, Stanford, CA: Stanford University Press.

Oakes, Timothy (2000) 'China's provincial identities: reviving regionalism and reinventing "Chineseness"', *Journal of Asian Studies*, 59(3): 667–92.

Peoples Daily (2010) 'Statues older, more numerous than terracotta warriors found in Hunan' August 18, 2010, available at http://english.people.com.cn/90001/90782/ 90873/7108783.html, accessed on January 9, 2011.

Rawski, Evelyn S. (1996) 'Presidential address: re-envisioning the Qing', *Journal of Asian Studies*, 55(4): 829–50.

Reed, Christopher A. (2004) *Gutenberg in Shanghai: Chinese Print Capitalism, 1876–1937*, Vancouver: UBC Press.

Ropp, Paul (2010) *China in World History*, Oxford: Oxford University Press.

Schwartz, Benjamin I. (1985) *The World of Thought in Ancient China*, Cambridge, MA: Belknap Press.

Skinner, G. William (1977) 'Regional urbanisation in nineteenth century China', pp. 211–52 in Skinner *The City in Late Imperial China*, Stanford, CA: Stanford University Press.

Teng, Emma (2004) *Taiwan's Imagined Geography: Chinese Colonial Travel Writing and Pictures, 1683–1895*, Cambridge, MA: Harvard University Asia Center.

Wang Ting (2009) 'Understanding local reception of globalized cultural products in the context of the international cultural economy: a case study in the reception of *Hero* and *Daggers* in China', *International Journal of Cultural Studies*, 12: 299–318.

Related novels and autobiographies

Chang, Jung (1991) *Wild Swans: Three Daughters of China*, London: Simon and Schuster.

He Liyi (2002) *Mr China's Son: A Villager's Life*, London: Perseus.

Liang, Heng, and Judith Shapiro (1983) *Son of the Revolution*, New York: Knopf/ Random House.

Lu Xun (2009) *The Real Story of Ah-Q and Other Tales of China: The Complete Fiction of Lu Xun*, London: Penguin.

Ma Jian (2002) *Red Dust*, London: Vintage.

Films/documentaries

Chen Kaige (1993) *Farewell My Concubine*
China: a century of revolution Part I
China: a century of revolution Part II
China: a century of revolution Part III
Zhang Yang (1999) *Shower*
Zhang Yimou (1994) *To Live*

3 Rituals and the life cycle

Lucy Xia Zhao

Studying rites (or rituals) in the life cycle facilitates our understanding of a society. Different societies have developed distinctive rituals to demarcate, regulate, and commemorate the different stages of life. In this chapter, I consider rites as social behaviour that is determined by society and where individuals have little choice about their definitions and execution. I do not seek the root(s) of a popular rite or rites in China. Nor do I try to explain why some traditional rites have faded away whereas others are still being practised. Rather, I introduce readers to some major rituals that are related to some key milestones in the life cycle among Han Chinese, who represent roughly 91 per cent of the total population in the People's Republic of China (see Chapter 9): birth and childhood, entry into adulthood, marriage, retirement and old age, and death and memorial ceremonies.

Birth and childhood

For many centuries considerations were given to childbirth before the marriage ceremony, and proactive measures were taken to boost the fertility of the wife after the marriage. In some parts of China, married couples went to the temple to pray to *songzi guanyin*, a goddess who was believed to decide if a couple deserved to have a child or children and made sure that the couple received the child or children. It was considered to be very important for a married couple to produce children to carry the family name into the next generation. In fact, having a child was the most important criterion to judge if a woman was a virtuous wife and if a man was filial. As a Chinese saying goes, *bu xiao you san, wu hou wei da* ('there are three types of upmost un-filial behaviour, among which the worst one is to produce no heir') (Liu and Li 2008: 2). A woman with wide hips was considered to be fertile and hence a desirable bride. A son was much preferred to a daughter to the extent that only the names and achievements of sons were recorded in their family log and clan chronology. Although these beliefs and practices have ceased to prevail especially among the educated urban population, the influence is still sufficient for hospitals not to disclose the gender of the foetus to would-be parents for fear that a female foetus would be aborted.

Unlike the West, it is uncommon in China to throw a baby shower before he or she is born. As a matter of fact, many consider such practice as being a possible jinx. Traditionally, the maternal grandmother prepares the whole layette for the baby before the due date. In some parts of China, she sends a package to her daughter one month before the due date to speed up the delivery, inside which she places a piece of white cloth. After the baby is born, the mother is supposed to wrap the baby in it.

Nowadays, the delivery usually takes place in the hospital. The mother and the new born baby will stay in the hospital from three to seven days. Most Chinese believe that labour greatly weakens a woman's health, and the first month after birth is essential to the health of the mother for the rest of her life. A Chinese woman is encouraged to *zuo yuezi* for one month after childbirth, during which she is supposed to mainly rest and to refrain from all household chores (Liu and Li 2008: 2–4). The paternal grandmother or the maternal grandmother normally comes to help during this critical period of time. Hiring a *yuesao* (women professionally trained to take care of the new mother and the baby) to help is gaining popularity in China. There are a lot of taboos during this month. Traditionally, the new mother was not supposed to shower or wash the hair during *yuezi* for fear that she was too weak to handle the water and that it would result in long-term migraines. She could instead be sponged with certain herbal water. The use of cold water by the mother was prohibited. Modern Chinese women tend to take a mid-way solution. They shower during *yuezi*, but will take extra care not to expose themselves to any cold air. Food is also carefully chosen and prepared for the mother. Cold drinks and uncooked food (such as fruit) are off limits. Food such as fish soup and pig-trotter soup is often prepared, as it is believed that it will help the mother to produce plenty of milk for the baby.

The general practice is that only close relatives such as paternal parents and maternal parents can visit the mother and her baby during the month of *yuezi*. The more distant relatives and friends visit the mother and the baby after the first month, although they probably send gifts beforehand. It used to be the grandparents' responsibility to dispatch cooked eggs dyed with red paper to friends and relatives to celebrate the birth of the child, but this practice is dying out. In many places, new parents hold a large party at the end of the first month and invite all their family and their friends to eat out in a good restaurant.

The baby's first jewellery from his/her parents or grandparents is often a gold or silver necklace called *changeming suo* ('longevity lock'), and bangles around the wrist and/or around his or her ankles. In ancient times, it was difficult for babies to survive due to harsh living conditions and insufficient medical care. Yet infant mortality was often attributed to evil spirits who took life away. Symbolically, the longevity lock was supposed to hold the baby in this world and keep evil spirits away. This practice is observed even in urban China, and the longevity lock is still used today to express the parents' wish that the child will live a long life.

The parents host a large banquet to celebrate the child's first birthday with relatives and friends. It is a tradition to give the child a bowl of *changshou mian* ('longevity noodles') on the birthday as a goodwill gesture that the child will live a long life. The child has his/her longevity noodle again on every birthday for years to come. Another important ritual on the child's first birthday and in fact the highlight is *zhuazhou* ('the choosing ceremony on the first birthday') (Liu and Li 2008: 5–6). The parents prepare an assortment of articles including seal, brushes, abacus, and so on for the child to pick after the birthday banquet. Each of the articles symbolizes a unique career ambition and future occupation. If the baby picks an abacus, for example, the parents and their guests will assert that he/she will be an accountant in adulthood. If the baby picks a seal, the parents and their guests will assert that he/she will become a government official when grown up. This is because the government officials used seals for official documents in ancient China. If the child selects a brush, the parents and their guests will assert that he/she will become a scholar in the future. In one of the Chinese classics, *A Dream of the Red Mansions*, the main male character (Jia Baoyu) picked rouge and powder at his *zhuazhou* ceremony. Later in life, he grew up to be a person who loved mingling with girls. It is said that Mr Qian Zhongshu, the late renowned writer in China, picked a book at his *zhuazhou* ceremony, much to his father's delight. Therefore, he was named *Zhongshu*, meaning 'to like books'. His later achievements made him a strong example for the believers of *zhuazhou*. Today, *zhuazhou* is mostly for fun and the result of *zhuazhou* is no longer taken seriously. The assortment of articles used to vary between boys and girls. Nowadays, boys and girls get the same assortment in most places.

Entry into adulthood

As most Chinese mothers work full time, children are normally sent to kindergartens at a young age. In some families that do not have the help of the grandparents for various reasons, the child can be sent to a kindergarten at one or two years old. Most children go to primary school at the age of six. They stay in the education system for at least nine years. When a child gets admitted to a university, his/her family's friends congratulate his/her parents with gifts in the form of money in a red packet. The parents treat their friends to a big banquet in return. These banquets can go on for several days, if the family is very well connected. Therefore it is difficult to book a table in good restaurants in August when the results of the university matriculation exams are announced.

There used to be rituals marking the passage from childhood to adulthood in imperial China, i.e. the *guan* and the *ji* ceremonies (Liu and Li 2008: 10–11). The *guan* ceremony took place when a young man reached the age of 20. It was organized by a respectable senior relative in his clan's ancestral temple on a carefully chosen, auspicious day. The senior member would coil the young man's hair into a bun, place three caps on his head, and give him an adult name with a nice connotation. The young man was regarded as an adult man and given both responsibilities and rights accordingly after the *guan* ceremony. For example, he would be eligible for marriage and in some cases he would be given or asked to manage part of the family business as an adult member of his family. The equivalent event for a young girl was the *ji* ceremony, which took place when she reached the age of 15. On the day, her hair would be gathered up and fastened with a *ji* ('hairpin'), and she would be given a grown-up name. The young girl was regarded as an adult woman after the *ji* ceremony and would be eligible for marriage. Of course, poor families were less likely than well-off families to hold the *guan* and the *ji* ceremonies for their sons and daughters. Ethnic minority groups in China have their own adulthood ceremonies and many are kept today.

For Han Chinese, the *guan* and *ji* ceremonies are long gone. With the recent interest in Confucian traditions, there have been voices advocating reviving the *guan* and *ji* ceremonies. But an important point is that there are no commonly accepted ceremonies to mark the coming-of-age for Han Chinese today. This has created a major problem for people to identify an age which signifies the entry into adulthood. According to the Chinese Constitution, individuals can cast their votes when they reach 18. However, individuals are not socially regarded in China as independent adults until they are married. The legal age to get married in China is 22 for men and 20 for women. But the legal marriage age cannot be used to indicate the entry into adulthood. Few people actually get married when they reach the legal age for marriage. More and more people marry quite late. This is due to high real estate prices and intense competition for jobs in China. For many Chinese parents, their children are not adults until they are financially independent and have their own dwellings.

Marriage

Marriage is one of the most important events for individuals worldwide. China is no exception. For a woman in traditional China, marrying the right man was considered to be 'as important as a man choosing the right occupation', as a Chinese saying goes. Marriage involves a lot of rituals. It is one of the aspects where traditional rituals in China are rigorously observed in contemporary society.

Match-making was a key partner selection method in traditional China. Since the beginning of the twentieth century, free choices, love, and romance have increasingly become the criteria for partner selection (Chapter 4). However, match-making has not been totally phased out, although it is arranged between the seekers themselves rather than their parents and it takes a more subtle form than before on many occasions. For example, a matchmaker may gather a group of people together with the match seekers to liven up the atmosphere and make the occasion less awkward for them.

In some occasions, even though the couple has already decided to get married, the groom's parents still find a matchmaker to visit the bride's parents to officially ask for their permission for the couple to marry. The matchmaker arranges for the two families to meet and get to know each other over a meal. The groom's family then send betrothal gifts to thank the bride's parents for their efforts in raising the bride. The kinds and amount of betrothal gifts have changed over time. The gifts traditionally included tea, poultry, and so on. Later they became things such as furniture that the couple could use after marriage. When televisions and refrigerators were introduced to China, it was fashionable to use them as the betrothal gifts. At one point, gold jewellery was very popular. Cash has been used for betrothal gifts for some time, and the amount has been on the increase. By accepting the gifts, the bride's parents pledge her to the groom. The bride's parents prepare the dowry for their daughter. This may take the form of a wardrobe in which there are red duvets that normally have phoenix and peony patterns (Liu and Li 2008: 17). The betrothal gifts and the dowry vary a lot from place to place. In most cases it is the outcome of negotiations between the groom's family and the bride's family. Theoretically, the larger betrothal gift is, the more 'face' (respect and esteem) it gives to the bride's family. It is also used by the groom's parents to publicize their wealth and enhance their status in local society. The dowry from the bride's family performs similar social functions.

If the bride and groom choose to join a collective wedding ceremony organized by professional wedding planners, they and their parents have little say over the dates. However, most couples tend to organize their own ceremonies and select their own wedding dates. If both the bride and groom are working professionals, it is likely that they pick a public holiday so that they can have a longer honeymoon combined with their marriage leave. Some couples or their parents check the lunar calendar and select an auspicious day for the wedding. Once the date is set, the two families work out a guest list and send out the wedding invitations which are often in red and gold, but seldom in white. White is the colour of mourning and it does not symbolize purity in traditional Chinese culture. Not everyone in China is ready to embrace the Western tradition of wearing white for weddings. Even if white is worn, it is often toned down by pink or other colours.

The wedding is a very good opportunity to maintain social relations for the families of the bride and the groom. Gifts are given to the groom's parents in the form of a red packet with cash in it. The amount of cash in the red packet varies from a nominal amount to a large sum. It is not deemed as inappropriate to send the gifts before one receives the invitation. The groom's family makes a detailed record of the people from whom they receive gifts, as gift-exchanging is strictly reciprocal in China. They will give gifts of at least the same value back when there is an occasion. As in other cultures, the arrangement of the guests' tables is always a painstaking process as it requires detailed attention to the status of the guests in making seating arrangements. It is common to seat people who know each other or are from the same firm at the same table.

There has been an increasingly popular practice of having one's wedding photos taken by a professional photographer after the marriage is agreed on but normally before the actual wedding ceremony is held. The couple makes an appointment with a photographic studio, which provides makeup artists, hairdressers and a whole selection of costumes for the couple to choose from. The photo-shoots are done both inside the studio and in scenic places recommended by the photographer or chosen by the couple.

The couple must register their intention to marry with the local Bureau of Civil Affairs to make their marriage legally binding. Most couples do so before the wedding ceremony. Two marriage certificates with the couple's photos will be issued. At that point the marriage becomes legal and is fully protected by the Marriage Law of the People's Republic of China. However, most couples, their parents, and other people would like to think that the couple are properly married after the wedding ceremony.

Traditionally, a groom met the bride with a sedan and horse during the wedding day. Some grooms still do so, but this practice is a rarity nowadays. The modern wedding ceremony is a combination of traditional Chinese wedding elements and Western wedding elements. It normally takes place in a grand restaurant. It is a tradition for the groom or his family to prepare and pay for the wedding ceremony. A professional wedding firm is hired to help decorate the restaurant, the wedding car and the marital home. This includes putting up double happiness cut-paper on the doors, windows and other places of the marital home. The traditional colour for weddings is red, so the decorations are mostly in red. The wedding car is also decorated with red rose bouquets and ribbons. But increasingly other colours are also used. The seats in the restaurant have covers which often feature red, pink and gold shades. Since people like to get married on an auspicious day, a restaurant often holds several weddings on the same day. Thus, a big poster with a photo of the bride and the groom and their names is placed in front of a dining hall to make sure the guests arrive at the right venue. There is often a pink arch or a flower arch either outside the restaurant or in front of the platform of the dining hall. The wedding firm will put a triangle-shaped or heart-shaped rack of wine glasses or candles in front of the platform.

Everything on the wedding bed is supposed to be new. The groom's parents will make the bed with red duvet covers, pillowcases and linen. In some places, there is the practice of putting dates, peanuts and walnuts under the corners of the linen because they resemble the words that express good wishes. The dates are there to convey the wish for the new wife to conceive soon. The peanuts signify that both boys and girls will be born and many children will be born out of this marriage. The walnuts symbolize harmony and happiness. On the night before the wedding ceremony, the groom's parents also let boys and girls roll on the bed, again as a good omen that the couple will have both boys and girls.

The wedding ceremonies in China often start in the morning. The bride either has her hair done the night before, or gets up early to have her hair and make-up done. The groom and his attendants including the best man set off early in the wedding car to collect the bride from her parents' home, followed by a procession of cars of the same colour. It is a big show and a matter of 'face' for the bride and the groom, so the groom tends to hire the best cars he can afford. The groom normally arrives at the bride's home at around 10.00am. Firecrackers are set off when he arrives. He will be stopped by the bride's friends including the bridesmaids at the door, who do not 'give away' the bride until they are satisfied by the groom's answers to their questions or requests and until they get red packets of sufficient cash. This is the occasion of much good-natured playing with words and haggling before the two parties can reach an agreement (Liu and Li 2008: 17–18). Once the groom is let into the bride's room, the bridesmaid prepares tea for the couple to serve the bride's parents as a way of showing respect and gratitude to them. The bridesmaid also gives sweet soup to the couple, signifying that they will have a sweet life together. The bride's brother or relatives traditionally carry the bride out of the house, as an indication that the bride is sent away from her maiden home. Now it has gradually become the groom's privilege. In many places, the bride's feet are not supposed to touch the ground all the way from her parents' home to the marital home. Unlike the Western tradition, the bride and the groom are both seated in the wedding car in China.

In the old days, the bride was supposed to be in tears when she left her parents' home, but this is rarely observed nowadays. The wedding costume for the groom is a black suit with a red tie. The traditional costume is in red for the bride, but this has been replaced by a white wedding dress for some brides at the beginning of the wedding ceremony. There is no taboo that the groom shall not see the bride's wedding dress before the wedding ceremony. As a matter of fact, the bride and the groom are very likely to choose the dress together. Unlike the Western tradition, the bride and groom arrive at the restaurant before their guests. They stand at the restaurant door with their parents to greet the guests. The wedding ceremony is hosted by a professional master of ceremonies (MC). After the guests arrive and are seated, the ceremony begins. Rose petals or coloured ribbons will be thrown at the bride and the groom when they walk to the platform. There can be various procedures during the ceremony, according to the MC. One of the activities is that the bride and the groom pour wine into the rack of wine glasses or light candles. This is a new ritual for Chinese weddings, possibly inspired by the cake-cutting ritual at the wedding ceremonies in the West. During the ceremony, the bride serves tea to the groom's parents and addresses them as parents. When this happens, the parents-in-law give the bride a red packet with cash inside. An honoured guest then delivers a congratulatory speech. The ceremony finishes at noon and then the feast starts. This is when the groom's drinking ability is put to test. By then, the bride has changed to a traditional Chinese wedding dress or another type of dress that is more comfortable to walk in. The bride and the groom, accompanied by the brides-maid and the best man, go to each table and make a toast. The bridesmaid

_____ : best man are expected to come to the rescue if the bride and the __n have too much to drink.

After dinner, some young relatives and friends will go to the marital house and start to *nao dongfang*, i.e. 'tease the bride and the groom and play practical jokes on them'. One activity that often occurs is to dangle an apple on a thread, and the bride and the groom are supposed to bite it at the same time. Another one is that the bride and groom give wine to each other at the same time. Traditionally *nao dongfang* was a ritual that was used to gather healthy young people to liven up the room, so that evil spirits would be driven out of the marital house and it would be ready for the wedding night.

Years of calamity

Like the Western Zodiac, Chinese have a cycle of twelve guiding animals: rat, ox, tiger, rabbit, dragon, snake, horse, goat, monkey, rooster, dog, and pig. Unlike the Western Zodiac, the twelve guiding animals rotate on a yearly basis (Wang and Lu 2008: 5–6). The year of one's own guiding animal is one's *benmingnian*. Therefore, people encounter their *benmingnian* at the ages of 12, 24, 36, 48, 60, 72 and so on. It is a common belief that life is not going to be smooth for people in their *benmingnian*. They are more vulnerable to illness and/or other misfortunes, and need to be especially cautious. People are often recommended to wear something red around their waists for protection during their *benmingnian*. A piece of red underwear and a red belt are popular items. Some people also visit the Buddhist or Taoist temples to pray to gods and obtain amulets. Some Taoist priests carry out rituals for people in their *benmingnian* or give instructions for them to conduct certain rituals to eliminate potential misfortunes. With rapid economic growth and rising living standards, Chinese people pay increasing attention to personal health so more and more people are vigilant in their *benmingnian*. The older they are, the more likely they take measures they can afford to protect themselves from potential misfortunes.

Retirement and old age

The majority of the population in China lives in rural areas. They do not have a retirement age since they do not have a pension and are not protected by the government welfare system. Urban workers in the private sector retire from work if they save a sufficient amount of money or if they cannot find a job. Urban employees in state enterprises and government agencies retire at the age of 60 if they are men and at the age of 50 or 55 if they are women. The younger retirement age for women is based partly on the assumption that men are providers and women are homemakers. The Chinese Ministry of Human Resources and Social Security will soon review the retirement age for women in the state sector considering factors including employment situation, gender equity, and social security (Xinhua 2011) for the sake of equality and fairness.

When some state workers retire, they try to find a new job to get some extra income. Others prefer to spend time on leisure activities. A lot of retired people in urban China take the important responsibility of taking care of their grandchildren and doing household chores for their children who work full-time and cannot afford or do not want to hire a maid. For some female senior citizens it is fashionable to practise dancing with a dance group in parks early in the morning and/or in senior citizen entertainment centres in the evenings. Some male senior citizens kill time by learning Chinese chess strategies, tactics and rules, or drinking tea with their friends. There are senior citizen entertainment centres in many cities in China. They provide a good venue for the activities mentioned above. Many retired people, men or women, attend senior colleges. Chinese painting is a popular subject, as it is believed to be able to nurture the soul and help develop a calm temperament. Some retired people take part in charity events and other activities.

The sixtieth birthday is considered a very important one in China. The children will organize a grand dinner to which relatives and some close family friends are invited. Possibly due to the collective nature of Chinese culture, the interests of the parents and the children are closely related to each other. People who wish to maintain a good relationship with the children often send them gifts on their parents' birthdays.

Death and memorial ceremonies

The burial of the deceased is a serious business. Wrong conduct makes the family of the deceased a laughing stock in the local community, and it is even believed to bring bad fortune to the family. Age has an important effect on the choice of the form of the funeral service. If a baby or a child dies, he/she will be buried in silence. No funeral rites will be performed at all. The same applies to an unmarried bachelor. In comparison, a proper funeral is called for when an elderly person dies. His/her children can be accused of being un-filial otherwise. This is where Confucianism still has great influence. The children are supposed to show their complete devotion to their deceased parents by arranging an impressive funeral (Ministry of Culture 2003).

When it is judged that a person has reached his/her last breath, the children or relatives will change him/her into the *shouyi* ('funeral wear'), which has been prepared by the person or his/her children long before the death occurs. *Shouyi* is traditionally brown or blue, but nowadays people accept other colours. Before the burial day, the family decorates the mourning hall in white and black. The deceased's black and white picture is hung on the wall. Bright colours or jewellery are not appropriate for the funeral. The family and relatives wear white linen over their clothes on the burial day. Friends of the deceased and of his/her family come to pay their final respects and express their condolences to the family. When the guests leave, the family and the relatives accompany the urn to the burial place. In some rural places, the procession to the burial place can be a big scene. The family and relatives wrapped in white linen walk in a single file. They are accompanied by musicians that play sad funeral music. In some urban areas, funeral parlours provide places for the urns (Liu and Li 2008: 19–20).

Burial places figure strongly in Chinese *fengshui* culture. A burial place with good *fengshui* is supposed to be able to protect and bring good fortune to the descendants for years to come. There have been numerous stories in Chinese history that people striving to get the throne attempted to demolish the tomb of their rival's ancestor to stop him/her from getting to power. After the urn is buried, the family may burn some coarse white or yellow paper that is supposed to be the currency of the other world. This tradition is kept especially in the rural areas of China. Food and fruit are placed in front of the burial place as a sacrifice.

After the funeral, the family makes a sacrifice every seven days for forty-nine days, which is called *zuoqi* ('to do the sevens'). The fifth seven-day sacrifice is when most rituals take place (Liu and Li 2008: 20–1). During this period, the family hosts a meal for relatives and friends. The family hires Buddhist monks to pray for the deceased's soul. Some people prefer Taoist priests to perform rituals. Another round of sacrifice takes place a hundred days after the death. Then the frequency of the sacrifice reduces to once a year for three years. Most people visit and clean their parents' graves on the annual *Qingming Festival* or *Tomb Sweeping Day*, which varies slightly year by year, but is usually around 4th–6th of April (Liu and Li 2008: 116–18; Wang and Lu 2008: 29–31).

Before 1949, the deceased was buried. Now he/she is normally cremated in a state-run crematorium partly because it is very expensive to buy the burial ground and partly because the government has promoted cremation as a clean and relatively inexpensive way to dispose of the body. Cremated remains are to be buried or immured in memorial sites or cemeteries, or retained by surviving children. All crematoria are run by the government and cremation has become a big business and can be very expensive nowadays.

Conclusion

In this chapter I briefly introduce readers to some milestones in the life cycle among Han Chinese: birth and childhood, entry into adulthood, marriage, retirement and old age, and death and memorial ceremonies. I would like to point out that I discuss the rites in China at a general level. There were different rites for the same life events in China during different historical periods. In addition, rites change over time. Some traditional rites have been handed down, while others such as the *guan* and *ji* ceremonies have faded away from daily life. New rites appear due to exposure to other societies and cultures. It is equally important to point out that not everyone in China observes the same rites. Some people practise some rites but not others, and certain rites are commonly practised in some places but not in others. Differences also exist in terms of age, gender, class, and so on. Ethnic minority groups in China perform different rituals. Nevertheless, it is hoped that this chapter helps readers improve their understanding of Chinese people with some information of the main rituals in Chinese society.

Bibliography

Liu, Fei and Kaiping Li (eds) (2008) *Talk about China in English: Folklore*, Shanghai: Shanghai Popular Science Press.

The Ministry of Culture, People's Republic of China (2003) 'Chinese funeral customs', available at http://www.chinaculture.org/gb/en_chinaway/2004–03/03/content_46092.htm, accessed on March 14, 2011.

Wang, Dejun and Lu Yunfang (eds) (2008) *Talk about China in English: Culture*, Shanghai: Shanghai Popular Science Press.

Xinhua (2011) 'China to review women's retirement age', 2011-02-28, available at http://www.chinadaily.com.cn/china/2011–02/28/content_12084830.htm, accessed on March 14, 2011.

Further reading

Ahern, Emily M. (1973) *The Cult of the Dead in a Chinese Village*, Stanford, CA: Stanford University Press.

Johnson, David (2009) *Spectacle and Sacrifice: The Ritual Foundations of Village Life in North China*, Cambridge, MA: Harvard University Asia Center.

Jones, Stephen (2007) *Ritual and Music of North China: Shawm Bands in Shanxi*, Aldershot: Ashgate.

McLaren, Anne E. (2008) *Performing Grief: Bridal Laments in Rural China*, Honolulu, HI: University of Hawaii Press.

Watson, James L. and Evelyn S. Rawski (eds) (1988) *Death Ritual in Late Imperial and Modern China*, Berkeley, CA: University of California Press.

Wolf, Arthur P. and Chieh-shan Huang (1985) *Marriage and Adoption in China, 1845–1945*, Stanford, CA: Stanford University Press.

Zhou, Shaoming (2009) *Funeral Rituals in Eastern Shandong, China: An Anthropological Study*, Lewiston, NY: Edwin Mellen Press.

Documentaries

Jones, Stephen (2007) *Doing Things: Ceremonial and Music in Rural North China*, SOAS, University of London Arts & Humanities Research Council.

4 Family and marriage

Xiaowei Zang

Chapter 3 discusses some aspects of marriage (especially wedding ceremonies) in China. This chapter examines other aspects of marriage, such as partner selection and divorce. In addition it studies the family institutions in China. There have been profound changes in the family and marriage since the nineteenth century thanks to industrialization, urbanization, the influence of the West, and the political campaigns carried out by the Chinese Communist Party since 1949. Nevertheless, the family has remained a fundamental social unit in Chinese society. Chinese people have continued their reliance on the family to meet the basic human needs of mating, reproduction, the upbringing of children, and the care of the elderly and to respond to new trends in employment, education, housing, etc. The Chinese family institution has been a main research subject in Chinese studies. This chapter introduces readers to some major issues and recent developments in the study of the family and marriage in China.

Family structure and fertility transition

It is widely believed that in traditional China many people lived in large, multi-generation families. A typical extended household is thought to have consisted of five generations living together under one roof, sharing one common purse and one common stove, under one family head. Some scholars have claimed that 'the so called large, extended, or joint form of the family was commonplace' in China (Cohen 1976: xiii). Wolf (1985) found that in nine districts in northern Taiwan between 1906 and 1946, more than 70 per cent of the population lived in stem families in which parents lived with a son, his spouse and his children. Wolf's findings are supported by research on mainland China by Lee and Gjerde (1986) and Lee and Campbell (1998).

Other scholars however have argued that in reality, extended families with five generations living together were rare. Eastman (1988: 16) estimated that the proportion of such extended households might have reached 6 or 7 per cent in the past. Lang (1946: 10) claimed that 'the joint family is not and never was the "normal" type of Chinese family'. Freedman (1979: 235) asserted that the large joint family 'could not have existed as a common form of the family because of the statistical fact that the average size of the domestic family was between five and six souls'. Goode thus contended (1963: 296) that in China, the large multigenerational family appeared to have been 'the ideal exception' and 'a luxury'.

A major reason for the different assessments is data limitation and deficiencies in methodology (Zhao 2000: 266–7). Recent computer microsimulation using both cross-sectional and longitudinal approaches shows that in traditional China, at all specified ages, proportions of individuals who could live in a five-generation household were well below 5 per thousand. Ten per cent of them could live in a household with four or more generations at the time of their birth. Living in a four-generation household seemed rather difficult to achieve (Zhao 2000).

Despite the above-mentioned difficulty, large extended households have persisted into contemporary Chinese society. This is remarkable given the rapid social changes and the family revolution in China since the nineteenth century. Indeed, most urban Chinese have lived in nuclear families since the 1930s. Increasing urbanization and industrialization since 1949 contributed further to the movement towards conjugal family structure. By 1900, over half of urban Chinese families took the nuclear form; by the 1980s this had grown to two-thirds (Zang 1993). Yet extended families with three generations have still constituted a substantive proportion of the households in China: 18.3 per cent and 19.5 per cent in 1990 and 1995, respectively. In 2000, 20.1 per cent of all family households in China had at least one elderly member aged 65 or above (Zeng and Wang 2003). These households have existed because of their usefulness in the provision of care for the elderly by adult children and of childcare and family services by elderly parents.

Despite the persistence of extended households, there has been a reduction in family size since 1949. Households in traditional China are thought to have been fairly large partly because some of them were extended and partly because of high fertility rates. There was a gradual movement towards small family size after 1949 due to the increase in the number of nuclear families. Yet the major change in family size apparently took place after the 1970s. It is found that the average household shrunk in size from 4.5 in 1982 to 3.5 in the early 2000s. One of the main reasons is the rapid and sharp fertility decline – from total fertility rates of approximately six births to two – between 1970 and 1990. At the national level, family size declined to around 1.7 children in 2006; the number is even lower in major metropolitan areas where one child is now the dominant mode of ideal family size. Because of the post-1970 demographic transition, China's fertility has reached a level well below replacement (Cai 2010: 422, 434; also Liu and Zhang 2009; Zheng *et al.* 2009; Retherford *et al.* 2005)

The degree of fertility decline in the 1990s is a subject of controversy, however. According to China's 2000 census, the total fertility rate (TFR) in the year 2000 was 1.22 children per woman. Yet it is widely believed that this estimate is too low, and this underestimate is attributed to fertility underreporting that has plagued China's censuses (Morgan, Guo, and Hayford 2009: 605). Some scholars have asserted that the TFR in 2000 was 1.8 children per woman (Retherford *et al.* 2005: 57). The estimate by the National Bureau of Statistics of China was 1.4 children per woman (Morgan, Guo, and Hayford 2009: 605). Retherford *et al.* (2005) have applied the own-children method of fertility estimation to China's 1990 and 2000 censuses and found that the true level of the TFR in 2000 should be between 1.5 and 1.6 children per woman. Morgan, Guo, and Hayford (2009) found that the TFR was most likely in the range of 1.4 to 1.6 per woman at the turn of the twenty-first century, using data from the 1997 National Population and Reproductive Health Survey and from the 2001 Reproductive Health and Family Planning Survey.

There have also been debates on the main causes of China's demographic transition. Some scholars have argued that China's fertility transition took a different course from that of other societies because of heavy-handed government intervention. In December 1973, the Chinese government introduced a *Wan, Xi, Shao* (晚, 稀, 少) policy that promoted late marriage and low fertility among Chinese people. In 1979–80, it officially launched the one-child policy that each Chinese couple is entitled to only one birth. The one-child programme has been supported by routine surveillance and vigorous enforcement by local governments in both urban neighbourhoods and rural villages (Scharping 2003). Retherford *et al.* (2005) argue that about two-fifths of the decline in the conventional TFR between 1990 and 2000 was accounted for by later marriage, and three-fifths by declining fertility within marriage. Their analysis also included estimates of trends in fertility by urban/rural residence, education, ethnicity, and migration status. Over time, fertility has declined sharply within all categories of these characteristics, indicating that the one-child policy has had large across-the-board effects. It is thus argued that government intervention has played an important role in fertility decline (also Liu and Zhang 2009). It is problematical to discuss the demographic transition without reference to the power and determination of the Chinese government to control China's population growth.

Other scholars, however, have argued that China's current low fertility is not simply a prescribed result of the one-child policy (Chen *et al.* 2009; Zheng *et al.* 2009). For example, China's fertility transition shows the rapid fertility decline under the *Wan, Xi, Shao* programme in the 1970s. Yet when the one-child policy was vigorously enforced in the 1980s, the observed fertility level in China hovered above the replacement level without visible ups and downs, a clear reflection of the difficulties in implementing such a draconian policy. Only in the 1990s did China's fertility drop below the replacement level, where it has remained (Cai 2010: 422; Coale 1989: 834, 839; Morgan, Guo, and Hayford 2009: 608–9).

As another example, Jiangsu province and Zhejiang province have had different fertility policies, yet the pronounced policy difference has not translated into a substantial difference in observed fertility levels between these

Figure 4.1 An urban Uyghur couple with their singleton daughter taken by Xiaowei Zang.

two provinces. Development factors explain a much larger proportion of fertility variation in Jiangsu and Zhejiang than policy factors. After controlling for other factors, the fertility difference between these two provinces is small. The two provinces also have similar variability in fertility at the county level. TFRs in Jiangsu range from 0.69 to 1.49, with a mean of 1.01; and TFRs in Zhejiang range from 0.68 to 1.87, with a mean of 1.15 (Cai 2010: 428, 433). Thus, it is argued that the one-child policy has had some effect on birth rates, but structural changes brought about by socioeconomic development and shifts in values and norms on family behaviour have played a key role in China's fertility reduction. Below-replacement fertility in China, as in other societies, is driven to a great extent by social and economic development (Cai 2010: 422, 435; Morgan, Guo, and Hayford 2009: 624).

China's below-replacement fertility has attracted attention from scholars given its social costs and the long-term demographic effects such as accelerated population aging, distorted sex ratios, and changes to the Chinese family and kinship system. For example, China has experienced an unprecedented rise in the sex ratio at birth (ratio of male to female births). There are simply far more male live births than female live births as compared to the numbers expected in most other human populations. The sex ratio at birth in China was 106.32 in 1975. It rose to 111.14 after 1990, and then climbed to 116.86 after 2000, and reached 120.49 in 2005. The rise of the sex ratio at birth is attributed to fertility decline, the one-child policy, a strong parental desire to have at least one son, and the increasing availability of sex-selection technology (Bhattacharjya *et al.* 2008: 1,832–3; also Liu and Zhang 2009). In a study of two groups of pregnant women in rural Anhui in 1999, it is found that the sex ratio at birth was 152 males to 100 females as reported by the first group of women and 159 males to 100 females as reported by the second group of women. It also found that the risk of death for girls was almost three times that for boys during the first twenty-four hours of life. The study compares the estimated number of missing girls by parity and pregnancy approval status with the abortions and stillbirths. Selective abortions of female foetuses may contribute most to the extremely high sex ratio of males among newborns (Wu, Viisainen, and Hemminki 2006).

A large-scale study of 4,764,512 people in all of China's 2,861 counties showed that sex ratios were high across all age groups, but they were highest in the 1–4 years age group, peaking at 126 in rural areas. Six provinces in China had sex ratios of over 130 in the 1–4 age group. The sex ratio at birth was close to normal for first order births but rose steeply for second order births, especially in rural areas, where it reached 146 (143 to 149). Nine provinces in China had ratios of over 160 for second order births. The highest sex ratios were observed in the provinces that allow rural inhabitants a second child if the first is a girl. Sex-selective abortion accounts for almost all the excess males. One particular variant of the one-child policy, which allows a second child if the first is a girl, leads to high sex ratios. In 2005, males under the age of 20 exceeded females by more than 32 million, and more than 1.1 million excess births of boys occurred (Zhu, Li, and Hesketh 2009). It is estimated that there were 22 million more men than women in the birth cohorts born between 1980 and 2000. Model-based simulations show that 10.4 per cent of these additional men will fail to marry. There will be some 28 million men in 2055 without female partners during their sexually active stages (Ebenstein and Sharygin 2009; Pan and Wu 2009).

There are consequences of the high sex ratio and large numbers of unmarried men such as the well-being of the elderly unmarried men, China's ability to care for its elderly unmarried men, and the prevalence of prostitution and sexually transmitted infections. Research using demographic and behavioural data shows the combined effect of sexual practices, sex work, and a male surplus on HIV transmission across developed parts of China's urban areas. Surplus men could become a significant new HIV risk group in China (Li, Holroyd, and Lau 2010: 402; Zhang *et al.* 2007: 456–7; also Tucker *et al.* 2005). Recent population-based survey estimates suggest levels of untreated chlamydia infection in urban China are as high as or higher than in urban areas in Western developed countries, and levels in rural China are similar to those in rural Africa (Parish *et al.* 2003). Chlamydia is often asymptomatic and goes untreated, which can lead to pelvic inflammatory disease and secondary sterility in China (Morgan, Guo, and Hayford 2009: 620).

Marriage

In most historical Chinese populations, virtually all women were married by age 30 (Coale 1989: 834). In contrast, not all men were married and their marriage age varied widely depending on their financial status. Marriage was not based on love and romance. It was instead conceived as the transfer of a woman from her family to that of her husband. There were widespread practices of buying and selling of women into marriage, forced marriage of widows, and purchasing young girls as future daughters-in-laws (Johnson 1983: 61–87; also Wolf 1980). Another major form of marital union was arranged marriages in which young people had very little say, either about timing or about partners. The bride and the groom did not meet each other until the wedding day. All this gave parents effective control over the marriages of their offspring (Parish and Whyte 1978).

There have been significant changes in the marriage institution in China since the early twentieth century. One study found that the mean age at first marriage increased from about 17.5 years around 1930 to 18.5 in the 1940s, about 20 in 1970, and about 23 in 1980 (Coale 1989: 834). Another study found that about 10 per cent of the Chinese brides during the 1930s were less than fifteen years of age; by 1950 early marriages were reduced significantly. In 1994, the average marriage age for women at first marriage was twenty-three years. Freedom of choice in choosing one's partner has also increased in China since 1900. Proceedings dominated by parents arranged more than half of all marriages between 1900 and 1938; by 1982, arranged marriages almost disappeared. By then, four in every five couples married of their own volition. Many young people found their mates themselves. For others, introduction by co-workers, supervisors, friends, and kin was an important way of getting to know the opposite sex before 1978. These changes have been brought about by the forces of industrialization, urbanization, mass education, and government policy (Zang 1993). Globalization, the Internet, etc. have strengthened the trend towards free love and romance among young people in China. Today, young Chinese men and women enjoy much more freedom in selecting mates than their parents.

However, it is important to point out that love and romance are a necessary but not a sufficient precondition for a lasting relationship in China. One study (Jackson, Chen, Guo, and Gao 2006) found that fairytale ideals were a major theme for young American adults but not for young Chinese adults. Another study (Buss *et al.* 1990) examined thirty-seven countries and found that the Chinese sample differed from other international samples in paying more attention to health, chastity, and domestic skills but giving less value to traits such as mutual attraction, dependability, and sociability. One plausible explanation is that in collectivistic cultures such as China, family-related or group-related characteristics of the potential partner were more important than romantic love (Dion 1993). Not surprisingly, family influence is still important in one's marriage decision in China (Pimentel 2000). A recent study found that parents and friends still had a great influence on marriage decision-making for young Chinese in dating relationships. Young Chinese would place more weight on their family's and friends' opinions rather than on their own views. They agreed that approval by parents, friends, and other family members was important for them to decide if they wanted to marry their lovers (Zhang and Kline 2009).

Status similarity is also an important factor in the choice of a marriage partner. Matchmaking in traditional China was based on the principle of 'one door matches another door'. Today, many marriages are same-status matches. One study found that after the 1980s, individuals increasingly married others similar to them with respect to education. The percentage of couples with the same number of years of schooling increased monotonically from 50 per cent to 65 per cent between the 1985–9 marriage cohort and the 1995–2000 cohort. At the national level there was an overall 15-point increase in the percentage of educational homogamy from 1970 to 2000. The odds of crossing two or three educational barriers were cut in half between 1980 and 2000. For college graduates in urban areas, the odds of marrying junior high school graduates (i.e. crossing two educational barriers) shrank from 0.11 to 0.02, and the chances of marrying a person with less than six years of schooling (i.e. crossing three educational barriers) in the late 1990s were only one tenth of the odds in the late 1970s. There was a greater degree of social closure among college graduates than among other educational groups. Rising spousal resemblance has increased as China's economy has boomed. Increasing rates of resemblance between spouses occur a decade earlier and at a higher level in urban areas than in rural areas (Han 2010).

Sexual norms and behaviour

Similarly, there have been significant changes in sexual norms in China. Sex is no longer a taboo topic as it was before the 1980s. For example, premarital sex was widely opposed and rare before 1978. A high premium was placed on premarital virginity. If an individual was caught in premarital sex, he or she would face serious punishments: mass criticisms and public humiliations, forced confessions, demotions, dismissal, or even a court sentence of imprisonment on a verdict of hooliganism or rape (Cui 1995: 15–18). The rigid control over premarital sex has been gradually undermined since the 1980s thanks to increased exposure to the sex norms of the West and employment in the private sector that does not police employees' private life as the state sector and public educational institutions did before 1978. Today, living together has been accepted as a way of life in urban China. In a large survey conducted on university students in Shanghai (N = 5,067), only 17.7 per cent of the sampled students opposed premarital sex (Chen *et al.* 2008). A study found that of the 4,769 female university students in Ningbo, 29.3 per cent of them admitted having sexual intercourse, and among them 5.3 per cent reported having multiple sex partners (Yan *et al.* 2009). Another study investigated 1,304 out-of-school youths in Shanghai in 2000–2 and found that the majority of them (60 per cent) held favourable attitudes towards premarital sex. Young men were more likely to have favourable attitudes compared with young women. Young men generally did not communicate with either parent about sex, whereas one-third of female youths talked to their mothers about sexual matters. Both young men and women chose their friends as the person with whom they were most likely to talk about sexual matters. About 18 per cent of the sampled respondents reported having engaged in sexual intercourse. One quarter of them had been pregnant or had impregnated a partner (Wang *et al.* 2007).

One main reason why unexpected pregnancy occurs is the limited knowledge of contraception young Chinese women received from their parents, teachers, and society at large. A 2007 study conducted in Beijing found that the majority of the pregnant teenagers scored less than 10 on a 20-point scale on contraceptive knowledge. Only 24.5 per cent of them obtained contraceptive knowledge from school or parents; the most common source of contraceptive information came from their friends, the Internet, and the media. Some 11.3 per cent of the pregnant teenagers considered it unnecessary to obtain contraceptive knowledge. Less than 53 per cent of the pregnant teenagers reported using contraceptives at their first sexual encounter (Wu 2010).

Another example of the changes in sexual norms in China is the official attitude towards homosexuality in the post-1978 era. Sexual behaviour among members of the same sex (mostly among men) was suppressed after the establishment of the People's Republic in 1949. It was officially defined as a mental illness, and the individuals who had been caught engaging in homosexual acts were publicly prosecuted as criminals before 1978. Partly because of the influence from the West, Chinese society has become more tolerant towards homosexuality (Li, Holroyd, and Lau 2010: 406, 410). In 1997, the Chinese criminal code was revised to eliminate the vague crime of 'hooliganism'. The *Chinese Classification of Mental Disorders* formally removed homosexuality from its list of mental illnesses on April 20, 2001. One mass survey conducted in 2000 found that among the 10,792 respondents, less than 31 per cent were against homosexuality; the rest were either indifferent towards or in favour of it.[1]

An article published on China.org.cn in 2001 suggested that the total number of homosexuals in China was between 360,000 and 480,000, with the majority of them being men.[2] However, an article published in *The China Daily* in 2004 claimed that male homosexuals, seen in public places such as gay bars, parks, and public baths, accounted for 0.9 per cent of all grown men between 15 to 55. The number of male homosexuals in China was estimated to be between 5 million and 12.5 million (the number of female homosexuals is unknown, but it is likely to be fewer than that of males).[3] One possible explanation of the two different estimates is that more and more Chinese gays and lesbians have come to terms with and thus publicly acknowledged their sexual identities. For example, a study conducted in Harbin between 2002 and 2006 reported an increased trend towards more people identifying as homosexual in the city during the period of the study (Zhang *et al.* 2007).

Drawing on her research over the past two decades among urban residents and rural migrants in Hangzhou and Beijing, Rofel (2007) argued that the emergence of homosexual identities and practices in China is tied to transnational networks of gay men and lesbians in certain critical respects. Chinese homosexual identities materialize in the articulation of transcultural practices with intense desires for cultural belonging or cultural citizenship in China. However, Rofel was critical of the Western developmental narrative which suggests that gay men in China will soon 'catch up' with the level of liberation and politicization of gay men in the West. Rofel argues that gay identities in China emerge in relation to specific desires for cultural citizenship within China. In other words, national and cultural context are inextricably tied to articulations of gay identity.

Li *et al.* (2010), heterosexual marriage is still regarded as a cultural imperative in China. There is still a lack of political sensitivity towards sexual minorities despite increasing tolerance towards homosexuality. Chinese gay men's understanding of their gender, sexual identity and sexual practices is not radically divorced from discourse on heterosexuality in China. Being a Chinese man is normatively culturally accorded to marriage and procreation to maintain the family bloodline. How do Chinese gay men construct their sexual identities to maintain sexual and emotional attraction to men in an overwhelmingly heterosexual environment? How do they cope with the cultural imperative of heterosexual marriage, normative family obligations, socially desired gender roles, emotional experiences and a need for social belonging? A study conducted in Guangzhou found that Chinese gay men had developed four types of sexual identities: establishing a non-homosexual identity, accumulating an individual homosexual identity, forming a collective homosexual identity, and adopting a flexible sexual identity. They practised different levels of involvement in same-sex activities and emotional attachment, social belonging to homosexual groups, and independent homosexual lifestyle. The more they got involved, the clearer homosexual identities appeared to be articulated. For these Chinese gays, sexual identity was both fluid and fragmented, derived from highly personalized negotiations between individualized needs and social and cultural constructs.

Marital breakdown

In imperial China, a husband could expel his wife or terminate his marriage to her on several grounds: barrenness, wanton conduct, neglect of husband's parents, loquacity, theft, jealousy, and chronic illness. The wife's legal protection derived from first, the claims to full membership of her marital family after observing three years of mourning for her parents-in-law, second, the fact that a wife had gone through adversity with her husband (e.g. from rags to riches), and third, the fact that a wife had no natal home to return to. The wife could apply to the courts for the dissolution of her marriage on a limited list of grounds: if her husband had deserted her for a prolonged period, seriously injured her, forced her into illicit sex, or tried to sell her to another man. But she could never terminate the marriage on her own in the manner her husband could. A traditional Chinese saying goes: 'If a woman marries a rooster, she follows the rooster for her lifetime; if she marries a dog, she follows the dog for her lifetime.' Although only men were entitled to initiate divorce proceedings, they were not always ready to do so due to strong cultural norms and associated social pressures, which were reinforced by the high costs associated with divorce and remarriage (Huang 2001).

After 1949, new marriage laws altered the legal context for divorce and empowered women, and social change redefined the social nature of married life. In 1953, China experienced a major surge in divorces, probably due to the promulgation of the Marriage Law in 1950. It was popularly maintained that many government officials, who had been penniless peasants before joining the communist revolution, divorced their rural wives to marry urban women. Yet more importantly, the 1950 Marriage Law allowed women to initiate divorce proceedings for the first time in Chinese history. Some married women, who were urban residents, had more education, and had their mar-riages arranged by parents, used divorce as a way out of their marriages. In southern China, for example, 49 per cent of the divorce applicants were between 18 and 25 years old. In 1950, three-quarters of the divorce cases in Shandong were brought by the wives. In 1951, women took the first step in 76 per cent of the divorce applications in thirty-two cities and thirty-four rural countries. There were '186,167 divorces in 1950, 409,500 in 1951, and 398,243 in the first half of 1952.' The courts handled 1.7 million peti-tions in 1953. The 1950 Marriage Law was thus called 'divorce law' (Platte 1988: 430–2, 441–2). After the mid-1950s, divorces became less frequent. For example, divorce suits handled by the courts in Beijing remained at around 7,000 per annum until the mid-1960s (Platte 1988: 433).

Another major surge of divorces occurred during the Cultural Revolution (1966–76). The impact of the Cultural Revolution on divorce is difficult to assess with accuracy because of the lack of data. The extraordinary social upheavals and fear of persecution often led one partner to ask for a divorce when the other got into political trouble. The implications for the whole family of one member's political wrongdoing were potentially disastrous. Divorce proceedings were initiated not because of a lofty sense of ideological outrage against the offending spouses but for the purpose of social survival and protection of the children's future (Conroy 1987: 55–6; Liang and Shapiro 1983).

Divorce has been on the upswing in China after economic reforms started in 1978 (Platte 1988). Nationwide, the divorce rate was 0.03 per cent in 1979, 0.07 per cent in 1990 and roughly 0.1 per cent in 2000, climbing to 0.21 per cent in 2003.[4] The number of couples divorcing has been rising steadily after the revised Regulation on Marriage Registration took effect in 2003. Couples now can seek divorces at civil affairs offices instead of dealing with complicated court procedures The Ministry of Civil Affairs in June 2010 reported an annual rise of 7.6 per cent in the number of divorces from 2005 to 2009, with 2.47 million couples divorcing in 2009.[5] Some 800,000 Chinese couples got divorced during the first half of 2010. During the same period, an average of 5,000 couples separated each day.[6]

There are three major forms of marriage dissolution in China today. The first one is divorce by mutual consent, or divorce by agreement, by registering at civil affairs bureaus. The second form is divorce by court mediation. The third is divorce by court verdict. The government in general and the court in particular seek to preserve the conjugal family against light-hearted decisions to separate. A court verdict is used as the last resort when all other efforts to mediate the couple are exhausted and fail (Platte 1988: 435–6). But it has become increasingly difficult for the court to mediate and persuade the couple to withdraw their divorce application.

The main causes of marital breakdown in China include the failure to deliver emotional support or a gratifying sexual relationship, family violence, the fading of romantic love after marriage, extramarital affairs, etc. All these are said to have contributed to the rising divorce rate. Some scholars have argued that social changes will lead to a further increase in divorce rates in China. Others however have claimed that Chinese cultural traditions and the laws concerning divorce would contribute to the low divorce level in China, relative to Western countries, at least for the foreseeable future.

Conclusion

This chapter outlines family and marriage institutions in China. It examines the post-1949 changes in family structure, family size, marriage, partner choices, sexual norms and practices, and marital breakdowns. While industrialization, economic growth, the spread of mass education, and urbanization in the post-1949 era have been partly responsible for these drastic changes, political campaigns and legal reforms carried out by the CCP to transform Chinese society have also played a major role in the transformation of family and marriage institutions in the PRC. China's market reforms and integration into the global capitalist system have allowed an increasing impact of globalization on Chinese society. Future changes in the family system are anticipated.

Notes

1 'Chinese Society More Tolerant of Homosexuality', available at http://www. china.org.cn/english/2001/Oct/21394.htm, accessed on November 20, 2010.
2 Ibid.

3   Zhang Feng, 'Male homosexuals estimated up to 12.5m', 2004-12-02, available at http://www.chinadaily.com.cn/english/doc/2004–12/02/content_396559.htm, accessed on November 22, 2010.
4   'Divorce cases in China skyrocketing', October 4, 2010, *Thaindian News*, available at http://www.thaindian.com/newsportal/south-asia/divorce-cases-in-china-skyrocketing_100438879.html, accessed on November 28, 2010.
5   'Rise of divorce cases in China alarming: Report', October 4, 2010, *The Times of India*, available at http://timesofindia.indiatimes.com/world/china/Rise-of-divorce-cases-in-China-alarming-Report/articleshow/6683163.cms, accessed on November 28, 2010.
6   'Divorce on the Rise in China', 2010-10-05, CRIENGLISH.com, available at http://english.cri.cn/6909/2010/10/05/1461s597782.htm, accessed on November 28, 2010.

Bibliography

Bhattacharjya, Debarun, Anant Sudarshan, Shripad Tuljapurkar, Ross Shachter, and Marcus Feldman (2008) 'How can economic schemes curtail the increasing sex ratio at birth in China?' *Demographic Research*, 19(1): 831–50.
Buss, David M. *et al.* (1990) 'International preferences in selecting mates', *Journal of Cross-Cultural Psychology*, 21(1): 5–47.
Cai, Yong (2010) 'China's below replacement fertility', *Population and Development Review*, 36(3): 419–40.
Chen, Bin, Yong-Ning Lu, Hong-Xiang Wang, Qing-Liang Ma, Xiao-Ming Zhao, Jian-Hua Guo, Kai Hu, Yi-Xin Wang, Yi-Ran Huang, and Pei Chen (2008) 'Sexual and reproductive health service needs of university/college students', *Asian Journal of Andrology*, 10(4): 607–15.
Chen, Jiajian, Robert D. Retherford, Minja Kim Choe, Xiru Li, and Ying Hu (2009) 'Province level variation in the achievement of below-replacement fertility in China', *Asian Population Studies*, 5(3): 309–27.
Coale, Ansley J. (1989) 'Marriage and childbearing in China since 1940', *Social Forces*, 67(4): 833–50.
Cohen, Myron (1976) *House United, House Divided*, New York: Columbia University Press.
Conroy, Richard (1987) 'Patterns of divorce in China', *Australian Journal of Chinese Affairs*, 17: 53–75.
Cui, Lili (1995) 'Sex education no longer taboo', *Beijing Review,* April 3–16: 15–18.
Dion, Karen K. and Kenneth L. Dion (1993) 'Individualistic and collectivistic perspectives on gender and the cultural context of love and intimacy', *Journal of Social Issues,* 49(3): 53–9.
Eastman, Lloyd E. (1988) *Family, Fields, and Ancestors: Constancy and Change in China's Social and Economic History, 1550–1949*, New York: Oxford University Press.
Ebenstein, Avraham and Ethan Jennings Sharygin (2009) 'The consequences of the "missing girls" of China', *World Bank Economic Review*, 23(3): 399–425.
Freedman, Maurice (1979) 'The Chinese domestic family: Models', pp. 235–9 in Maurice Freedman, *The Study of Chinese Society*, Stanford, CA: Stanford University Press.
Goode, William (1963) *World Revolution and Family Patterns*, New York: Free Press.

Han, Hongyun (2010) 'Trends in educational assortative marriage in China from 1970 to 2000', *Demographic Research*, 22: 733–70.

Huang, Philip C. C. (2001) 'Women's choices under the law: marriage, divorce, and illicit sex in the Qing and the Republic', *Modern China*, 27(1): 3–58.

Jackson, Todd, Hong Chen, Cheng Guo, and Xiao Gao (2006) 'Stories we love by', *Journal of Cross-Cultural Psychology*, 37(4): 446–64.

Johnson, Kay Ann (1983) *Women, the Family, and Peasant Revolution in China*, Chicago: University of Chicago Press.

Lang, Olga (1946) *Chinese Family and Society*, New Haven, CT: Yale University Press.

Lee, James Z. and Cameron D. Campbell (1998) 'Headship succession and household division in three Chinese banner serf populations, 1789–1909', *Continuity and Change*, 13(1): 117–41.

Lee, James and Jon Gjerde (1986) 'Comparative household morphology of stem, joint, and nuclear household systems', *Continuity and Change*, 1(1): 89–111.

Li, Haochu, Eleanor Holroyd, and Joseph T. F. Lau (2010) 'Negotiating homosexual identities', *Culture, Health & Sexuality*, 12(4): 401–14

Liang, Heng, and Judith Shapiro (1983) *Son of the Revolution*, New York: Knopf/Random House.

Liu, Tao and Xing-yi Zhang (2009) 'Ratio of males to females in China', *British Medical Journal*, 338, article number: b483.

Morgan, S. Philip, Guo Zhigang, and Sarah R. Hayford (2009) 'China's below-replacement fertility', *Population and Development Review*, 35(3): 605–29.

Pan, Yuanyi and Jianhong Wu (2009) 'Population profiling in China by gender and age: implication for HIV incidences', *BMC Public Health*, 9(S9): Suppl. 1.

Parish, William and Martin Whyte (1978) *Village and Family in Contemporary China*, Chicago: University of Chicago Press.

Parish, William L., Edward O. Laumann, Myron S. Cohen, Suiming Pan, Heyi Zheng, Irving Hoffman, Tianfu Wang, and Kwai Hang Ng (2003) 'Population based study of chlamydial infection in China', *Journal of the American Medical Association*, 289(10): 1265–73.

Pimentel, Ellen Efron (2000) 'Just how do I love thee?' *Journal of Marriage and the Family*, 62(1): 32–48.

Platte, Erika (1988) 'Divorce trends and patterns in China: Past and present', *Pacific Affairs*, 61(3): 428–45.

Retherford, Robert, MinjaKim Choe, Jiajian Chen, Xiru Li, and Hongyan Cui (2005) 'How far has fertility in China really declined?' *Population and Development Review*, 31(1): 57–84.

Rofel, Lisa (2007) *Desiring China: Experiments in Neoliberalism, Sexuality and Public Culture*, Durham, NC: Duke University Press.

Scharping, Thomas (2003) *Birth Control in China, 1949–2000*, London: Routledge.

Tucker J. D., Gail Henderson, Tian Wang, Ying Huang, William Parish, Sui Pan, Xiang Chen, and Myron Cohen (2005) 'Surplus men, sex work, and the spread of HIV in China', *AIDS*, 9(6): 539–47.

Wang, Bo, *et al.* (2007) 'Sexual attitudes, pattern of communication, and sexual behavior among unmarried out-of-school youth in China', *BMC Public Health*, 7: 189.

Wolf, Arthur P. (1980) *Marriage and Adoption in China, 1845–1945*, Stanford, CA: Stanford University Press.

Wolf, Margery (1985) *Revolution Postponed*, Stanford, CA: Stanford University Press.

Wu, Liping (2010) 'A survey on the knowledge, attitude, and behavior regarding contraception use among pregnant teenagers in Beijing, China', *Clinical Nursing Research*, 19(4): 403–15.

Wu, Zhuochun, Kirsi Viisainen, and Elina Hemminki (2006) 'Determinants of high sex ratio among newborns', *Reproductive Health Matters*, 14(27): 172–80.

Yan, Hong, Weiqi Chen, Haocheng Wu, Yongyi Bi, Miaoxuan Zhang, Shiyue Li, and Kathryn L. Braun (2009) 'Multiple sex partner behavior in female undergraduate students in China', *BMC Public Health*, 9: article number 30.

Zang, Xiaowei (1993) 'Household structure and marriage in urban China: 1900–1982', *Journal of Comparative Family Studies*, 24(1): 35–43.

Zeng, Yi and Zhenglian Wang (2003) 'Dynamics of family and elderly living arrangements in China', *The China Review*, 3(2): 95–119.

Zhang, Dapeng, (2007) 'Changes in HIV prevalence and sexual behavior among men who have sex with men in a northern Chinese city: 2002–6', *Journal of Infection*, 55(5): 456–63.

Zhang, Shuangyue and Susan L. Kline (2009) 'Can I make my own decision?' *Journal of Cross-Cultural Psychology*, 40(1): 3–23.

Zhao, Zhongwei (2000) 'Coresidential patterns in historical China: a simulation study', *Population and Development Review*, 26(2): 263–93.

Zheng, Zhenzhen, Yong Cai, Wang Feng, and Gu Baochang (2009) 'Below-replacement fertility and childbearing intention in Jiangsu province, China', *Asian Population Studies*, 5(3): 329–47.

Zhu, Wei Xing, Li Lu, and Therese Hesketh (2009) 'China's excess males, sex selective abortion, and one child policy', *British Medical Journal*, 338: article number b1211.

Related novels and autobiographies

Fu, Shen (1983) *Six Records of a Floating Life*, Harmondsworth: Penguin Classics.

Mo Dun (1992) *Rainbow*, University of California Press.

Pa, Chin (1972) *Family*, New York: Anchor.

Films and documentaries

Jones, Stephen (2007) *Doing Things – Ceremonial And Ritual In North China*, Department of Music, School of Oriental and African Studies, University of London.

Yang, Mayfair (1997) *Through Chinese Women's Eyes*, Women Make Movies, 462 Broadway, Ste. 500W, New York.

Zhou, Xiaoli and Brent E. Huffman (2006) *The Women's Kingdom*, Women Make Movies, 462 Broadway, Ste. 500W, New York.

5   Gender and sexuality

Jieyu Liu

Following the mainstream acknowledgement of the Feminist movement in the early 1970s, gender is now widely recognized as one of the key concepts in understanding society. Whilst difficult to define, gender in social science is generally acknowledged to be 'denoting a hierarchical division between women and men embedded in both social institutions and social practices' (Jackson and Scott 2002: 1). Gender significantly influenced the way in which Chinese society was organized in pre-modern China and continues to do so today. Gender shapes various aspects of life in China, such as family (see Zang Chapter 4), work, education and political participation.

Sexuality, whilst closely affected by the gender system in a society, focuses upon a more specific aspect of life, i.e. organization and experiences around sex. Rather than being a 'natural' construct, it is widely accepted that sexuality is socially organized through various institutions such as family and education, and maintained by various discourses (such as religion and science) that tell us what sex is, what it ought to be and what it could be (Weeks 1986).

Since gender and sexuality are experienced as social structural phenomena, as well embodied and lived in everyday interactions, the examination of these concepts sheds light onto various aspects of Chinese lives in both public and private domains. This chapter starts by examining the historical context of gender and sexuality in China; then focuses upon gender transformation in the twentieth century with a close examination of gender relations at work; finally the chapter explores sexuality in contemporary China including issues such as intimacy, sex and economy, and homosexuality.

Historical context of gender and sexuality

Throughout much of pre-modern history Chinese rulers adopted Confucianism as the core principle for regulating society, that is, everybody should know and behave in accordance with their position in society to achieve a harmonious and hierarchical order. Unfortunately for women, they were located at the bottom of this hierarchy. The idea of *Nanzunnübei* (that 'women are inferior to men') served as the code for women's conduct in society, exemplified by prescriptions such as the *Sancong* (the 'Three Obediences'), which dictated that women were subject to the authority of their father when young, their husband when married and their son when widowed (see Min 1997). In essence, Confucianism prescribed a patriarchal, patrilineal, and patri-local family system where men officially dominated women (Ebrey 1993; Mann 2001).

For the male patriarch it was important to maintain familial lineage where the living respected ancestors and present elders, and familial continuity was maintained by producing male heirs. To continue a family line, if the first wife failed to produce a son, a concubine might be purchased in the hope she would bear a male heir (in many wealthy families concubinage was a common part of family life) (Mann 2001). The cornerstone of this system was that marriage and sexuality existed to build future generations, with love and pleasure secondary to this (Barlow 1991).

Whilst it was accepted that a man would have various sexual partners throughout his life, female fidelity was crucial because one of the best feminine virtues prescribed by Confucian writings was for a woman to have only one man in her life. Widows who refused to remarry, even when pressured by their parents or parents-in-law, were singled out for praise in contemporary accounts of exemplary women, published either as independent volumes or as chapters in dynastic histories (Mann 1987). Indeed, even if a woman was raped, suicide was an accepted approach for the maintenance of her virtue.

The subordination of women was considered essential for the preservation of social stability and civilization itself in pre-modern China (Watson and Ebrey 1991). One of the ways in which gendered norms of sexual control were structurally reinforced was through the segregation of boys and girls from the middle years of childhood. Whilst females were confined to the 'inside'/domestic sphere, excluded from public life, and denied access to education or eligibility for examinations, males were given free rein to explore and dominate the 'outside'/wider world. As a result of this distinction, *nei ren* ('inside person') came to be the common term for a wife (Watson and Ebrey 1991).

Some have argued that in reality the Confucian patriarchal arrangement was less negative than feminist historical interpretation might imply (Mann 2001; Wolf 1985; Watson and Ebrey 1991). The husband gained sexual access to his wife and his patriline gained claims to her labour and the children she would bear. The wife gained financial security via a claim to her husband's estate and also a place of honour in ancestral rites. A few women of the largest, wealthiest families were even able to have significant influence through management of household funds and control over female relatives and servants (Mann 2001). More commonly, when a wife successfully gave birth to a male heir, her status in her family would rise, or when her son got married she would earn the right to oversee her daughter-in-law. It is noted, however, that whatever powers women obtained in pre-modern China, these were not theirs by right but delegated to them by men and circumstance (Wolf 1985). For example, whilst imperial legal codes granted a mother the same authority over her children as a father, the mother derived this right through her capacity as a wife; and if there was a conflict of views the father's will would always prevail (Mann 1987). Such power dynamics were also demonstrated in the film *Raise the Red Lantern* (Zhang 1993).[1] Although the background was set in the early twentieth century, the film offered a view of life in a closed patriarchal household of wealth in pre-modern China. The film described the shifting balance of power between various concubines in their struggle to improve their standing in the household. While the film showed how easily the master could be manipulated by his concubines, it was evident that the power a concubine could command was closely derived from her capacity to gain the master's favour. Further, bearing a male child played a more critical role than a woman's beauty and sexual appeal in her position in the household.

Gender transformation in the twentieth century

At the start of twentieth century, many contemporary intellectuals began to question Confucianism as they sought to explain China's constrained modernization and the inferiority which had allowed European powers to take effective control of key parts of the country. These intellectuals regarded the unequal status of women as one of the key obstacles to Chinese development and promoted ideas such as free marriage and women's education.[2]

At the same time, the engagement with Western scientific discourse persuaded many Chinese intellectuals to prioritize a biological determinist approach to the understanding of gender (Zheng 2009). As a result of the alleged superiority of modern science, the belief that gender roles were determined by biological differences and gender hierarchy was 'natural and progressive' was firmly legitimized (Dikotter 1995: 9). This biological determinist understanding persisted in the Mao and post-Mao eras (Evans 1997; Gilmartin *et al.* 1994; Jacka 1997; Ko and Wang 2006; Liu 2007; Zheng 2009).

The founders of the Chinese Communist Party (CCP) tried to promote the liberation of women. Whilst the rural focus of Party campaigns from the 1930s onwards meant that liberation was often subordinated by other revolutionary goals (e.g. campaigns to end wife-beating and ban arranged marriages needed to be carefully weighed against the need to win the support of peasant men) the CCP firmly believed that women's emancipation would be realized through their full-time participation in paid work outside the home (Davin 1976). Indeed, when the CCP came to power in 1949, to introduce a new ideology of gender equality, it legislated on issues such as marriage, labour, and land. The All-China Women's Federation, a government department, was set up specifically to deal with women's issues (Croll 1983; Davin 1976). It is widely acknowledged that these actions genuinely improved women's status and quality of life.

In keeping with Marxist theory, which locates gender issues within class struggle (Landes 1989), the CCP's attempt to uphold women's interests was subordinated to an extent by other prioritized efforts in building the socialist nation. For example, women were called upon to return home and be good housewives in the early 1960s when there was mass unemployment (Andors 1983). As a result of competing interests, the Women's Federation often struggled with its role of assistant to the CCP's central work and with the role of protector of women's interests (Jin 2001). During the Cultural Revolution (1966–76), class issues took precedence and, despite slogans such as 'women hold up half the sky' and 'what men can do, women can do', hardly any official attention was given to women's issues (Honig 2002).[3] After Chairman Mao's death in 1976 China adopted an approach to socialist construction that was centred on economic modernization and, with gender equality subsumed by this priority, discrimination against women proliferated (Honig and Hershatter 1988), as discussed below.

Gender and work

Gender has been shaping various aspects of life in China, such as family (see Chapter 4), work, education and political participation. Since the mobilization of women into paid work was among the top gender campaigns after 1949, this section will focus upon the changes in the workplace to critically evaluate the gender transformations in the latter half of the century. As a result of the state's mobilization, paid employment became a normative feature of urban women's lives in the Maoist era (Wang 2000).[4] Research has shown that women born under socialism (post-1949) established a full-time working identity and that for these women it was far less acceptable to be a housewife (Liu 2007; Wang 2001). Moreover, by earning a wage that was central to the family budget, urban women were able to more readily achieve parity with men in the family decision-making process (Jankowiak 2002). Similarly, in rural areas, women were expected to join in with collective labour and such work relationships equipped them with wider social networks that went beyond their own family (Hershatter 2002).

Despite redefining the boundary between household and social production, a focused examination of employment conditions found that gender segregation persisted in workplaces. For example, in urban areas the division between 'heavy' industry and 'light' industry was formulated along the gender line: according to the 1990 census, in light industries (e.g. leather-making and textiles) women comprised 70 per cent of workers, but less than 20 per cent in heavy industries (e.g. construction and metal processing) (Liu Dezhong and Niu Bianxiu 2000). Given the wages of light industries were much lower than those in heavy industries (Liu 2007) such segregation had gendered economic consequence. National representative data (from 1988 to 1994) also confirmed that overt wage discrimination between men and women performing similar work was limited, and that the main source of wage inequality was the concentration of women workers in low-paying sectors of China's economy (Maurer-Fazio *et al.* 1999). In rural regions, men received more work points[5] because they were considered to be undertaking 'heavy work' despite the fact that the division between heavy labour and light labour could be flexible and arbitrary (Jacka 1997). This gendered division of labour was premised upon a 'natural' difference between men and women and that women's 'weak' physique was best suited to 'light' work and so links back to the biological determinist understanding that gained attention during the republican era and was noted above.

The mobilization of women into the workplace did not exempt them from their more traditional duties, such as being a good wife and mother. Although men were called upon to do a share of domestic work, research has shown that women continued to spend far more time undertaking domestic tasks (Research Institute of All China's Women's Federation *et al.* 1998: 473, Table 9.1). The stronger cultural association of women and family meant that women entered social production on unequal terms to male workers, and through a vicious circle of devoting more time to domestic duties, reinforced the workplace gender hierarchy. Contemporary narratives of urban industrial women workers show that, unlike their male counterparts, women suffered from time poverty, juggling work and family duties, and this made it difficult for them to invest time in cultivating social connections that would benefit their career (Liu 2007). Rural studies demonstrated the double burden upon women affected their ability to earn work points and be active in political campaigns (Andors 1983; Hershatter 2004).

The *danwei* was the work and residential unit fundamental to social organization in urban China prior to the 1990s and has continued to be an important organizer of work and life in the post-1990 era. The distinctive familial organization of the *danwei* played a special part in perpetuating gender ideology and practices (see Lui 2007). For example, the *danwei* maintained the traditional practice of men providing the house in marriage as only male workers were eligible for housing application. Such gendered housing allocation reinforced the traditional idea of female dependency in family life and made marriage materially necessary for women. It also made women more vulnerable if any marital problems arose. Although theoretically rendered obsolete by socialism, Confucian familial protocols were in fact 'redeployed in various forms in daily practice of *danwei*'s control' (Liu 2007: 141). The gender inequalities which women workers had experienced eventually exploded into overt discrimination during the reform period. Without the state's rhetorical protection, women were thrown into the market. Middle-aged and older women workers in particular were more prone to lose their jobs and bore the brunt of economic restructuring (Liu 2007; Wang 2000).

In the countryside, from the 1980s collective farming was displaced by a return to family farming, which meant that women's labour was once again controlled by the head of the household (Davin 1999; Jacka 1997). Because restrictions on rural-urban migration reduced, men and young women left the countryside for better paid jobs in cities. Older and married women continued to run low-profit agricultural businesses whilst having limited access to the micro-financial loans initiated by the government (see Jacka 1997; Judd 1994).

Among the rural-urban migration of today, gender continues to play an important role. As a result of the gendered expectation in marriage and family, marriage cut short women migrants' working life whilst enabling men to migrate since the wife was expected to look after the household in the countryside (Fan 2007). Further, male migrants are mainly found working on construction sites, whilst young migrant women mainly work as domestic workers, waitresses and assemblers in foreign-owned factories (Tan 2000). Overall, economic reforms have improved living standards immensely; however, the effects of these reforms have been felt differently according to age, location, social hierarchy and their intersections with gender.

Sexuality in contemporary China

The Confucian emphasis on family and lineage meant that in pre-modern China sexuality was prioritized to ensure procreation of the next generation. The communist revolution in 1949 brought many challenges to Confucian ideologies and rearranged many aspects of social life, including sexual relations. Whilst journalistic reports tend to view the Mao regime as puritanical and the following reform era encompassing a sexual revolution (Jeffreys 2006), research findings question a simple dichotomy between the repression of the Maoist era and the apparent liberalization of the post-Mao period (Hershatter 1996; Evans 1997, 2000). In order to capture the changes and continuities in organization and experiences around sex that have taken place in China, the following section discusses issues such as sexuality in intimate relations, sex and economy and homosexuality to unfold the complexity of the sexuality picture.

Sexuality in intimate relationships

The 1950 Marriage Law outlawed concubinage and arranged marriages; free-choice marriage became the expected norm for families in socialist China (Chapter 4). Pan (1994) highlighted that as a result of this law, the role of love became gradually important in marriage. With the introduction of the one-child policy in 1979, the traditional equation of sex with procreation was fundamentally undermined. Sigley (1998) showed that with the aim of promoting the one-child policy, there was abundant official literature to highlight the pleasurable aspects of marital sexual relations.

Free-choice marriage and family were promoted and established as the main site where sexual equality might be achieved. Whist the heterosexual marital unit became normalized in terms of sexual relations, this excluded and deviated other forms of relationship such as premarital sex and homosexuality (Jeffreys 2006). Evans (1997, 2000) discussed the significant gendered consequences of the official discourses on sexuality. Despite the rhetoric of equality, women were still defined in 'scientific' terms as essentially different from and less sexual than men. In this monogamous picture, women were represented as the principal targets and agents of sexual morality and reasonability; and so the double standard implicit in the Confucian principle of female chastity was recast in gender-specific identification of female responsibility for the maintenance of social and sexual morality (Evans 1997, 2000). Despite the abundance of sexual representations since the 1980s, neither the popular nor official discourses have tackled sexuality as a gender issue and so the view that 'nature subjects women to lives dominated either by male or reproductive concerns continues to permeate' (Evans 1997: 219–20).

Although a wife is obligated to support her husband's interests and serve his needs, sexuality can also function as a site to enact resistance. During an ethnographic study of an urban setting in the 1980s, Jankowiak (1993) found that women had some say in the frequency of intercourse in marriage. If a wife felt satisfied with her marriage, she was more than cooperative to her husband's advances; if not, she rejected the advances either directly or with excuses (e.g. sleeping with a child in order to avoid her husband). Jankowiak (2002) also pointed out the variation of male sexual techniques by social class with the educated men putting more emphasis upon women's enjoyment in sexual acts. Finally, it is noteworthy that while Chinese women regarded sexual relations as a marital duty, male identity is equated with sexual performance (Jankowiak 2002). If a husband is impotent, a Chinese woman is within her rights to request and immediately receive a divorce.

Over the last two decades newspaper and media coverage of extramarital love has rocketed (Chapter 4). While extramarital affairs allow the expression of romance and exchange of sex unspoiled by economic factors, such affairs coexist with a continuance of fulfilling family responsibilities by the philandering spouses (Farrer and Sun 2003). Public discussion of divorce has also risen considerably. Many divorce cases are filed by women, often on grounds of incompatibility; however, at the same time, divorce was often portrayed as disadvantageous to women (Honig and Hershatter 1988). As a result of the implicit standard of female chastity, divorced women were often pitied or looked down upon, subject to stigma in natal family networks, and in public domains such as the workplace (Liu 2007).

The post-Mao period has also witnessed the emergence of new sexual discourses in the popular domain, exemplified in the proliferation of novels and online blogs about personal sexual experiences. When these accounts were written by a woman, controversy arose particularly. For example, when the woman writer Wei Hui published her novel *Shanghai Baby* in China in 1999, the graphic description of the heroine's sexual experiences attracted a lot of readers as well a public moral crisis.[6] It was officially banned as being decadent; nevertheless, the availability of the Internet enabled its wide non-official circulation. While some of these publications to some extent objectified women and satisfied the male's gaze, Wei and other young women writers who wrote about their sexual experiences were pioneering in the sense that they talked about sex publicly as women, which challenged the male's authority and control over sexual discourse. However, in public, these women writers were generally condemned as morally disreputable women.

Some mainland Chinese scholars feel that China's sexual revolution is more associated with the younger generation, though with a significant gender twist. Survey data show that young Chinese men increasingly view sex in a manner that is unrelated to romance, but young women are still constrained by traditional assumptions about female sexual behaviour with a high value attached to female chastity (Jeffreys 2006). By analysing sexual culture among Chinese youth, Farrer (2002) found that official sex education, by condemning premarital sex and reinstalling sexual morality, reproduced the importance of female chastity and traditional gender roles. With such strong gendered implications, despite the abundance of sexual representations in the post-Mao era, it seems problematic to use the term 'sexual revolution' to describe the transformations in China (Liu 2008).

Sex and the economy

Since the 1980s, China has pursued a policy of 'opening up' to the outside world and moving to a market economy – which has, among other things, led to the emergence of new sexual cultures in large coastal cities: for some young women in Shanghai, being 'sexy' and sexually more adventurous has become a badge of 'modern' status (Farrer 2002). 'Opening up' has also brought with it a growing deployment of a sexualized femininity in the market domain. The beauty economy is booming: commercial companies employ models to advertise their products and many local governments have sponsored beauty contests to boost local tourism (Xu and Feiner 2007). The sex industry has also proliferated as a result of the emergent consumerism, catering to the demands of the increasing numbers of wealthy businessmen whereby sexualized leisure activities have become normative business practices to maintain good relationships with clients.

The wider social economic background embedded in sexual consumption of women's bodies created particular problems for white-collar professionals, an occupation many university women graduates aspire to. Case studies show that women's sexuality has become a commercial resource deliberately initiated and developed by their organization; they are expected to engage in sexual labour during interactions with clients in work and in leisure venues are vulnerable to sexual harassment and exploitation (see Lui 2008). Despite the desexualization of women in the market economy, past restrictions on sexual expression and discussion have given 'reputable' women little or no opportunity for sexual autonomy. While men happily consume women's sexuality, women who are actively engaged in sexual activities are considered decadent; women's sexuality is still strictly moralized. This has challenged white-collar professional women as they attempt to negotiate the sexualized work culture whilst maintaining their sexual reputation. In view of the close link between morality and women's sexuality, it seems to be impossible to excel in a sexualized business world as well as to be a reputable woman. Either women ignore the sexual gossip when adapting to business-related leisure in venues designed for men's sexual pleasure or miss out on networking opportunities that might be vital to the effective performance of their jobs. These white-collar professional women seemed to walk a fine line between respectability and disreputability (Liu 2008).

At another end of the labour market are the sex workers involved in prostitution which re-emerged in the post-Mao era. Prostitution was rampant prior to 1949. When the CCP took over, eradicating prostitution was regarded as a sign of the moral superiority of socialism. As a result, prostitution became non-existent (Sigley 2006). In the post-Mao years, despite government efforts to ban commercial sex to ensure a healthy social environment, the sex industry has boomed, serving the increasing number of wealthy businessmen (Jefferys 2004). Government intervention is considered questionable by some scholars, since research shows that the policing of commercial sex is generating corruption and social injustice to sex workers (Pan 1994).

As a result of a strong association between morality and female sexuality, sex workers are widely regarded as decadent in public and viewed as causing a crisis to national morality. While subject to extensive institutional and social discrimination in the city, sex workers negotiate an urban identity through 'their consumption practices and through exploiting the superior social, cultural, and economic resources possessed by their clients' and act as 'brokers of modernity' in the countryside (Zheng 2009: 5). Unlike the white-collar women stuck in a dilemma between maintaining a morally high reputation and excelling in a sexualized business culture, sex workers assumed an entrepreneurial ownership of their own bodies, and 'reclaimed the commodification of their bodies as an empowering practice'. By disregarding their reproductive duties to the families and the state, these sex workers 'subverted the gender and social hierarchy' (Zheng 2009:12). Women working in the Pearl River Delta felt that the term 'sex work' placed too much emphasis on 'sex' at the expense of other aspects of their 'work' – the emotional and embodied labour (Ding and Ho 2008).

Homosexuality

While there was no mention of homosexuality in the official publications in Maoist years, homosexuality entered into both popular and official discourse in the reform era when it became closely associated with AIDS, crime, sickness and abnormality (Evans 1997). The aversion to homosexuality is dissimilar to homophobia in the West. Homosexuality and lesbianism are not merely objects of moral outrage – they challenge the foundations of the Asian patriarchal family. To live as a gay man is to 'renege on the paramount filial duty of continuing the family line and ensuring parents' future status as ancestors; to live as a lesbian refuses women's part in this project, brings shame on the family, and flies in the face of all tenets of feminine virtue' (Jackson, Liu, and Woo 2008: 24). Historians found that in the late Qing legal code from the mid-eighteenth century on, homosexuality was thrown together with other kinds of extramarital sex and considered undesirable because it did not lead to legitimate procreation within marriage (Dikotter 1995). Aggravated by the assimilation of Western concepts of biological science in the earlier twentieth century, homosexuality became further condemned as a form of sexual pathology (Hinsch 1990).

In such a hostile environment, homosexuals' lives are not easy. Although Chinese law makes no specific mention of homosexuality, narratives of male homosexuals show that they are subject to brutal treatment including beatings by police in public (Evans 1997). Lesbians are also found to be subject to administrative detention and re-education as 'hooligans' (He and Jolly 2002). In recent years, some Chinese researchers played important roles in exposing the discrimination and pleading for greater tolerance for homosexual people. Gay clubs have been established in some of the larger cities (Li and Wang 1992). Although homosexuals 'are talked to, or talked about', they are effectively 'denied a voice in public discourses about sexuality' (Evans 1997: 208). Further, the pleading for public tolerance and recognition among Chinese scholars co-existed with a persistent understanding of homosexuality as a deviant or diseased behaviour, a result of a naturalized view of heterosexuality and sexual difference (Evans 1997: 208–9).

Conclusion

This chapter outlined the ways that gender and sexuality affected the organization of Chinese society in both public and private domains. In the past century, various national projects have challenged Confucian ideologies and practices and re-arranged the relations between men and women. Due to an inadequate understanding of gender in the socialist modernization project, inequalities between men and women persisted. For example, although the boundary between inner space and outer domain has been refined, the gender segregation based upon 'heavy' labour and 'light' labour still predominated at work. The gendered division between domestic sphere and social production was maintained despite the fact that women were mobilized into the workplace. Further, due to the intersection of gender with other social categories, attention needed to be paid to urban/rural location, social hierarchy, and generational differences to understand the complexity of gender transformations in China.

Sexuality, while traditionally serving the need to produce the next generation, has undergone great changes in the last five decades. Maoist years were not a puritanical era as people might have expected: sexuality was closely regulated rather than repressed (Evans 1997). In the post-Mao era, even when the government tried to limit access to knowledge about 'decadent' sexual practices, new communications technologies as well as the demands of a market economy have begun to make it easier to evade censorship and to exchange sexual information. Although the abundance of the sexual discourses more often than not re-sexualized women, studies show that, in the case of sex workers, women could subvert the gender and social order by claiming the ownership of their own bodies (Zheng 2009). Despite hostile public attitudes, homosexuality is also becoming gradually more visible in some urban areas.

Further, it is important that we recognize that sexuality is 'embedded in wider social relations and in non-sexual aspects of social life; in particular, it is enmeshed with gender relations' (Jackson, Liu, and Woo 2008: 18). The gendered implications of current changes around sexuality are significant. For example, women's sexuality is still strictly moralized, which leaves women who are engaged in sexual pleasure or discourses morally decadent (Liu 2008). An entrenched biological determinist belief of gender not only normalizes heterosexuality thereby making other sexual alternatives deviant but also limits the liberating effects of such sexual transformations for women.

Notes

1 The film follows the sad life of a young woman who married into household as the master's fourth concubine. The name of the film is of the practice in the household, that is, a red lantern will be raised concubine's room when the master spends the night at her place.
2 In reality, because of social and political disorder during the early p century, these practices were constrained to a privileged few (Barlow
3 Although embedded in inner-party politics, the 1973 campaign to Confuciansm offered a rare moment for gender inequality to be openly in the context of a political campaign (Andors 198   Johnson 1983; Cr
4 In pre-Communist China, women were already   id to be working mills in industrial centres such as Shanghai   Tianjin (Hershatte However, large-scale women's employment be   n Maoist years.
5 This practice was used during the collective agri   e period: the worke input was first calculated in points and then re
6 It is supposed to be a semi-fictionalized account   xp love and sex in Shanghai.

Bibliography

Andors, Phyllis (1983) *The Unfinished Revolution of Chinese Women*, Bloomington, IN: Indiana University Press.

Barlow, Tani E. (1991) 'Theorizing woman: Funu, Guojia, Jiating', *Genders*, 10: 132–60.

—— (2004) *The Question of Women in Chinese Feminism*, Durham, NC and London: Duke University Press.

Brownell, Susan and Jeffrey N. Wasserstrom (eds) (2002) *Chinese Femininities/Chinese Masculinities: A Reader*, Berkeley, CA: University of California Press.

Croll, Elisabeth (1980) *Feminism and Socialism in China*, London: Routledge and Kegan Paul, 1978. Reprint, New York: Schocken.

—— (1983) *Chinese Women since Mao*, London: Zed Books.

—— (1985) *Women and Rural Development in China: Production and Reproduction*, Geneva: International Labour Office.

Davin, Delia (1976) *Woman-work: Women and the Party in Revolutionary China*, Oxford: Clarendon Press.

—— (1999) *Internal Migration in Contemporary China*, New York: St Martin's Press.

Dikotter, Frank (1995) *Sex, Culture, and Modernity in China*, Honolulu, HI: University of Hawaii Press.

Ding Yu and Ho Sik-Ying (2008) 'Beyond sex work: an analysis of Xiaojies' understandings of work in the Pearl River Delta Area, China', pp. 123–40 in Jackson, S., Liu, J. and Woo, J. (eds), *East Asian Sexualities: Modernity, Gender and New Sexual Cultures*, New York and London: Zed Books.

Ebrey, Patricia Buckley (1993) *Chinese Civilization: A Sourcebook*, New York: The Free Press.

Evans, Harriet (1997) *Women and Sexuality in China: Dominant Discourse on Female Sexuality and Gender since 1949*, London: Polity Press.

—— (2000) 'Marketing femininity: images of the modern Chinese woman', pp. 217–44, in Timothy B. Weston and Lionel M. Jensen (eds), *China beyond the Headlines*, Lanham, MD: Rowman and Littlefield.

Fan, C. Cindy (2007) *China on the Move: Migration, the State, and the Household*, New York and London: Routledge.

Farrer, James (2002) *Opening Up: Youth Sex Culture and Market Reform in Shanghai*, Chicago, IL: University of Chicago Press.

Farrer, James and Sun, Zhongxin (2003) 'Extramarital love in Shanghai', *China Journal*, 50: 1–36.

Gilmartin, Christina, Gail Hershattter, Lisa Rofel, and Tyrene White (eds) (1994) *Engendering China: Women, Culture, and the State*, Cambridge, MA: Harvard University Press.

He, Xiaopei and Susie Jolly (2002) 'Chinese women tongzhi organizing in the 1990s', *Inter-Asia Cultural Studies*, 3(3): 479–91.

Hershatter, Gail (1986) *The Workers of Tianjin, 1900–1949*, Stanford, CA: Stanford University Press.

—— (1996) 'Sexing modern China', pp. 77–96 in Gail Hershatter, Emily Honig, Jonathan N. Lipman, and Randall Stross (eds), *Remapping China: Fissures in Historical Terrain*, Stanford, CA: Stanford University Press.

—— (2002) 'The gender of memory: rural Chinese women and the 1950s', *Signs*, 28(1): 43–72.

—— (2004) 'State of the field: women in China's long twentieth century', *The Journal of Asian Studies*, 63(4): 991–1,065.

Hinsch, Bret (1990) *Passions of the Cut Sleeve: The Male Homosexual Tradition in China*, Berkeley and Los Angeles, CA: University of California Press.

Honig, Emily (2002) 'Maoist mappings of gender: reassessing the red guards', pp. 255–68 in Susan Brownell and Jeffrey Wasserstrom (eds), *Chinese Femininities/ Chinese Masculinities: A Reader*, Berkeley, CA: University of California Press.

Honig, Emily and Gail Hershatter (1988) *Personal Voices: Chinese Women in the 1980's*, Stanford, CA: Stanford University Press.

Jacka, Tamara (1997) *Women's Work in Rural China: Change and Continuity in an Era of Reform*, Cambridge: Cambridge University Press.

Jackson, Stevi and Sue Scott (eds) (2002) *Gender: A Sociological Reader*, London and New York: Routledge.

Jackson, Stevi, Liu Jieyu, and Woo Juhyun (eds) (2008) *East Asian Sexualities: Modernity, Gender and New Sexual Cultures*, pp. 85–103, New York and London: Zed Books.

Jankowiak, William R. (1993) *Sex, Death, and Hierarchy in a Chinese City: An Anthropological Account*, New York: Columbia University Press.

—— (2002) 'Proper men and proper women: parental affection in the Chinese family', pp. 361–80 in Susan Brownell and Jeffrey Wasserstrom (eds), *Chinese Femininities/ Chinese Masculinities*, Berkeley, CA: University of California Press.

Jeffreys, Elaine (2004) *China, Sex and Prostitution*, London: Routledge.

—— (2006) 'Introduction: talking sex and sexuality in China', pp. 1–20 in Elaine Jeffreys (ed.), *Sex and Sexuality in China*, London: Routledge.

Jin Yihong (2001) 'The All China Women's Federation: challenges and trends', pp. 123–40 in Ping-Chun Hsiung, Maria Jaschok, Cecilia Milwertz, and Red Chan (eds), *Chinese Women Organizing: Cadres, Feminists, Muslims, Queers*, Oxford and New York: Berg.

Johnson, Kay Ann (1983) *Women, the Family, and Peasant Revolution in China*, Chicago, CA: University of Chicago Press.

Judd, Ellen R. (1994) *Gender and Power in Rural North China*, Stanford, CA: Stanford University Press.

Ko, Dorothy and Wang Zheng (2006) 'Introduction: translating feminisms in China', *Gender and History*, 18(3): 463–71.

Landes, Joan B. (1989) 'Marxism and the "Woman Question"', pp. 15–29 in Sonia Kruks, Rayna Rapp, and Marilyn B. Young (eds), *Promissory Notes: Women in the Transition to Socialism*, New York: Monthly Review Press.

Liu Deizhong and Niu Bianxiu (2000) 'Chinese occupational segregation and women's employment', *Journal of Women's Studies*, 4: 18–20 (in Chinese).

Liu Jieyu (2007) *Gender and Work in Urban China: Women Workers of the Unlucky Generation*, London and New York: Routledge.

—— (2008) 'Sexualized labour? "White-collar beauties" in provincial China', pp. 85–103 in Stevi Jackson, Liu Jieyu, and Woo Juhyun (eds), *East Asian Sexualities: Modernity, Gender and New Sexual Cultures*, New York and London: Zed Books.

Li Yinhe and Wang Xiaobo (1992) *Their World: A Perspective on China's Male Homosexual Community*, Taiyuan: Shanxi Renmin Publishing House (in Chinese).

Mann, Susan (1987) 'Widows in the kinship, class and community structures of Qing Dynasty China', *Journal of Asian Studies*, 46(1): 37–56.

—— (2001) *Under Confucian Eyes: Writings on Gender in Chinese History*, Berkeley, CA: University of California Press.

Maurer-Fazio, Maggie, Rawski, T. G. and Zhang, Wei (1999) 'Inequality in the rewards for holding up half the sky: gender wage gaps in China's urban labour market, 1988–94', *China Journal*, 41: 55–88.

Min, Dongchao (1997) 'From asexuality to gender differences in modern China', pp. 193–203 in Eileen J. Yeo (ed.), *Mary Wollstonecraft: And 200 years of Feminism*, London and New York: Rivers Oram Press.

Pan Suiming (1994) 'A sex revolution in current China', *Journal of Psychology and Human Sexuality*, 6(2): 1–14.

Pan, Suiming (2006) 'Transformations in the primary life cycle: the origins and nature of China's sexual revolution', pp. 21–42 in Elaine Jeffreys (ed.), *Sex and Sexuality in China*, London and New York: Routledge,

Research Institute of Women's Federation, Department of Social Science and Technology Statistics and State Statistical Bureau (1998) *Gender Statistics in China 1990–1995*, Beijing: China Statistical Publishing House (in Chinese).

Sigley, Gary (ed.) (1998) 'Getting it right: marriage, sex and pleasure', A Special Issue of *Chinese Sociology and Anthropology*, 31.

—— (2006) 'Sex, politics and the policing of virtue in the People's Republic of China', pp. 43–61 in Elaine Jeffreys (ed.), *Sex and Sexuality in China*, London and New York: Routledge.

Tan, Shen (2000) 'The relationship between foreign enterprises, local governments, and women migrant workers in the Pearl River Delta', pp. 293–309 in Loraine A. West and Yaohui Zhao (eds), *Rural Labor Flows in China*, Berkeley, CA: Institute of East Asian Studies, University of California.

Wang, Zheng (2000) 'Gender, employment and women's resistance', pp. 62–82 in Elizabeth J. Perry and Mark Selden (eds), *Chinese Society: Change, Conflict and Resistance* (1st edn), London and New York: Routledge.

—— (2001) 'Call me "Qingnian" but not "Funü": a Maoist youth in retrospect', pp. 27–52 in Xueping, Zhong, Zheng, Wang, and Di, Bai (eds), *Some of Us: Chinese Women Growing up in the Mao Era*, New Brunswick, NJ and London: Rutgers University Press.

Watson, Rubie S. and Patricia Buckley Ebrey (eds) (1991) *Marriage and Inequality in Chinese Society*, Berkeley and Los Angeles, CA: University of California Press.

Weeks, Jeffrey (1986) *Sexuality: Key Ideas*, London: Routledge.

Wolf, Margery (1985) *Revolution Postponed: Women in Contemporary China*, Stanford, CA: Stanford University Press.

Xu, Gary and Susan Feiner (2007) 'Meinu Jingji/China's beauty economy: buying looks, shifting value, and changing place', *Feminist Economics*, 13(3–4): 307–23.

Zheng Tiantian (2009) *Red Lights: The Lives of Sex Workers in Postsocialist China*, Minneapolis, MN and London: University of Minnesota Press.

Related novels and autobiographies

Wei Hui (1999) *Shanghai Baby*, Shenyang: Chunfeng Wenyi Publishing House (in Chinese).

Films and documentaries

Stanley Kwan (2001) *Lan Yu* (蓝宇)
Zhang Yimou (1993) *Raise the Red Lantern* (大红灯笼高高挂)
Zhang Yuan (1996) *East Palace, West Palace* (东宫西宫)

6   Contested ground

Community and neighbourhood

Chunrong Liu

An extraordinary consequence of China's market reforms is the fundamental change within rural villages and urban neighbourhoods where signs of grass-roots autonomy seem to alter the pre-existing pattern of social infrastructure and pose a challenge to the Chinese state. Indeed, revival of communal groups, emergence of property-based organizations as well as collective actions have tempted many observers to interpret villages and neighbourhoods as spring-boards of civil society, in sharp contrast to organized dependence during the pre-reform era (Derleth and Koldyk 2002; 2004; Lei 2001; Lin 2002; Xu 1997; Pekkanen and Read 2003).

This chapter discusses the complexity of Chinese grassroots society with reference to market reforms, social change, and state adaptation. Rapid market-oriented reforms have spawned rich social fabrics in local communities. Meanwhile, persistent demands for stability and governability have generated community-based welfare and governance programmes such as villager committee (VC) elections, the 'New Socialist Countryside Building' campaign (NSCB) and the push for 'Urban Community Building' (UCB). These drastic movements have restructured the grassroots society, resulting in a patterned cellular solidarity with limited mobilization capacity against the state.

Grassroots society in Mao's China

Traditional Chinese grassroots society was composed of semi-autonomous local units, each of which was structured around the kinship system as its core (Yang 1959). Rural community was governed by highly indigenous leadership based on the solidarity groups of kinship, and social control was based upon the collective principles of joint-responsibility and mutual surveil-lance. The imperial state limited its formal bureaucratic power at the magis-trate level, engaging the local community from within through the agency of gentry as well as the *Baojia* system, which was a community-based system of law enforcement and civil control with one *jia* consisting of ten families and ten *jia* (or one hundred families) making a *bao* (Hsiao 1960).

The kinship-based community order was demolished by the Chinese Communist Party (CCP) after 1949. Land reforms, agriculture collectivization and the creation of people's commune system in the 1950s restructured natural villages, turning them into production brigades and production teams. Village life was penetrated by state authorities. Parish and Whyte (1978) observed that through administrative sanctions (coercion, material sanctions, etc.) and normative influence (communications, childhood socialization, and mobilized social pressure), the government was able to induce changes in rural life. As a result, traditional moral bonds, such as kinships, clans, and religion that had long governed the vast countryside were largely destroyed. Gone also were armed bandits, lineage, and ethnic feuds. A new governance system in which loyalty to kin, village and lineage was replaced by loyalty to the production team and brigade, has emerged to dominate peasant community life (Potter and Potter 1990).

The Maoist urban authority similarly shaped neighbourhood society. The socialist distribution system including the public allocation of housing and jobs produced a unique quality of rootedness in urban life (Whyte and Parish 1984). Guided by the socialist ideology of 'production first and life second', work-unit (i.e. *danwei*) compound and residential community became the prevailing form of urban neighbourhood. The principle of socialist communal living was extended to the neighbourhood, and 'most urban residents would rarely have any need to travel beyond the walls of their work-and-living unit' (Gaubatz 1999: 1,497; also French and Hamilton 1979). While there were some differences in housing consumption (Logan, Bian, and Bian 1999), people working for the same *danwei* often lived in the same *danwei* compound, shared similar housing conditions and amenities, and enjoyed no independent location choices. This made urban neighbourhoods more hetero-geneous in social status than was the case in other countries (Whyte and Parish 1984: 237).

Residents' committees (RCs), an elaborate state-sponsored social organ-ization, were established to incorporate, assist, mobilize, and monitor the population. Invented in the early 1950s as an 'autonomous mass organization' to replace the *Baojia* system, native-place associations, and lineage organiza-tions, the RCs helped organize urban residents who did not belong to *danwei* (Salaff 1971). Under the jurisdiction of each street office, and relying on small groups and individual activists in the neighbourhoods, the RCs coordinated a broad range of activities, promoted and organized citizen participation in political campaigns, and supervised public services (Gaulton 1981; Dixon 1981; Read 1999).

Despite the extensive state penetration and organized control (Walder 1986), some traditional aspects of community life survived in both urban and rural contexts, and some unintended consequences occurred. Davis and Harrell (1993) observed that family loyalty and obligation had not been totally destroyed in rural areas. There were clientelist authority relationships between village leaders and villagers and some scope for bottom-up interest articula-tion (Oi 1989; Burns 1988). In urban areas, the low rate of residential mobility, shared living spaces, and the same *danwei* affiliation generated considerable neighbourhood solidarities, which served as a buffer between individuals and government campaigns (Whyte and Parish 1984). Bringing residents together, the RC-led neighbourhood mobilizations might facilitate the cultivation of 'a sense of neighbourliness' (Chan 1993).

The changing rural community

Tremendous changes have occurred in the village community since the end of Mao era. *Decollectivization* took place as the result of the market reforms that swept rural China in the late 1970s. The household contract responsibility system produced systematic changes in the rural community (Oi 1999; Unger 2002). With the dissolution of the pre-1978 collective structures and control organs, rural farmers have witnessed significant social differentiation and geographic mobility (Chapter 8). More importantly, *decollectivization* and market-oriented rural reforms have reduced the relevance of state agents in the community and therefore created spaces for new forms of community life. In the organizational vacuum left by *decollectivization*, two notable social dynamics have emerged: solidarity groups and social mobilizations. They have drastically transformed the village community from an organized political space into a contentious social setting where state power is constantly challenged.

Solidarity groups

These are spontaneous, self-governing, and village-based social organizations, large in number and of great diversity, which constitute the most daunting social dynamics in the post-reform village. A nationwide village-level survey in 2005 estimated that the overall number of rural grassroots social organizations had reached 3.16 million. Among the surveyed 552 organizations, over 18 per cent were churches, temples, and other religious organizations; 16.7 per cent were cultural, sports, and health organizations; 14 per cent were civil dispute mediation organizations; 13.8 per cent were engaged in community security control or patrol activities; and another 13.8 per cent were related to technical assistance and mutual-aid in production (Pesqué-Cela *et al.* 2009).

In this grassroots associational sphere, especially prominent is the revival of lineage and religious groups. Although they were suppressed in the Mao era, lineage forces have re-emerged in the post-1978 era and are manifested in the enthusiasm for re-compiling genealogical records, the renovation of the ancestral house, and the revival of lineage rituals and sentiments (Wang 1991). Along with this change is the explosion of cults of folk-faith and religious activities, including church attendance, pilgrimages, geomancy, temple building, and *qi gong* practice. These developments can be largely attributed to the state's retreat from the ban on religious activity, a decline in the appeal of the official ideology, and individuals' psychological needs for security amidst rapid commercialization and increasing social dislocation (Dean 2003; Madsen 2010).

The socio-political consequences of the renewed social spaces are perplexing. Solidarity groups have functioned as a main source of social identification and differentiation in post-1978 rural China. They have inculcated an extraordinary sense of obligation to the group and created informal accountability for local state agencies, and made village elections more competitive (Tsai 2007; Pesqué-Cela *et al.* 2009; Thurston 1998). As Dean (2003) noted, the revival of religion-based communal networks may indicate a gradual development towards community autonomy because there is a process of merging local governance with religious activities.

Conflict and mobilization

Post-reform policies have not only created spaces for community solidarity accumulations but also altered the substance of conflicts both within the rural community and between the community and the local state. On one hand, while there has been a seemingly close association between the local lineage structure and the degree of social cohesion, inter-clan rivalry and violence have apparently become important sources of community conflict in some areas, particularly in southern China (Chiang 1995). When the rival clans rejected the intervention and mediation of the local government, the disputes often led to large-scale armed battles and harmed community social cohesion.

On the other hand, due to the weakening of Maoist collective organs and the deteriorating provision of public goods and services, conflicts between the rural population and representatives of the local state were intensified (Bernstein and Lü 2003). No longer dependent on the collectives for a living, villagers became much more ready to defend their interests against local cadre impositions and state policies such as birth control, grain procurement, and local taxes and levies. Since the 1990s, excessive tax burdens, widespread official corruption, land expropriation and the degradation of the environment have been major sources of rural conflicts.

Interestingly, pre-existing informal social networks in the rural community have played an important role in resisting state control. O'Brien and Li (2006) have applied the term 'rightful resistance' to peasants' strategic use of both formal and informal institutions in their conflicts with the state. Recent rural resistance has been organized with more sophisticated activists and leaders. By setting up various types of community-based organizations, both formal and informal, community leaders have been able to mobilize the constituencies and lodge complaints. The emergence of mobilization agents signifies a further change in the rural community as they can robustly shape collective claims, recruit activists and mobilize the public, devise and orchestrate acts of contention, and even organize cross-community efforts (Li and O'Brien 2008).

China scholars have disputed the causes, nature, and implications of resistance that have arisen from the rural community. Some have argued that peasant claims represented a nascent 'rights consciousness' which could precipitate a fundamental change in the state-society relationship (Li 2010). Others have argued that rural resistance represented a historically familiar pattern of 'rule consciousness', which undergirded rather than undermined the political system (Perry 2009). In any case, the post-1978 rural community has become a fertile soil for active, self-conscious mobilizations that are reconfiguring community power and affect the making and implementation of public policies.

State interventions

The collapse of the pre-1978 commune structure has altered the distribution of power and social infrastructure in the rural community. However, the village community should not be treated as a unified and autonomous entity which is insular to state penetration. The Chinese authoritarian system has a strong interest in controlling local society in order to avoid alienation and the resulting political and social crisis (Ding 1994). The regime is wary, at best, and hostile, at worst, to any organization that functions outside its direct or indirect control (Saich 2000). Since the 1980s, stability mentality and a growing demand for governability have triggered many community-oriented interventions. Among them, two of the most strategic are VC elections and the recent 'New Socialist Countryside Building' (NSCB) programme, which are profoundly reconstituting social solidarity in the rural community.

Village democracy

The VC was initially organized by community-spirited cadres as a community response to the decline of social control due to the withdrawal of the people's commune system. With the support of some top leaders, this bottom-up initiative was legitimated as a basic-level mass organization of self-government in the 1982 Constitution. The progressive political climate for popular participation in the early 1980s further contributed to the experiment of VC elections (O'Brien and Li 2000). Since the implementation of the Organic Law of the Village Committees (experimental) in 1987, elections have been gradually institutionalized, with approximately 6–7 rounds being held in most parts of rural China by 2009. VC elections have come along with other community-based institutional designs such as village assemblies and village representative assemblies, which were intended to encourage villager participation in public deliberations. There was also the cadre responsibility and evaluation system to enforce local officials' compliance with central government policies.

Despite the many problems afflicting VC elections, this invention has redefined the state-society relationship in the countryside. By providing an educational opportunity for the peasant population to learn about the concepts, procedures, and organization of the democratic processes, VC elections have enabled villagers to demand citizenship rights that they have never enjoyed (Li 2003). As Thurston (1998) observed, one unintended consequence of village elections is the restoration of the sense of community after the collapse of the communes. Manion (1996) found that competitive elections had shortened the distance between village leaders and their constituents, resulting in the increasing congruence between the two. It follows that such congruence between the elected village government and rural residents would help reconstruct social order and strengthen communal bonds.

VC elections have also established a legal-rational type of authority in the village by exposing village leaders to elections based on voluntary participation. The peasant community during the Mao era was organized with state control and mobilized participation. Yet it failed to develop a true sense of community as it was based on state regimentation rather than self-organization and voluntary participation from within. By gradually turning 900 million rural peasants into participatory citizens, VC elections have rationalized the community power structure, shifting its base from top-down coercion to bottom-up participation for the common good of the community.

Welfare programmes

The community-oriented welfare programmes have also been a key form of state intervention in the reform era. After 1949, rural welfare provisions were revolutionized. Family networks were largely destroyed and the concept of rural mutual aid was encouraged in which neighbours assisted each other in times of need. With the redistribution of land and the collectivization movement came along the invention of the rural welfare system. Under the rural commune system (1958–77), welfare responsibility was formally shifted to the commune away from the family, and social support was based on a universal approach (Dixon 1982). In the post-1978 context, the end of collective agriculture and the virtual demise of the collective have left many villages without public welfare provision. The urgency of rural welfare issues is compounded by rapid demographic changes. The problem of pensions and care for the elderly are the critical issues among other rural challenges that have caused peasant resistance and social instability.

The Chinese government has perceived that social benefits matter for community belonging and regime support and has adopted many policy measures such as poverty alleviation programmes and tax reduction initiatives since the 1980s. One of the most recent and comprehensive initiatives is the New Socialist Countryside Building (NSCB) programme, which was part of the eleventh Five-Year Plan (2006–10). The NSCB programme not only prioritizes the goal of rural modernization but also embraces social policy reforms and addresses growing disparities and discontents in rural society. Key components of the project include developing modern agriculture, increasing peasants' income, conducting rural environmental protection, promoting rural healthcare and sanitation, and developing the rural education and the social security system (NDRC 2005). A new insurance system was to be established in the countryside with the premiums paid by the beneficiaries and the collective and government subsidies.

The introduction of the NSCB programme signifies that the state is committed to taking a more active role in rural economic development and social welfare provision, with an implicit goal of ensuring social stability in the countryside. Since the beginning of the NSCB, access to health care, education, infrastructure and a safety net has been expanded. The programme has constituted more than a political slogan and has the potential to successfully overcome rural poverty as well as rural marginalization (Ahlers and Gunter 2009). Arguably, welfare policies matter for the production of social capital (Kumlin and Rothstein 2005). Exposure to social benefits and entitlements in the Chinese rural community may condition social interactions among peasants and remould elite-mass relationships and the community power structure.

The changing urban neighbourhood

This section discusses the changing grassroots society as well as state responses in the urban setting. Neighbourhood dynamics are grounded in two major social and spatial transformations that have distinguished Chinese urban society since the market reforms. The first was the stratification of urban space stemming from rapid urban development, urban gentrification, and housing commoditization. In particular, housing reforms since the 1990s have privatized much of the publicly owned housing stock and promoted home-ownership investments, which have directly led to changes in residential pattern and neighbourhood forms and growing residential segregations (Wang and Murie 2000)[1]. In contrast to the dominant and homogeneous form of *danwei* compounds, private residential buildings have mushroomed and become an established form of accommodation in cities.

The second dynamics are state enterprise reforms or *dedanweilization*, which have created millions of unemployed industrial workers who 'find themselves in the painful process of adjusting to a way of life that centres on their community rather their workplace' (Pan 2002: 6). *Dedanweilization* has stimulated community governance by shifting social functions and responsibilities for occupational welfare from *danwei* to the local community (You 1998: 23–8; also Lee 2000; Derleth and Koldyk 2004; Chan 1993; Wong 1998). The crucial question confronting the urban government and its grassroots agent is whether and how they can maintain stability by re-engaging urban residents and meeting the enormous demand of localized public provisions.

Figure 6.1 An urban wet market (Xiaowei Zang).

New neighbourhood space

Rapid urban transformations are responsible for the differentiation of organizational infrastructure in the neighbourhood, and the growth of neighbourhood-based collective actions for community space. Dynamics in these two dimensions have combined to demonstrate a greater social autonomy in the urban grassroots.

Organizational structure

While urban neighbourhoods were firmly organized by the state-led RCs in the Maoist era, two market-based innovations including management companies and homeowner associations (HA) have assumed the obligations that had previously been held by the RCs in commercialized residential estates. Management companies and HAs originated in residential neighbourhoods built by Hong Kong and Singaporean developers in 1994, which have been extended into commercial estates throughout China subsequently (Read 2003b). The contract-based management companies are responsible for fee-charging businesses that provide sanitation services, routine building maintenance, and ground/lawn care. HAs are defined as homeowners assembly's 'executive body' by the 'Codes of Property Management in People's Republic of China' issued on June 8, 2003. Each HA has between five and fifteen committee members, and is empowered to set up discussion agendas in the

Figure 6.2 Gated Community in Urban China (Chunrong Liu)

neighbourhood, choose and employ a management company, and raise and manage neighbourhood maintenance funds.

HAs have faced dual constraints from both the government and real estate developers. Yet they have gradually become institutionalized in neighbourhood society and been regarded as one of the most dynamic signs of China's nascent civil society. As Read (2008: 1241) commented, 'The more active of these organizations constitute a startling break from the practices of Communist Party-sponsored groups and afford residents significant space in which to meet, debate, take action at their own initiative, and manage their neighbourhoods in a democratic fashion.' It raises questions on community governance. For example, how can new governing forces cooperate with the official self-governing organization of the RC as well as the CCP's neighbourhood branch?

Another new player in neighbourhood life is the 'community mass groups' (*shequ qunzhong tuandui*). Differing from property-based homeowner associations and RC-led sub-groups, community mass groups are mostly self-empowered, volunteer-run, and organized with an informal leadership. As an indigenous ingredient of community infrastructure, their growth has been extremely phenomenal.[2] For example, in Shanghai, there were more than 18,000 community mass groups with over 450,000 participants by 2009, which provided their members with rich information, stimulations, opportunities for self-expression, social support, fellowship, and mutual aid (Li 2010). Despite their limited resources and external reach, their impacts cannot be underestimated. They have significantly diversified the organizational life of neighbourhood society, and frequently contributed to problem solving and community identity building at the urban grassroots.

Neighbourhood activism

The emergence of competition for community space, which ranges from disputes on housing management quality to mobilization against state policies, has constituted a further change in the urban neighbourhood. Among them, homeowners' contestations over housing management issues have been growing strikingly since housing reforms. The disputes that reached the courts were about 166,000 nationwide in 2000, a 42 per cent increase since 1997 (Tomba 2005). Ironically, these types of collective claim are largely an unintended consequence of housing privatization, which has contributed to the accumulation of neighbourhood common interests and fostered the awareness of homeowners (Davis 2006).

In addition to housing management issues, many neighbourhoods have also acted on local governance problems with a NIMBY (Not In My Back Yard) orientation, such as the damaging effects that development can have to air quality and the danger of noise pollution. An extraordinary case is the battle against the Shanghai Maglev extension project in 2006, which would link the new airport at Pudong to the old Hongqiao airport if it got its way. Another key event was the spontaneous mobilization of the *Tiantongyuan* neighbourhood in greater Beijing in 2008, which was an effort to modify the route plan of line no.5 of the Beijing subway system so that the neighbourhood could be more conveniently connected. Unlike the Maoist state-mobilized collective action for policy implementation, bottom-up activisms are constantly associated with the pursuit of enhanced life quality and constituted by the property-based organizations. By activating neighbourhood residents, they have contributed to local identity building and urban policy dynamics (Tomba 2005; Zhu 2008).

Neighbourhood-oriented reforms

Local authority in urban China is active in figuring out community governance reforms to accommodate the unprecedented changes in neighbourhood society. In the general scheme of 'urban community building' (UCB) since the mid-1990s, state intervention has decisively shaped the characteristics of neighbourhood society with community-based service and neighbourhood self-governance programmes.

Community services

As an emerging functional need of post-*danwei* urban society, community services are regarded as localized, self-administered, welfare-oriented, and diversified and able to serve the variety of needs in neighbourhoods. To install community service programmes, a new organizational structure has been innovated in the national UCB scheme. In 1994, the Ministry of Civil Affairs (MCA) issued a circular to promote *Shequ* (community) construction. A joint document emphasizing urban community as a basic unit for service delivery was released by the office of the CCP central committee and the State Council in 2000. Since then, the MCA has explored several models of *Shequ* (community) building based on local initiatives and experiments in Shenyang, Shanghai, Wuhan and Qingdao. The concept of *Shequ* (community) varies in different localities in terms of the degree of scale, autonomy, and government control over communities (Derleth and Koldyk 2004). In the Shenyang Model, for example, it was felt that neighbourhood-based residents' committees were too small to operate effectively while street offices were too large to function as effective grassroots organizations. These communities were rescaled larger to be larger geographically than an RC-organized neighbourhood. The MCA called the new social infrastructure organizations 'community residents committees' (*shequ jumin weiyuanhui*).

The formulation of *Shequ* (community) has paved ways for the government to initiate and sponsor community service centres and programmes. Meanwhile, the RC has been adapting and changing its traditional role in the community. As a result of a reformed urban welfare framework and decentralized urban administration, the RCs have developed and implemented a range of service programmes for community residents, such as daily elderly care and child care, morning exercise teams, evening social events, and cultural gatherings (Xu *et al.* 2005). The community-based comprehensive and efficient delivery of social services has been established to meet the diverse needs of local residents, and also helped achieve greater political and social integration (Bray 2006).

Democratic governance

Absorbing the RC into a localized service network creates a dilemma in which the RC is strongly engaged by the administrative agencies of the government. As a result it has gradually lost relevance to social space within the neighbourhood. In many newly established gated communities, resident autonomy is comparatively stronger than in the previous work unit compounds. Since the late 1990s, considerable efforts have been made to revitalize the RC in neighbourhood life by showcasing citizenship and promoting community elections and self-governance. In 1998, the *Sifang* district of Qingdao City in Shandong province organized the first RC direct election. This was followed by several experiments in several other cities. In Shanghai, the first round of RC direct elections in 1999 was piloted by two street offices. The latest election in 2009 showed that 84 per cent of RCs were directly elected with an average voting rate of 86 per cent (SBCA 2009).

To reconstruct neighbourhood participatory space, the post-election admin-istration of urban neighbourhoods is typically reinvented with the principle of 'separation of deliberation and administration' (*yixing fenli*). Under this arrangement, a RC shall be staffed by 3–9 elected and voluntary representatives as the 'deliberative force' which works on participatory issues. Full-time professional social workers who are contracted by a street office are regarded as the 'administrative force' and take care of government assigned adminis-trative affairs. With this division of labour, top-down policy implementation and bottom-up participation are expected to be balanced. A further reform is to establish a grassroots deliberative institution as an advisory body to the RC. In many neighbourhoods, the deliberative institution takes the shape of the 'deliberative assembly' (*yishi hui*), which is appealing to many community residents and is networked by the HAs and other community organizations (Lin 2002). In contrast to the earlier stage of community building featuring administrative integration and top-down public service delivery, these new strategies of community organizing can be viewed as a process of grassroots democratic empowerment. They have made the RC more inclusive and less hierarchical, and enabled the RC as a source of localized civic community (Liu 2007; 2008).

Concluding remarks

This chapter shows the growth of social solidarity at the local level of Chinese society. The Maoist pattern of community social infrastructure, marked by a high degree of organized dependence, has been significantly eroded with the explosive growth of new social fabrics such as rural solidarity groups, urban property-based organizations, and spontaneous bottom-up activisms. Diversifi-cation and proliferation of grassroots social fabrics portend that Chinese society has grown more autonomous if not contentious. Despite great variations, there is a general direction pointing towards 'a substantial renegotiation of state-society relations at the grassroots level' (Perry and Goldman 2007: 13–14).

The rise of community autonomy is deeply associated with market-oriented reforms including rural *decollectivization*, urban *dedanweilization*, and hous-ing privatization. This implies that the waning of socialist social control and the collective regime has opened up new horizons for grassroots reorganizing and shaped the social infrastructure of local communities. The growth of new social fabrics confirms that, as the government has further withdrawn from many aspects of citizens' social life, some degrees of autonomy would sooner or later emerge (Sullivan 1990; Davis *et al.* 1995).

Without underestimating the role of state power withdrawal in the creation of civic spaces, many changing aspects of the neighbourhood and the com-munity must be viewed as a result of deliberative interventions and strategic institutional choices by the state. Indeed, confronted by grassroots power vacuums and social fabrics associated with market transformation, and realizing that the previous pattern of organized control is losing relevance, the state is striving to validate and re-validate its authority (Shue 2004). In both the rural community and the urban neighbourhood, state re-validation for stability and governability, which is processed by embracing village democracy, designating comprehensive rural welfare programmes, promoting community services and neighbourhood-level democratic governance, has largely decentralized the opportunities, resources as well as boundaries for the making of grassroots associational space.

Notes

1 While less than 15 per cent of the urban population had lived in privately owned dwellings at the end of the Mao era, the homeownership rate reached a remarkable level of 71.98 per cent in 2000 (*China Real Estate News,* 19 May, 2000).
2 Mass community groups are deeply rooted in the *dedanweilization* reform, which shifts leisure space and social interactions from occupation-based *danwei* to neighbourhood communities and creates a particular association demand. They also develop because of a non-transparent ambiguous regulation environment. The Regulation on the Registration and Administration of Associations (revised in 1998) considers groups operating within the urban neighbourhood and community as "internal" organizations, which are not required to register with MCA administrations.

Bibliography

Ahlers, Anne and Gunter Schubert (2009) 'Building a new socialist countryside – only a political slogan?' *Journal of Current Chinese Affairs*, 38(4): 35–62.

Bernstein, Thomas P. and Xiaobo Lü (2003) *Taxation without Representation in Contemporary Rural China*, New York: Cambridge University Press.

Bray, David (2005) *Social Space and Governance in Urban China: the Danwei System from Origins to Reform*, Stanford, CA: Stanford University Press.

Burns, John (1988) *Political Participation in Rural China*, Berkeley, CA: University of California Press.

Chan, Cecilia L. (1993) *The Myth of Neighbourhood Mutual Help: The Contemporary Chinese Community-based Welfare System in Guangzhou*, Hong Kong: Hong Kong University Press.

Chiang, Chen-Chang (1995) 'The resurgence of clan power in mainland China', *Issues & Studies*, 31(5): 64–75.

Davis, Deborah (2003) 'From welfare benefit to capitalized asset', pp. 183–98 in Ray Forrest and James Lee (eds), *Chinese Urban Housing Reform*, London: Routledge.

—— (2006) 'Urban Chinese homeowners as consumer-citizens', pp. 281–99 in Sheldon Garon and Patricia Maclachlan (eds), *The Ambivalent Consumer*, Ithaca, NY: Cornell University Press.

Davis, Deborah, Richard Kraus, Barry Naughton, and Elizabeth J. Perry (1995) *Urban Spaces in Contemporary China: The Potential for Autonomy and Community in Post-Mao China*, New York: Cambridge University Press.

Davis, Deborah and Stevan Harrell (eds) (1993) *Chinese Families in the Post-Mao Era*, Berkeley, CA: University of California Press.

Dean, Kenneth (2003) 'Local communal religion in contemporary Southeast China', *China Quarterly*, 174: 338–58.

Derleth, James and Daniel R. Koldyk (2002) 'Community development in China', pp. 64–74 in Qineng Chen and Fan, Jiang (eds), *Community Development in China and Canada*, Beijing: The Ethnic Publishing House (in Chinese).

—— (2004) 'The *Shequ* experiment: grassroots political reform in urban China', *Journal of Contemporary China*, 13(41): 747–77.

Ding, Xueliang (1994) *The Decline of Communism in China: Legitimacy Crisis, 1977–1989*, Cambridge: Cambridge University Press.

Dixon, John (1981) *The Chinese Welfare System 1949–1979*, New York: Praeger.

—— (1982) 'The community-based rural welfare system in the People's Republic of China: 1949–79', *Community Development Journal*, 17(1): 2–12.

French, Richard and F.E. Ian Hamilton (1979) 'Is there a socialist city?' pp. 1–12 in Richard French and F.E. Ian Hamilton (eds), *The Socialist City*, Chichester: John Wiley.

Gaubatz, Piper (1999) 'China's urban transformation: patterns and processes of morphological change in Beijing, Shanghai and Guangzhou', *Urban Studies*, 36(9): 1,495–521.

Gaulton, Richard (1981) 'Political mobilization in Shanghai, 1949–51', pp. 35–65 in Christopher Howe (ed.), *Shanghai: Revolution and Development in an Asian Metropolis*, Cambridge: Cambridge University Press.

Hsiao, Kung-Chuan (1960) *Rural China, Imperial Control in the Nineteenth Century*, Seattle, WA: University of Washington Press.

Kumlin, Staffan and Bo Rothstein (2005) 'Making and breaking social capital: the impact of welfare-state institutions', *Comparative Political Studies*, 38(4): 339–65.

Lee, Ming-Kwan (2000) 'Chinese occupational welfare in market transition', *China Quarterly*, 164: 1,084–85.

Lei, Jieqiong (ed.) (2001) *Urban Community Building during Transformation*, Beijing: Beijing University Press (in Chinese).

Li, Lianjiang (2003) 'The empowering effect of village elections in China', *Asian Survey*, 43(4): 648–62.

—— (2010) 'Rights consciousness and rules consciousness in contemporary China', *China Journal*, 64: 47–68.

Li, Lianjiang and Kevin J. O'Brien (2008) 'Protest leadership in rural China', *China Quarterly*, 193: 1–23.

Li, Xueju (ed.) (2010) *Civil Affairs: 30 Years in Retrospect* (The Shanghai Volume), Beijing: China Society Press (in Chinese).

Lin, Shangli (ed.) (2002) *Case Studies on Community Democratic Governance*, Beijing: Social Science Literature Press (in Chinese).

Liu, Chunrong (2006) 'Social changes and neighbourhood policy in Shanghai', *Policy and Society*, 25 (1): 133–55.

—— (2007) 'State intervention in the creation of neighbourhood social capital' *Sociological Studies* [*Shehuixue Yanjiu*], 2: 60–79 (in Chinese).

—— (2008) 'Empowered autonomy: the politics of community governance innovation in Shanghai', *Chinese Public Administration Review*, 5 (1–2): 61–71.

Logan, John R., Bian Yanjie and Bian Fuqin (1999) 'Housing inequality in urban China in the 1990s', *International Journal of Urban and Regional Research*, 23: 7–25.

Madsen, Richard (2010) 'The upsurge of religion in China', *Journal of Democracy*, 21(4): 58–71.

Manion, Melanie (1996) 'The electoral connection in the Chinese countryside', *American Political Science Review*, 90(4): 736–48.

NDRC (National Development and Reform Commission) (2005) *The Outline of the 11th Five-year Plan for National, Economic, and Social Development of the People's Republic of China*, Beijing: China Statistics Press (in Chinese).

O'Brien, Kevin J. and Lianjiang Li (2000) 'Accommodating "democracy" in a one-party state', *China Quarterly*, 162: 465–89.

—— (2006) *Rightful Resistance in Rural China*, Cambridge: Cambridge University Press.

Oi, Jean. C. (1989) *State and Peasant in Contemporary China*, Berkeley, CA: University of California Press.

—— (1999) 'Two decades of rural reform in China', *China Quarterly*, 159: 616–28.

Pan, Tianshu (2002) 'Neighbourhood Shanghai: community building in Five Mile Bridge', PhD dissertation, Department of Anthropology, Harvard University.

Parish, William L. and Martin K. Whyte (1978) *Village and Family in Contemporary China*, Chicago, IL: University of Chicago Press.

Pekkanen, Robert J. and Benjamin L. Read (2003) 'Explaining cross-national patterns in state-fostered local association', paper presented at the American Political Science Association Annual Meeting, Philadelphia, August 27–31.

Perry, Elizabeth J. (2009) 'A new rights consciousness?' *Journal of Democracy*, 20 (3): 17–20.

Perry, Elizabeth J. and Merle Goldman (eds) (2007) *Grassroots Political Reform in Contemporary China*, Cambridge, MA: Harvard University Press.

Pesqué-Cela, Vanessa, Ran Tao, Yongdong Liu and Laixiang Sun (2009) 'Challenging, complementing or assuming "the mandate of heaven"?' *Journal of Comparative Economics*, 37(1): 151–68.

Potter, Sulamith H. and Jack M. Potter (1990) *China's Peasants: The Anthropology of a Revolution*, Cambridge: Cambridge University Press.

Read, Benjamin L. (1999) 'Revitalizing the state's urban "nerve tips"', *China Quarterly*, 163: 806–20.

—— (2003a) 'State, social networks, and citizens in China's urban neighbourhood', PhD dissertation, Department of Government, Harvard University.

—— (2003b) 'Democratizing the neighbourhood? New private housing and home-owner self-organization in urban China', *The China Journal*, 49: 31–59.

—— (2008) 'Assessing variation in civil society organizations', *Comparative Political Studies*, 41(9): 1240–65.

Saich, Tony (2000) 'Negotiating the state', *The China Quarterly*, 161: 124–41.

Salaff, Janet (1971) 'Urban neighbourhood committees in the wake of the Cultural Revolution', pp. 298–324 in John W. Lewis (ed.), *The City in Communist China*, Stanford, CA: Stanford University Press.

SBCA (Shanghai Bureau of Civil Affairs) (2009) 'Reports on residents committee election and grassroots democracy building: 10 years in retrospect' (in Chinese), unpublished report on file with Shanghai Bureau of Civil Affairs.

Shue, Vivienne (2004) 'Legitimacy crisis in China?' pp. 24–49 in Peter Hays Gries and Stanley Rosen (eds), *State and Society in 21st Century China*, New York: Routledge.

Sullivan, Laurence R. (1990) 'The emergence of civil society in China', pp.126–44 in Tony Saich (ed.), *The Chinese People's Movement*, Armonk, NY: M.E. Sharpe.

Tang, Wenfang and William L. Parish (2000) *Chinese Urban Life under Reform*, Cambridge: Cambridge University Press.

Thurston, Anne F. (1998) *Muddling toward Democracy: Political Change in Grassroots China*, Washington, DC: United States Institute of Peace.

Tomba, Luigi (2004) 'Creating an urban middle class: social engineering in Beijing', *The China Journal*, 51: 1–26.

—— (2005) 'Residential space and collective interest formation in Beijing's housing disputes', *The China Quarterly*, 184: 934–51.

Tsai, Lily L. (2007) 'Solidarity groups, informal accountability, and local public goods provision in rural China', *American Political Science Review*, 101(2): 355–72.

Unger, Jonathon (2002) *The Transformation of Rural China*, Armonk, NY: M. E. Sharpe.

Walder, Andrew G. (1986) *Communist Neo-traditionalism*, Berkeley, CA: University of California Press.

Wang, Huning (1991) *A Study of Village Family Culture in Contemporary China*, Shanghai: Shanghai People's Press (in Chinese).

Wang, Ya Ping and Alan Murie (2000) 'Social and spatial implications of housing reform in China', *International Journal of Urban and Regional Research*, 24(2): 397–417.

Whyte, Martin King and William L. Parish (1984) *Urban Life in Contemporary China*, Chicago, IL: University of Chicago Press.

Wong, Linda (1998) *Marginalization and Social Welfare in China*, New York: Routledge.

Xia, Huigan and Li Bingmei (2010) 'The reform and development of housing management in Shanghai', available at http://www.shfg.gov.cn/fgdoc/kjqkxb/200910/t20091023_328989.html., accessed on December 15, 2010 (in Chinese).

Xu, Qingwen, Jian Guo Gao and Miu Chung Yan (2005) 'Community service centres in urban China', *Journal of Community Practices*, 13(3): 73–90.

Xu, Yong (1997) *Villager Self-government in Rural China*, Wuhan: Huazhong Normal University Press (in Chinese).

Yang, Ching-kun (1959) *The Chinese Family in the Communist Revolution*, Cambridge, MA: MIT Press.

You, Ji (1998) *China's Enterprise Reform: Changing State-Society Relations after Mao*, London: Routledge.

Zhu, Jiangang (2008) 'Space, power, and the construction of community identity: a case study of residents' movement in Shanghai neighbourhood', *Chinese Sociology and Anthropology*, 40(2): 65–90.

Related novels and autobiographies

Cao, Jingqing (2005) *China along the Yellow River: Reflections on Rural Society*, New York: RoutledgeCurzon.

Chen, Guili and Chun Tao (2004) *An Investigation of China's Peasantry*, Beijing: The People's Literature Publishing House.

Films and documentaries

Antonioni, Michelangelo (1972) *Chung Kuo*, a production of Radiotelevisione Italiana (RAI), which presents urban and rural life in Mao's China.

Duan Jinchuan (1996) *No. 16, Barkhor South Street*, a documentary about the Barkhor street residents' committee in Lhasa.

Yi, Jian (2006) *The Quiet Revolution* – a documentary about China's village self governance.

7   Education

Gerard A. Postiglione

This chapter introduces the education system and prospects for education in China. As a social institution, education promotes continuity more than social change. For most of China's history, education has been a conservative force (Elman and Woodside 1994; Lee 2000). Confucian ideology emphasized the diligent study of books containing moral principles underlying social order, and passing examinations was a path to officialdom in traditional China. With the exception of student activism during the Cultural Revolution of 1966–76, education was a stabilizing force in Mao's China. In the post-1978 era – aside from transmitting a state-defined cultural heritage – the function of education is to reproduce social order and unify a multiethnic and rapidly developing nation with growing social and economic inequalities. The education system succeeds in the eyes of each social group and community to the extent that it can deliver on the promise of a better economic future (Postiglione 2006). The state's task is to orchestrate educational reforms that lead the masses down the path to a better life. In addition, education has to make China's economy more globally competitive, and to present China to the world community as a highly relevant civilization for the twenty-first century. The latter is to be accomplished through cultural diplomacy, media presence, and hundreds of Confucian Institutes (Wang 2009, Yang 2010). Yet the more formidable task is apparently domestic – making education respond to a diverse population: to rural as well as urban families, to migrants as well as an urban middle class, to ethnic minorities as well as poor rural Han Chinese, to those with disabilities as well as those who are gifted. If compared to education in many developed states, education in China has become less socialist in addressing inequalities. The impressive achievement of providing nine years of basic education in more than 95 per cent of the country has become overshadowed by growing inequalities. The richest 10 per cent of society was 23 times richer that the poorest 10 per cent in 2007, a rise since 1998 when it was 7.3 times (Jia 2010). While this may create upheavals in other societies, stability in China is preserved by its cultural heritage that has a preference for harmonious socio-political development. As economic indicators rise for a nation of one-child families, quality of life has become a priority and education is increasingly expected to be relevant to it.

The imperial legacy and education in the pre-1949 era

In imperial China, the state's direct involvement in learning was limited. It merely administered the examinations that were the means for selecting government officials. The main content of those examinations was Confucianism, a moral canon which idealized non-hereditary values. Confucius (551 to 479 BC) was a government official who saw growing disorder, chaos, and injustice in the system. He set himself to develop a new moral code based on correct behaviour (理), benevolence, humanity (仁), honesty (义), knowledge in the sense of moral wisdom (智), and faithfulness, integrity (信). He espoused social fairness and the maxims that 'In education there should be no distinction of classes' (有教无类).

The examination system dated from the Sui Dynasty (581–618). Emperors and their dynasties used the Confucian tradition to legitimize their power and the examinations played a key role in the development of China's bureaucratic state. It did this by enforcing objective qualifications, alongside existing forms of patronage, and allowed commoners to qualify for office by way of examinations. The main route to officialdom became degrees earned individually but bestowed by imperial authority. A ruling class of literati-bureaucrats emerged to guide decisions by the emperor. The trend continued virtually unchanged over centuries till 1905.

In fact, the imperial examination system did make possible a certain equality of opportunity, although the advantages were still in favour of those families who had wealth and power (Chang 1963). Although this system did create a pool of highly educated men, it was superimposed upon a mostly illiterate population. It was unfortunate that the examination system was part of a Chinese conservatism that calcified the system over many centuries and generated little new learning from within or the motivation to venture outward into the larger world. The Chinese tradition was even able to endure a half century of Western incursions, beginning in the nineteenth century. Western learning remained peripheral. However, at the turn of the twentieth century, important reforms began to bite, including the abolition of the imperial examination system in 1905. Though it has now been a little more than 100 years since its abolition, there is substantial residue even today of a system of learning by rote (Watkins and Biggs 1996).

The first government-run modern college was the Metropolitan College (1898) in Beijing, the predecessor of Peking University (Beijing University). Its first president, Cai Yuanpei, transformed the university according to the Western concept of a modern university with his principle of freedom of thought, by which he meant, make the most of Chinese and foreign things. In fact, Peking University today has instituted an experimental liberal arts education, called the Yuanpei Programme that is based on Harvard University's general education programme.

China's first modern school system was modelled on that of Japan. However, in 1921, with the influence of the New Culture Movement in China and the progressive education movement in the USA, the All-China Federation of Education Associations introduced a new schooling system patterned on the American 6-3-3-4 system. It was made official in 1922, also a time when Chinese students returning from overseas study in the USA became increasing influential. After 1927, universities were largely modelled on British and American ones, with few exceptions. There were also church schools run by foreign missionaries, and 207 universities (79 private and 21 church colleges; the rest were public/government institutions), with a total about 150,000 students by 1947.

The new education system was elitist when viewed from the perspective that China had a largely peasant-based and illiterate population. Founded in 1921, the Chinese Communist Party (CCP) appropriated the issue of inequality. The educational issue of illiteracy helped to define the Chinese communist movement. Schools and universities were created by the communists in their base area of Yennan in the 1940s and became a force of influence for education in the post-1949 era.

Education under Mao

The CCP defeated the Nationalist Party in the Third Civil War of 1946–9 and established the People's Republic of China in 1949. It decided to join the Soviet Bloc in the 1950s and learned from the Soviet Union. It reformed the education system in China including the nationalization of universities, university access for children of peasants and workers, ideological support for socialism, and a close link between education and labour. Students paid no tuition fees for higher education and they would be guaranteed a job after graduation. Colleges and universities were organized into *danwei* – the communist unit of society, sometimes referred to as an 'iron rice bowl' in which salary, accommodations, meals, health care, and other benefits were guaranteed to all employees for life. After the split in Sino-Soviet Union relations in the late 1950s, the CCP did not make major changes in higher education. It also learned from the Soviet Union how to curtail academic freedom. In the 1956 Hundred Flowers campaign, the government invited intellectuals to air their views, after which an anti-rightist campaign was launched to punish many intellectuals for their views.

Higher education expanded rapidly during the Great Leap Forward of 1958–60. Enrolments reached 680,000 in 434 colleges and universities by 1966 when Chairman Mao launched the Cultural Revolution. Examinations for university entrance were abolished. Good political performance became the main criterion for university admissions. The chaos had devastating results on all parts of the education system, and by 1977 enrolments in higher education had dropped to 273,000.

Education in the post-1978 era

The situation began to change in December 1978 when Deng Xiaoping introduced an era of economic reform and opening up to the outside world. University entrance examinations were reinstated. By 1985, the number of institutions of higher education reached 1,016 and reforms were introduced throughout the system that gave more autonomy to schools and universities in matters of curriculum, finance, student selection, and academic staff recruitment. The Tiananmen tragedy of 1989 slowed educational reform. By the mid-1990s the educational reforms regained speed as Deng Xiaoping rejuvenated China's economic reforms and further opened the way for market forces in society. This meant expanded access to education.

There has been a rapid expansion in educational opportunities in the post-1978 era. First, there has been an increased demand of individuals and employers for relevant knowledge and skills to boost their economic prospects. The state's response has been to popularize basic education and literacy for all, expand secondary and tertiary vocational-technical education for job skills in a burgeoning labour market, and increase university enrolments for higher learning. Second, the urbanization of Chinese society has seen a growing demand by the new middle class for higher cultural status. This creates intensified social competition for educational credentials in an elaborate system led by elite urban schools and universities, both domestic and international. Moreover, education helps ethnic minorities gain access into the national mainstream of social opportunities (Postiglione 2009). Third, there is the ubiquitous demand by the state for education as social control. Education takes on the responsibility to socialize a citizenry, unify the country ideologically, and prepare high-calibre leaders to reconcile communist precepts with market economics (Law 2006). These three overlapping demands – for practical skills, for status culture, and for social control, compete at different times for influence over educational reforms. Changing social context determines their pecking order. In times of rapid economic growth, the demand for practical skills is a top priority. In times of internal strife, the demand of the state for social control takes precedence. As the middle class expands, so does their demand for more status culture. However, most reforms in the structure and content of education are influenced by a combination of the three demands.

Equally important, the expansion in educational opportunities and educational reforms in China have to reconcile multiple polarities: foster high-quality learning not only in schools of the prosperous east, but also in the poorer west; ensure social stability but not stifle innovation and creativity; preserve aspects of cultural heritage while adhering to the ideological precepts of a socialist market economy; promote mainstream cultural capital while sustaining the cultural vitality of a 100 million ethnic minority population; learn from the outside world to spur high-level scientific and technological progress but temper the younger generation's attraction to negative aspects of globalization; and remain committed to a market economy while providing fair educational opportunities.

To achieve the above-mentioned goals, the Ministry of Education has set out a national plan and directed local authorities to design their own implementation strategies. The central government produces five-year education plans. However, educational reforms do not always conform to the stereotypical top-down authoritarian type in China. Localities are often busy finding ways to circumvent central policies. If educational policies from the central government appear unsuitable for local conditions due to financial or cultural reasons, rather than confront higher authorities, localities find alternative means of making progress. Non-adherence to central policies can result in trouble for local officials, especially if results are poor. Yet instituting alternative adaptations of a policy in innovative ways to improve local education can influence subsequent policy deliberations at the central level.

Primary and secondary schools in today's China

For all children in China, learning English begins in grade three of primary school. The main subjects are mathematics and Chinese language and literature, science, geography, history, and moral education. At the end of nine years of basic education, an examination determines the future path for students who continue on in school. About half of all students are tracked into the vocational/technical path, while the rest attend senior secondary school in preparation for the national entrance examination for college and university. Gifted and special needs students were not addressed until about 1985. There are an increasing number of special schools, and vocational training schools that have been established for special needs students. Inclusive education has become a leading topic in China, especially since 2000.

Except in ethnic minority schools in areas where the written language in common use is Uyghur, Tibetan, Mongolian, Korean, or other minority scripts, the standard medium of instruction is Chinese (Mandarin, known in China as *Putonghua*). For ethnic minority groups that have a common spoken language without a written language in common use, the medium of instruction can be their mother tongue for the first year or two of primary school, after which the transition to complete Chinese medium teaching takes place. The medium of instruction is a complex issue and varies across ethnic autonomous areas (Postiglione 2009; Postiglione and Beckett 2011). After completing the compulsory nine years of education, students who wish to continue to senior secondary school normally pay for further education.

Although most primary and secondary schools in urban China are state run, the private school movement has gained momentum. Private schooling has proved that it can provide a high-quality education, often superior to that in state-run urban schools. The government has encouraged the private school movement and is unwilling to fund public schools in which bureau-

Figure 7.1 The gate of a rural school in Gansu Province. The slogan on the wall reads: 'Give us a child, and we will return a pillar of the state.'

cracy and corruption are widespread. Instead, it has looked to 'social forces' (社会力量) or non-government groups and individuals to take a lead in establishing and running private schools. While good government schools have survived, less successful government schools may be converted to the private mode of finance and management to become more competitive (Hu *et al.* 2009). Unlike rural children, urban children have access to the burgeoning sector of private schools, including pre-schools, primary and secondary schools, as well as colleges and universities (Lin 1999).

In short, Chinese society is learning to adapt to a transformative education system. Markets have come to matter more than Marxism in educational provision, especially as more needed to be paid for quality education and choosing college and university courses that lead to employment. The government has tried to expand literacy and nine-year basic education to all, including the poorest segments of society. Indeed, Chinese society has reached a historical point of note – the first time that virtually all children are attending primary school. China has managed to push enrolment rates for primary and junior secondary schooling to levels above most other lower income countries. This is surprising because it has a low proportion of GDP allocated to education, as compared to other developing countries.

Figure 7.2 In the playground of a village primary school in a Muslim area of
western China, the teachers and village leaders are distributing learning
materials to returning students. The girls and boys (wearing white
prayer caps) are separated into two lines. The slogan on the wall says
'Dear students, did you study today?' (亲爱的同学，你今天学习了吗).
Three sentences on the blackboard are 'All students, for all students,
for students of all' (一切为了学生，为了一切学生，为了学生一切).
On the left-hand side of the blackboard it says 'Respect and love one
other, with virtue and honesty' (互尊互爱, 文明诚信), the right side says
'Know right and glory, construct a new atmosphere' (知荣辱, 树新风).

China's higher education

China has become the largest system of higher education in the world (Levin
2010). University enrolment experienced an unprecedented growth beginning
in 1998 (Postiglione 2005). Between 1999 and 2004, enrolment nearly quad-
rupled. In 1999, enrolment in higher education stood at 1.6 million, and in 2004,
enrolment was 4.473 million. According to the 2007 Ministry of Education
statistics, in 1990, less than 4 per cent of the 18–22 age group was enrolled as
students in higher education, compared to 22 per cent in 2005.

The decision to expand in 1998 was in response to pressure from below
resulting from the policy for universal basic education and the subsequent
increase in students graduating from senior secondary school. The government's decision to expand was also aimed at getting families to spend more

of their savings so as to stimulate the economy in the aftermath of the Asian economic crisis (and to keep more students in college and university during a period of rising unemployment). Education is the fastest growing focus of consumer spending by urban residents. This spending is increasing at an average rate of about 20 per cent annually. An average of 10 per cent of savings goes to education, which is higher than the 7 per cent put aside for housing.

The globalization of the Chinese economy is compelling universities to adapt and compete like never before. With the phasing out of a planned economy, Chinese higher education has moved towards reforms similar to those in other parts of the world, including a proliferation of nongovernment-supported institutions of higher education. Private (*minban*) colleges and universities were entering the scene for the first time since 1949, and their numbers were increasing rapidly. Between 2004 and 2006, the number of *minban* colleges and universities grew from 133 to 278, enrolling 319,800 students in 2004 and 1,337,900 by 2006. By 2004, independent colleges (*duli xueyuan*), a new type of institution came to prominence. By 2006, they numbered 318 with 1,467,000 students (Hu *et al.* 2009). Some independent colleges are established by public institutions of higher education that use

Figure 7.3 Chinese National Flag raising ceremony in a Middle School in Xiamen city (福建省厦门市大同中学) by Gerard A. Postiglione.

their own facilities and classrooms, but are self-supporting by charging higher fees. However, for both *minban* and independent colleges, quality remains a problem. Thus, while privatization may have improved the quality of many primary (6,161) and secondary schools (7,796) by 2006, the same cannot yet be said for higher education. The main accomplishment of private higher education has been to improve access for more students.

China has made great efforts to establish several world class universities that can stand alongside leading international universities. China has recently launched two programmes in higher education known as 211 Project and 985 Project. These two plans selected a group of top universities and provided financial support for them to attain world class standards. China's Beijing University and Qinghua University, both located in the capital, and Fudan University in Shanghai enjoy the highest reputations in the country. The Outline for 2010–20 calls for the government to release its monopolistic control on universities and permit autonomy by allowing presidents and faculty to run their institutions. However, the government will continue to provide funding for a major portion of state universities and to make policy frameworks at the macroscopic level for non-government higher education. Universities are to be governed by the institutions themselves. Student admission will no longer be determined only by the national college and university examination. Each university will aim to make admission criteria more diverse with an emphasis on whole person development. As the massification of higher education continues apace into the future, China's colleges and universities will become more of a leading force in the larger education system and, as has been the case in other countries, will inevitably become a major driver of the democratization of Chinese society.

However, rising unemployment of university graduates, something not seen before in China, has created an inflationary spiral that will have to be addressed sooner or later. China has to rapidly expand but also privatize much of its higher education system, raise the quality of undergraduate education while broadening the curriculum for more liberal thinking, provide jobs for 6 million graduates annually, and keep a lid on various forms of academic corruption. Finally, more and more women and members of ethnic minority groups are attending university but the proportion of women and members of ethnic minorities in top universities has not kept pace with the rate of expansion. Students from remote areas are more likely to find themselves unable to afford tuition fees, and lacking the study skills needed to survive and excel in a cosmopolitan university atmosphere. In short, challenges in access, equity, and quality education remain (Li, forthcoming).

The rural–urban divide

The degree of inequality is higher in basic education than in higher education in China. Inequality in basic education is mainly rooted in the rural–urban divide in China. China is commonly divided into rural and urban sectors, and there is a big difference between rural and urban education. Before the rural education finance reforms of 2007, less than a quarter of the funds for education went to rural areas, even though more than half of the national population was considered rural. China's new market economy has continued to favour the urban middle class, leaving the rural poor, peasant migrants, ethnic minorities, and girls lower access and high dropout rates.

The rural–urban gap is also reflected in the structure of the education system. The children of urban residents have access to three years of pre-school (the last year being kindergarten). Pre-schools emphasize basic training as well as the writing of Chinese characters, games, dance, singing, and emphasis on values such as kindness and beauty. Most rural students do not have the opportunity to attend pre-school. At age six, urban children begin six years of primary school, which is usually located in their neighbourhood. In rural and pastoral areas, some students do not begin school until eight years old because rural schools are far from home and roads are not safe for small children. Fewer girls attend school in rural areas and may also drop out of school earlier than boys (Ross 2006). There has been an effort to correct the impression in society that a boy is more valuable than a girl. The 2000 census shows 117 boys to 100 girls, while the world average is 105. In the city of Lianyungang, Jiangsu Province, the sex ratio for newborns aged zero to four reached 163.5 boys to 100 girls in 2005 (Xinhua 2007). The encouraging news is that since 1990, female illiteracy was slashed from 31 per cent to 13 per cent in 2000. In 2002, both boys and girls attended primary school in equal numbers for the first time, although girls had a lower attendance and graduation rate in secondary school than boys.

Many rural children attend a two or three year primary school in their village, then move on to board at a six-year primary school in the township to complete their primary education. Those going on would board at the secondary school in the county town, far from their home village. Urban children commonly attend a secondary school close to home that consists of three years of junior secondary and three years of senior secondary school. About a quarter to two-thirds of them attend senior secondary vocational-technical school. But in some rural areas, vocational-technical education begins as early as junior senior secondary school. In order to make better use of scarce resources, many village schools have been consolidated into township schools. Rural migrants have taken their children to urban areas for schooling, or left their children behind (*liushou ertong*) with relatives and friends in their villages. Children of migrants have diminished educational opportunities. New national guidelines have been proposed to eliminate this growing problem.

There are other issues related to education in rural areas. A free nine-year cycle of compulsory education is guaranteed by law. However, it is not unusual for there to be supplementary fees, especially in rural areas. Until recently, many children in poor rural counties were required to pay for school books.

However, since 2007, governments at central and local levels have instituted measures to prevent schools from charging exorbitant fees. Financial reforms in education since 2007 have improved the free provision of school textbooks and injected funds to assist schools in poorer rural regions (Lou and Ross 2008).

Indeed, as educational costs have risen, many poor households have found it increasingly difficult to cover the costs (Kong 2010). Some rural counties have struggled to fund nine-year compulsory education. Rural areas have lacked the basic conditions necessary for education, including desks, and teaching aids like chalk. While there have been improvements, the Sichuan earthquake of 2008 demonstrated the poor quality of school construction in rural areas. Teacher qualifications and salaries are on the rise but often not enough to keep good teachers in rural areas. Some remote areas have qualified teachers, new schools, adequate facilities and even libraries, while others endure shortages of each. Achieving a more balanced development remains an elusive priority.

Dropout trends have been a major problem in rural areas and have resembled viruses in that they move across the country following increases in primary school enrolments, then level off and move upward to junior secondary school. For example, in a study of three poor counties in Southwest China, Ding (forthcoming) found there were 214 persons in the seventh grade in 2007, 152 in eighth grade in 2008, and 104 in ninth grade in 2009. In this case, more than half dropped out. Although this is not a typical case, and Ding even called it an extreme case, it does demonstrate that high dropout rates still exist in some localities. Such a situation could be viewed as troubling since attendance is very high in urban schools. Ding concludes that the government's 2007 policy of free compulsory education and living expenses subsidies for boarding school students resulted in a decline of the dropout rates. This does not mean that merely increasing funding is the answer to improve education.

Another study of six counties in six provinces or autonomous regions shows that the dropout rates of rural junior high schools were between 3.66 per cent and 54.05 per cent. The study suggests that beyond food and clothing, dropping out is caused by a lack of confidence and interest in continuing their education, difficult textbooks, monotonous school life, tense relationships between students and teachers, poor food and lodging, inconvenient transportation, and rising costs of school lodgings (Sheng and Xue 2003).

Rural girls have constituted a high proportion of the drop-outs from primary schools. Municipalities like Beijing and Shanghai, and east coast provinces like Zhejiang and Jiangsu have lower dropout rates for girls (Ross 2006). Urban families with their only child being a girl are more likely to give as much attention to ensuring a good education as if she were a boy. While 16 provinces in eastern China had virtually full enrolment, the Northwest and Southwest have struggled to catch up. However, the statistics on school attendance and enrolment do not always match the reality because there is pressure on local officials to reach targets set by the central authorities. This can result in a sugar coating of educational statistics. However, such statistics are increasingly being challenged. A study in 2005 contended that enrolment figures were exaggerated. Some schools practised the art of borrowing students when inspectors were expected to visit (Ma 2005; Zhu 2005).

To overcome these problems, the Chinese government has set aside 15 billion yuan for rural education as a way to reduce educational inequality between rural and urban areas. The *Decisions of the State Council to Further Strengthen Education in Rural Areas* has proposed achieving the 'two basics' (literacy and basic education) and improving the educational quality in 372 rural western counties in China. By 2007 all poor students were exempted from miscellaneous fees and textbook charges, and would receive lodging allowances for boarding at school.

Finally, migrant children's education, which is related to the rural-urban divide, has become a major challenge to schools in urban China. The fifth national census of 2000, counted as many as 20 million such children with an average level of education below the norm in the areas where they live. This means that there are over 20 million children in China on the move or living parentless back in their native villages. They do not have the same educational rights as urban children. Many private schools established by migrants, often the only option for migrant children, have been closed by local governments for not meeting the basic standards of building and space. Public primary and junior secondary schools are supposed to educate migrant children and charge them the same amount for school fees as children of permanent residents. The education of migrants is also supposed to be included in the urban development plans. Yet these desirable objectives have yet to be fully achieved.

Ethnic minority groups

Another major dimension of educational inequalities is the gap in schooling between Han Chinese and ethnic minority groups in China. Only ten countries have total populations that surpass that of China's ethnic minorities, which now number about 110 million. The 55 minority groups live in 116 designated ethnic autonomous areas which cover half the country. In minority areas, the state has to ensure education promotes access and equity, economic development, cultural autonomy as set out in the constitution, and national unity. The education of ethnic minorities has thus become a key sector of China's education system (Zhu 2007; Chen 2008; Gao 2008; Yu 2008; Zhao 2009). The Ministry of Education has a large division dealing with their educational policy and practices. The State Ethnic Affairs Commission also has a division of minority education that oversees many of the ethnic colleges in China. Under the government's new curriculum reforms, minority education is supposed to reflect the cultural diversity of China's minorities and improve ethnic intergroup relations, as well as make schools more attractive to ethnic communities, thereby promoting a harmonious multiculturalism.

It is impossible to conceptualize China's ethnic minorities as a single entity due to cultural, regional, and developmental differences. However, the government's unified set of ethnic minority education policies are intended to be implemented flexibly so as to take account of the unique situation in each ethnic minority region. Ethnic autonomous regions became authorized to develop their own educational programmes, including levels and kinds of schools, curriculum content, and languages of instruction. Special funds for minority education were increased, and a portion of the annual budget for ethnic minority areas could be used for education. Funds for teacher training increased and various types of in-service training have been set up. Schools can be established according to the characteristics of the ethnic minorities and their regions; in rural, frontier, and cold mountainous regions, boarding schools were arranged and stipends provided for students. Special emphasis in education could be placed on ethnic minority language, culture and historical traditions. Several major universities have special remedial classes for minority students with preparatory programmes in the first year. University admission standards for minority students have been lowered or points added to ethnic minority students' examination scores to make admission easier to attain.

There are some troubling issues related to educational policies for ethnic minorities in China. Through state educational institutions, ethnic minority culture becomes transmitted, celebrated, transmuted, truncated, or in some cases eliminated. Formal education can become an instrument to broaden cultural sophistication beyond the ethnic community, or it can radically intensify ethnic identities and inequalities in cultural capital. In the case of China, the diversity that exists among its ethnic minority population is only partially reflected in the content of school textbooks, even though minority languages are emphasized in many regions.

In addition, multiethnic diversity is salient in propaganda but not highly encouraged in state education. Ethnic cultures are celebrated at national events, but cultural diversity in schools and society is carefully managed. It is prescribed within the context of the ruling ideology of 'ethnic plurality within the unity of the Chinese nation', and within the government's 'harmonious society' campaign. The debate over cultural preservation, ethnic autonomy, and state schooling has remained complex (Postiglione 1999). Schools can shape ethnic identity through the values they transmit. Making ethnic minorities into Chinese citizens is an educational task which has remained a work in progress. Culturally meaningful access to mainstream schools, colleges and universities has remained a major challenge for improving the quality of ethnic minority community life in China.

Furthermore, most minority groups have trailed Han Chinese in educational attainment. The notion of cultural backwardness has continued to be part of popular discourse about ethnic minorities, and has often been cited in China as the principal reason for educational inequalities between Han Chinese and ethnic minority groups. Cultural backwardness however is not a good argument since about ten of China's 55 minority groups have education levels above the national average. There is a key question regarding the extent to which school norms recognize and encourage diverse cultural groups and create a learning environment that reflects the ethnic diversity of the nation. The extent to which schools in China create an atmosphere that has positive institutional norms towards diverse cultural groups is limited by notions of cultural backwardness. Palden Nyima's research noted how mainstream education has led to a loss of self-esteem and interest in education, particularly in the case of Tibetans, and is reflected in dropout rates (Nyima 1997, 2000).

Conclusion

China's education system is confronting many challenging questions. Is it able to raise the quality of education and reduce the uneven balance in access and equity across regions and groups? Is it able to unite all its ethnic minorities into a mainstream cultural heritage? Will the higher education system continue to produce unemployable graduates or will it be able to foster enough high-level talent among the youth, most of whom are from one-child families, to support China's rapidly aging population in the near future? Can university autonomy and academic freedom become a reality in a one-party state? As the popular Western media is critical of many aspects of state and society in China, it is worth taking note of the unprecedented accomplishment of a developing country of 1 billion that managed in the short span of 30 years to bring most of that large population out of poverty, promote almost full literacy, provide access to basic education for all by 2015, have the largest university system with several world class universities, and be internationally competitive in mathematics and science education.

Bibliography

Chang, Chung-Li (1963) 'Merit vs. money', pp. 22–7 in Johanna M. Menzel (ed.), *The Chinese Civil Service*, Lexington, MA: D.C. Health and Company.

Chen, Yanqbin (2008) *Muslim Uyghur Students in a Chinese Boarding School*, New York: Lexington Press.

Ding, Yanging (forthcoming) 'The problem with access to compulsory education in China and the effects of the policy of direct subsidies to students.' An empirical study based on a small sample. Chinese Education and Society, 45, 1.

Elman, Benjamin A. and Alexander Woodside (1994) *Education and Society in Late Imperial China, 1600–1900*, Los Angeles, CA: University of California Press.

Gao, Fang (2008) 'What it means to be a "model minority"?' *Asian Ethnicity*, 9(1): 55–67.

Hu Wei, Xie Ximei and Chai Chunqing (2009) 'The development of private schools in China', pp. 289–94 in Yang Dongping, Chai Chunqing, and Zhu Yinian (eds), *The China Education Development Yearbook*, Leiden: Brill Press.

Jia, Chen (2010) 'Country's wealth divide past warning level', *China Daily*, May 12, available at http://www.chinadaily.com.cn/china/2010–05/12/content_9837073.htm, accessed on February 25, 2011.

Kong, P. (2010) 'To walk out: rural parents' views on education', *China: An International Journal*, 8(2): 360–73.

Law, Wing-Wah (2006) 'Citizenship, citizenship education, and the state in China in a global age', *Cambridge Journal of Education*, 36(4): 597–628.

Lee, Thomas H.C. (2000) *Education in Traditional China: A History*, Leiden: Brill

Levin, Richard (2010) 'The rise of Asia's universities', The Royal Society, London, http://opac.yale.edu/president/message.aspx?id = 91, accessed on February 25, 2011.

Li, Chunling (forthcoming) 'Socio-political change and inequality of educational opportunities', *Chinese Education and Society*.

Lin, Jing, (1999) *Social Transformation and Private Education in China*, New York: Praeger.

Lou, Jingjing and Heidi Ross (2008) 'The road to free and compulsory education', *Chinese Education and Society*, 41(1): 408.

Ma, Josephine (2005) 'Many rural children cheated of their right to schooling', *South China Morning Post*, January 15, p. 4.

Nyima, Baden (1997) 'The way out for Tibetan education', *Chinese Education and Society*, 30(4): 7–20.

—— (2000) *Wenming de kunhuo: Zangzu de jiaoyu zhilu* (The puzzle of civilization: The way out for Tibetan education), Chengdu: Sichuan Education Press.

Postiglione, Gerard A. (ed.) (1999) *China's National Minority Education: Culture, Schooling and Development*, London: Routledge.

—— (2005) 'Higher education in China', *Harvard China Review*, (Spring): 138–43.

—— (2006) *Education and Social Change in China*, New York: M.E. Sharpe.

—— (2009) 'Education of ethnic groups in China', pp. 501–11 in James Banks (ed.), *The Routledge International Companion to Multicultural Education*, London: Routledge.

—— (2009) 'Higher education since 1949', *Encyclopedia of Modern China*, Volume 1: 482–6.

Postiglione, Gerard and Gulbahar Beckett (2011) *China's National Minority Language Education*, London: Routledge.

Ross, Heidi (2006) 'Challenging the gendered dimensions of schooling', pp. 25–50 in Gerard Postiglione (ed.), *Education and Social Change in China*, New York: M.E. Sharpe.

Sheng Lianxi and Xue Kang (2003) 'Primary education in rural areas', in *Renmin Zhengxiebao* (CPPCCC post), June 26 (cited in Yang Dongping, 'Education from growth to reform', translated in *Chinese Education and Society*, 38(4): 1–45.

Wang Yan (2009) 'Confucian Institutes and international promotion of the Chinese language', pp. 289–94 in Yang Dongping, Chai Chunqing, and Zhu Yinian (eds), *The China Education Development Yearbook*, Leiden and Boston: Brill Press.

Watkins, David A. and John B. Biggs (eds) (1996) *The Chinese Learner: Cultural, Psychological and Contextual Influences*, Melbourne: Australian Council of Educational Research.

Xinhua (2007) 'China warned of risks of imbalanced sex ratio', *China Daily* http://www.chinadaily.com.cn/china/2007–8/24/content_6055339.htm, accessed on February 25, 2011.

Yang Rui (2010) 'Soft power and higher education: an examination of China's Confucius Institutes', *Globalisation, Societies and Education*, 8(2): 235–45.

Yu, Haibo (2008) *Schooling and Identity Among the Naxi*, New York: Lexington Press.

Zhao, Zhenzhou (2009) *Am I Privileged? Minority Mongol Students and Cultural Recognition in Chinese Universities*, New York: Lexington Press.

Zhu Qingshi (2005) 'Jiaoyu gongping jishu zhidu baozhang' (Educational equality news institutional guarantees), *Zhongguo qingnianbao* (China Youth News), www.news.ustc.edu.cn, accessed on March 5, 2011.

Zhu, Zhiyong (2007) *State Schooling and Ethnic Identity: The Politics of a Tibetan Neidi School in China*, New York: Lexington Press.

Films/documentaries

Yige buneng shao (Not one less) (1999), Directed by Zhang Yimou, Popular film in China and Hong Kong, also on DVD.

Zhongxue (Secondary School) (2005) Directed by Tammy Cheung, Hong Kong: Reality Film productions.

Children of Blessing (2007) Directed by Teng Xing, Minzu University, Beijing.

Sisters: Educating China's Future (2005) Directed by Seeberg, V., Jacobs, T.A. (2005) BZMedia, Available at http://www.guanlanscholarshipfoundation.org

Education in the Other China (2004), Seeberg, V., Jacobs, T.A. Cleveland: BZMedia.

8 Status and hierarchy

Qian Forrest Zhang

A society is differentiated and stratified in many ways; hierarchies can be formed and found along multiple dimensions: political power, social honour, economic wealth, cultural knowledge, and even skin colour. All hierarchies, however, do not have the same import. In any society, therefore, one can potentially identify a 'hierarchy of hierarchies' – different dimensions of social inequality and hierarchy form a hierarchy in terms of its importance in shaping people's lives and social relationships.

One useful way to understand this 'hierarchy of hierarchies' in a given society is to see it as determined by how economic activities are organized in that society. By 'economic activities' we mean, following Polanyi (1957: 248), 'interaction between man and his environment, which results in a continuous supply of want-satisfying material means', which, after all, are the main activities that have preoccupied most people's lives throughout human history. The most important social hierarchy is formed on the basis of the dominant *mode of production* (MOP) in an economy – the system of extracting, transferring and distributing economic surplus among different social groups. Although this hierarchy is formed in the processes of economic production and consumption, as we shall see, the basis of this hierarchy – the resource used to create and maintain this hierarchy – can be political power, social status or even religious quality.

Hill Gates (1996) contends that for the past 1,000 years, socioeconomic hierarchy in Chinese society was primarily structured by two different modes of production: the state-managed tributary mode of production (TMP) and the lineage-based petty commodity mode of production (PCMP). As Gates summarizes:

> For a thousand years in the late-imperial tributary mode, a class of scholar-officials has transferred surpluses from the various producer classes (peasants, petty capitalists, laborers) to themselves by means of direct extraction as tribute, taxes, *corvée*, hereditary labor duties, and the like. In the private markets that flourished in China from the Song forward, free producers transferred any remaining surpluses *among* the commoner classes by means of wage labor and a hierarchical kinship/gender system.
>
> (p. 7)

These two systems of organizing production and distributing surplus placed Chinese people within their reach into a two-tiered class structure. Under the TMP, extraction of surplus from producers by holders of political power created the most important status divide in the traditional society: officials vs. commoners. In the PCMP in imperial China, the main unit of petty-commodity production was *patricorporations* – household and lineage enterprises that owned or controlled properties and used mainly family labour to produce commodities to be sold on markets for profit (Gates 1996). Within these patricorporations, surpluses were transferred among members on the basis of the hierarchical kinship/gender relations. By resting ownership of properties, command over production process, and control of consumption patterns in the male, elder, and agnatic members of the patricorporation, the PCMP translated the relational hierarchy that existed among family members, which was culturally defined and politically enforced, into a socioeconomic hierarchy.

Despite a tumultuous century of confrontation with the outside world and internal societal transformation, the existence of some form of state-managed tributary mode of production and market-based petty commodity mode of production persisted to be the two dominant modes of production that shaped socioeconomic hierarchies in Chinese society. The real fundamental change came only after the founding of the People's Republic of China in 1949.

Hierarchies in socialist China

During the socialist era (1949 to 1978), the reach and strength of the TMP reached its apex, whereas the PCMP was suppressed to the point of near elimination. The new socialist state's two main policy goals – creating an egalitarian society on the basis of public ownership of means of production and industrializing an agrarian society with a war-torn economy – both required a transformation of the modes of production and their underlying property relations. The state embarked on an ambitious project of re-engineering the property relations and class structure of the society. Such transformation would then allow the state to penetrate into the lowest level of society and eliminate countervailing forces and local elites, both of which enabled the state to extend the reach and strength of its tributary extraction. To accumulate the capital needed for its plan of state-led industrialization, the state ratcheted up its tributary system to transfer surplus from rural producers to both building urban industries and creating new urban administrative and working classes. To further eliminate competition with the state and concentrate resources into the state's control, the state also suppressed the market-based PCMP to the point of near elimination.

By the mid-1950s, the new regime had already completed much of the socialist transformation of the national economy. A new socialist economy was in place, providing the basis for a new set of social hierarchies to emerge. Although the state had proclaimed creating an egalitarian society as its goal and indeed successfully transformed pre-existing social hierarchies, true equality turned out to be an elusive goal. New social hierarchies soon took shape on the basis of the transformed modes of production.

Socialist transformations of Chinese society

The transformation started in rural areas with the land reform in the early 1950s, when land and properties were seized from the landlord and rich peasant classes and redistributed to all rural households. But in less than a decade, the state started to push for collectivization in agriculture, transferring land ownership from individual households to collective brigades and communes and organizing production collectively. The PCMP was greatly reduced, as its material foundation – private land – was pulled from underneath it. Peasants were left with small plots of land to grow vegetables for self-consumption.

Although rural residents' private land ownership was short-lived, the rural social structure was nevertheless indelibly changed by the land reform and collectivization. The landed gentry, the political and economic elite in pre-socialist China, were eliminated as a class – in some extreme cases, even physically; the rural socioeconomic hierarchy was effectively flattened – the Chinese countryside became a sea of small peasant households under socialism.

Political status became a more significant dimension of hierarchy that set rural residents apart – in a way that reversed the previous hierarchy in rural society. The new regime entrusted local power – and the operation of surplus extraction – to political activists who rose from the lower and middle strata of the rural society: poor and middle-ranking peasants. As a class, these peasants gained not only economically through the redistribution of landlords' properties, but also politically the extractive power granted by the new state. The former landed gentry and other classes classified as counter-revolutionary, on the other hand, not only descended economically to the same level – if not worse – as other rural residents, but also regularly became subjects of political attack and public humiliation.

A similar social transformation swept Chinese cities. Private properties of urban capitalists were nationalized with modest compensations by the state and private enterprises turned first into public-private joint ventures and then publicly owned enterprises. As in rural areas, the PCMP declined, first, because private properties were seized; second, for those hold-outs, as more resources began to be included in the central-planned redistribution, markets for industrial inputs and consumer products both constricted, further squeezing the space for the PCMP. The state's direct control over the increasing number of public enterprises strengthened the TMP, allowing the state to extract surplus from these state-owned enterprises (SOEs) and collective-owned enterprises (COEs).

The establishment of state-owned enterprises gave rise to a new system of regulating urban consumption and workers' lives – the work units. These urban work units provided their employees with a cradle-to-grave system of social services that included housing, childcare, healthcare, education, pension, old-age care, and even on-site canteens and public bathing houses. The work units were also a part of the state's plan of managing urban collective consumption. Replacing markets for housing and other consumption needs with state-planned allocation helped the state to suppress labour wages and private consumption, so that more surpluses could be re-invested into industrialization.

With the establishment of a public enterprise system and state-planned allocation of resources, a new hierarchy emerged in the urban employment structure (Bian 1994). SOE workers became a new labour aristocracy, who enjoyed full benefits of the cradle-to-grave welfare system. COEs, in comparison, were usually smaller and had lower administrative ranks; their ability to provide for their employees was limited. The remaining petty-commodity producers, who struggled at the margin of the state-run economy and had no work units to provide for them, constituted the bottom rung of this urban employment hierarchy.

The urban–rural divide and official–commoner divide

The strengthened TMP erected new hierarchies in its own way. Hierarchies among different social groups based on their standings in the tributary mode of production intensified along two dimensions: urban vs. rural and officials vs. commoners.

Fundamentally, the rural–urban divide was created by the state's extraction of rural surplus, which was then invested in urban industries and social services. It had to be maintained by a politically defined status hierarchy that the state erected to segregate rural and urban residents. The existence of wide gaps between rural and urban living standards would have created a spontaneous city-bound migration by rural residents, which would then threaten to both reduce surplus created in the agricultural sector and divert industrial investment into more urban consumption. To prevent this and to keep rural producers within the reach of TMP, the state implemented strict residential control through the Household Registration System (HRS), which separated rural and urban residents into two distinct categories of citizens.

Rural residents, without urban registration, were not only denied urban employment opportunities, but also excluded from the rationed distribution of many basic consumption items, making it highly difficult for any unauthorized migrants to survive in cities. Except for a few channels of mobility, all managed by the state, which allowed for some rural residents to move to and settle in cities, a highly rigid status hierarchy, based on residential registration, separated urban and rural residents.[1] This urban–rural divide became a long-lasting legacy of the socialist era, shaping the trajectories of many later developments.

The subsuming of a great amount of economic activities under the TMP also strengthened another divide that had long existed in the Chinese society:

that between officialdom, who now were even more empowered with strong central-planning institutions, and commoners, who were further deprived of the opportunity to accumulate some economic wealth in a subordinate PCMP. The socialist officialdom, although now called by a different name, selected through different procedures, and proclaiming a different ideology, nevertheless shared one fundamental feature with the imperial ruling class of scholar-officials: they exercised state power in extracting tributes from commoners and received compensation from the extracted surplus.

Because the socialist state put almost all areas of society under its administration, this official–commoner divide and the administrative hierarchy within officialdom also penetrated and manifested themselves in all walks of life, far beyond just government bureaucracies or state-owned enterprises. The entire society became encompassed within the administrative hierarchy, with the great majority of the population merely commoners, at the bottom of the hierarchy and having no administrative rank, and a small officialdom on top, itself hierarchically organized in multiple ranks.

Entering the officialdom became a quantum leap in social mobility. And such entrance was strictly controlled by the state. Even the privileged urban SOE workers did not automatically have the 'cadre status'. Before an ordinary worker could be promoted to an administrative post – gaining a position in the administrative hierarchy – he or she first needed to be granted a 'cadre quota' and thus changing the status from a commoner to a cadre, a member of the officialdom. Thus, despite the profound social changes implemented by the new socialist regime to create a more egalitarian society, the 'new society' remained highly hierarchical.

Hierarchies in post-socialist China

With the reform starting in late 1970s, another round of profound social changes began, although this time in a more peaceful and incremental fashion than the Communist Revolution. In the first half of the Reform – or Post-Socialist – Era (1978 to present), the central-planned, redistributive economy had remained in force and the dominance of the TMP intact. However, on the margins of the redistributive economy and the TMP, markets started to revive and expand. The PCMP, which had been suppressed and dormant for at least two decades, re-emerged; a new mode of production, the capitalist mode of production (CMP), also rose.

Changes in the modes of production

Self-employment activities were again allowed in both the cities and the countryside at the beginning of the Reform, but were limited to taking on no more than seven employees. In cities, the return of sent-down youths from the countryside and the entry into the labour force by birth cohorts born during the peak birth rates in the 1960s created rampant unemployment. The state had to open up the private petty-commodity production to accommodate the growing demand for jobs.

Initially, self-employment mainly attracted disadvantaged groups – people who could not get jobs in the state sector. The growth of self-employment in cities increased sharply after 1992, when the speed of the reform was accelerated to promote the market economy and private entrepreneurial activities. The rise in self-employment occurred also because the state sector reform started to downsize SOEs and lay off redundant workers in the 1990s. As a result, an internal hierarchy appeared in the petty-commodity production sector. Those who entered to pursue entrepreneurial career opportunities brought with them greater capital and skills and usually had greater success and financial returns from self-employment. Others who were pushed into petty-commodity production by state-sector downsizing and were seeking a refuge from poverty had little more than their own labour to rely on and had many fewer chances of becoming prosperous.

In rural areas, however, the resurgence of the PCMP took a markedly different path. The rural reform disbanded rural communes and brigades as collective units of production, re-assigned land use rights to rural households, and, as a result, restored households as the unit of production and consumption in rural areas. The rural economy was again dominated by smallholding, household producers. Although many these small farming households remained subsistence producers, more and more were becoming commodity producers who produced both agricultural and non-agricultural goods for markets. Rural households were still within the reach of the TMP, subjected to the state's extraction in the form of obligatory grain quotas. However, they were allowed to engage in market-oriented petty commodity production, whether diversifying into non-farm employment or selling agricultural surplus in markets. The new rural economy resembled the pre-socialist formation, where both the TMP and PCMP existed.

Before long, the trickle of rural petty-commodity production turned into a gusher, especially in non-farm production. The growth of rural non-farm employment took different forms in different regions: in the southern coastal region, more in the form of small family-based enterprises, similar to the traditional patricorporations; in northern coastal and inland regions, more in the form of collective township-and-village enterprises (TVEs). For the first 15 years of the post-socialist transition, the growth of TVEs and rural household enterprises became the main force that drove China's rural industrialization and transfer of labour from farming to non-farming jobs. A new dimension in rural social stratification emerged: managers in TVEs, who were usually current or former village cadres, and the enterprising families became the new economic elite in rural society, accumulating wealth through market-based entrepreneurial activities that grew outside the reach of the TMP.

A novel development of the post-socialist era, especially from the 1990s onwards, is the emergence and rapid rise of a capitalist mode of production (CMP) in the economy. Unlike the PCMP, the CMP uses commoditized labour in non-family-based organizations. The extraction of surplus is based on ownership and control over means of production. A crucial event in the rise of the CMP in the Chinese economy is the legalization of domestic private enterprises through a constitutional amendment in 1988, which gave protection to private properties and allowed the employment of eight or more employees. As a result, domestic private firms started to grow, and joined the foreign-invested firms, which first brought in the CMP, in expanding the CMP in the economy. The growth of CMP was further fuelled by the privatization of collective rural TVEs and urban SOEs in the 1990s. The number of domestic private firms increased sharply and some large-size firms started to emerge. In recent years, the domestic private sector has grown to one-third of the national economy, while foreign-invested private firms and state firms each takes another one-third. With this rapid rise of the CMP, the transfer of surplus from commoditized labourers to capital owners emerges as a new and increasingly powerful process in creating social inequality and forming hierarchies.

Not surprisingly, the resurgence of PCMP and rise of CMP pushed the once dominant TMP into a retreat, as the reform opened up new markets and shifted more economic activities outside the reach of the TMP. In the increasingly marketized urban economy, the state withdrew its direct tributary extraction from the increasing number of non-state firms. Even in state firms, more management autonomy and property rights were devolved from governments to the firms themselves. Since the late 1990s, the accelerated pace of privatization in state sectors, especially of smaller-scale SOEs, further reduced the scale of the state-run economy and restricted the reach of the state-managed TMP.

In recent years, however, after the initial period of retreat, the remaining large-scale SOEs, albeit small in number, have experienced a revival and helped to ensure that the TMP remains a powerful force in the new economic system and in shaping social hierarchies. These large-scale SOEs gained strength not only from an influx of capital after being listed on domestic and overseas stock exchanges, but more importantly, from greater capacity of surplus extraction based on market monopoly (Huang 2008). These SOEs were concentrated in the so-called 'strategic sectors' of the national economy where entry by private firms was severely restricted: banking and finance, telecommunications, oil and petrochemicals, energy and resources, public utility, defence, and transportation.[2] Protected by such politically granted market monopoly and emboldened by the political power they had within the state system, these SOEs were able to extract surplus from consumers in the form of monopoly rent, sometimes in excessive amounts and through illegal means.

The corporate reform implemented in these SOEs and their participation in capital, labour and other markets, however, transformed them from traditional socialist firms into a new breed of state firms. Both the CMP and TMP are at work in these state monopoly firms: the state monopoly capital simultaneously extracts surplus from workers on the basis of control of means of production in the CMP and extracts surplus from consumers in the TMP through monopoly rent created and protected by the state's political power.

In rural areas, although the reform allowed households to diversify into farm and non-farm productions outside the reach of TMP and gradually did away with state-imposed mandatory quotas of production, the intensity of the TMP nevertheless expanded for a period of time. In the 1990s, fiscal reform and the privatization and decline of TVEs severely reduced local governments' revenue sources and local governments had nowhere to turn but to ratchet up their extraction of surplus from rural households. As a result, besides the agricultural tax levied by the central government, various levels of local government created a myriad of new types of taxes, levies, charges, and corvée labour to extract surplus from rural residents (Bernstein and Lu 2000). Excessive peasant burdens soon became a nationwide problem and led to the rapid deterioration of local governance in rural areas.

This trend was finally reversed when the Hu Jingtao and Wen Jiabao administration came into office in 2003. In 2004, the agricultural tax was abolished nationwide and, with it, the central state's direct surplus extraction from individual agricultural producers. A practice that had existed for over 2000 years in Chinese history and statecraft finally came to an end. Furthermore, the central government started a direct subsidy to farmers on the basis of farmland size. The central government also implemented strict restrictions on the type and amount of taxes, levies, and corvée labour that local governments could impose on rural residents. Although implementation varied across regions, the combination of these measures helped to curtail the power of the state-managed TMP in rural areas.

Changes in social hierarchies

Under socialism, the dominant mode of production, the TMP, was a political creation: the extractive power was based on the political power of the state, in turning private properties into state properties, in controlling farmers' harvest, in disciplining labour, and in restricting rural residents' exit from state extraction. The hierarchies it created in society, although they had clear social and economic consequences, were primarily based on politically defined statuses – urban vs. rural and officials vs. commoners. The society, thus, was a politically stratified society, or, in sociological terms, a status-stratified society.

In the PCMP and CMP of post-socialist China, the extraction of surplus is based on economic ownership rather than political power. Even the TMP, which remains powerful, now also mixes with and draws on the CMP in its operation in the hybrid form of state monopoly capital. Correspondingly, the hierarchical structure of the society changes, from comprising of primarily politically based hierarchies to a mixture of political and economic hierarchies, with the latter becoming increasingly significant. The most notable change in this process is, therefore, the emergence of economically based hierarchies

– class stratification – in contemporary Chinese society, which can be seen from changes in the rural-urban divide and the emergence of new classes.

To what extent the rural-urban divide has weakened and whether rural-urban inequality has declined or increased are still hotly debated topics. Overshadowed by these debates, however, is an important change: the source of rural-urban inequality is shifting from political to economic. The household registration system that used to create the differential statuses between rural and urban residents is, indeed, still in effect. However, its impact on people's life chances and living conditions has been considerably weakened.

As the institutional barriers erected under socialism to help maintain the TMP and transfer of rural surplus into urban industries were gradually dismantled, urban lives were no longer dependent on the rationed allocation of consumer goods and social services, tied with employment in work units and urban registration. In the past three decades, hundreds of millions of rural residents have migrated to cities – to either work temporarily or settle permanently. These rural migrants are indeed still poorly treated in cities, stigmatized by urbanites, and have difficulties in getting good jobs or permanently settling down; but these difficulties they encounter in cities are increasingly the result of their disadvantaged economic positions in the CMP and PCMP, especially in labour and housing markets, and less the result of a politically defined rural status.

A similar change is happening to the inequality between urban and rural areas. In the past, the 'rural' status was defined not because of one's occupation in agriculture in the economic division of labour, but because of one's position in a political classification – the household registration system. This rural status then simultaneously subjected one to the extraction of surplus under the TMP and excluded one from receiving transfer of surplus in the form of all kinds of urban social services. But nowadays, the rural registration status no longer has such an effect: rural producers are not only freed from the extraction by the central government, but also receive direct transfer of surplus in the form of farming subsidy. They can also freely migrate to cities and have gained access to many urban services.

Rural areas are still generally poorer than cities, but not because they are politically subjected to the tributary extraction by cities, but rather mainly because of their specialization in the less profitable agricultural production in the economic division of labour, which occupies a peripheral and subordinate position to the manufacturing and financial industries in cities. When a rural area upgrades its economy from agriculture into manufacturing, as many rural villages in peri-urban locations have done, it quickly improves its economic prosperity to a level comparable to similar urban areas, without ever changing its politically defined 'rural' status.

Another situation puts this new source of rural-urban inequality in even sharper relief: when rural residents manage to occupy advantageous positions in the economic system vis-à-vis urban residents, the urban-rural hierarchy can be reversed, without changing the political statuses. One can find such examples in the so-called 'villages-in-the-city', or *chengzhongcun* – rural villages encircled by the expanding city. Residents in these villages still have rural registration status – and thanks to that, property rights of land and houses located in these urban 'villages'. These property rights place them in an advantageous economic position as landlords; their rents allow them to live in material comfort and become the envy of many urbanites. On the other side of the equation, many well-educated urban residents – college graduates in Beijing, for example – find themselves in disadvantaged positions in both the labour and housing markets. Their situation has given rise to a new social phenomenon: the 'ants', or *yizu*: people who, like ants, struggle in low-paid, unstable jobs and live in cramped quarters – often rental houses located in peri-urban villages and villages-in-the-city and owned by 'rural' landlords. Clearly, for parties involved in this confrontation, the more important divide is not whether one has a rural or urban status in the political scheme, but whether one owns a property or not in the economic market.

The hierarchy that may still exist between rural and urban residents is now undergirded by different modes of production than before. While the TMP is still in effect, the central processes that create rural-urban disparities are both located in the rising CMP: first, the transfer of surplus from rural migrant labourers to urban owners of capital through the sales and use of commoditized labour; and second, the transfer of surplus from rural agriculture to urban manufacturing and financial industries, when capital and industry increasingly control and profit from both the inputs and outputs of agricultural production.

In both cities and rural areas, people's positions in the economic hierarchy are also gaining importance over positions in the hierarchies of social status and political classification. In cities, a new economic elite, comprised of private entrepreneurs and high-salaried professionals working for multinational and big state firms, not only has carved out an enviable position for themselves in the social hierarchy, but also made an indelible mark with their unprecedented wealth and extravagant lifestyles on the collective imagination of the new consumer society. In recent years, another group that has attracted lots of attention is the so-called 'rich second generation', or *fu erdai*: young adults who are born to large family wealth and are eager to flaunt it, often in an in-your-face manner that triggers strong reactions from the masses.

In rural areas, class-based stratification – a hierarchy based on economic assets and positions – is also gaining ascendance. Under socialism, rural stratification used to be based on two factors: access to political power and the demographic structure of the family. Since the 1980s, however, when, first, rural industrialization and then rural-to-urban migration unleashed the massive transfer of the labour force from agriculture to non-agricultural jobs, access to non-farm wage jobs has become the greatest source of household income inequality in rural China (Khan and Riskin 1998). Families with political connections are still doing better; but most cadre families get higher income because they are able to use their political power to either secure wage jobs for family members or to venture into private entrepreneurship (Walder and Zhao 2006).

In recent years, class-based stratification even started to emerge among agricultural producers. Up until the mid-1990s, income from farming was highly equitable among rural households in China. This is mainly because land was distributed within a village in a largely egalitarian manner. Another reason is that farming in general was not very profitable and could not generate much wealth even for families who have more labour and land engaged in farming. But profound changes have taken place in Chinese agriculture in recent years. New actors – in particular, entrepreneurial farmers and agri-business companies – have entered agriculture and started to organize agricultural production on a large scale with rented land and hired labour. A new hierarchy – one that is determined in this emerging CMP on the basis of one's economic position – is transforming what used to be a flattened and homogeneous peasant class into a host of unequal class positions (Zhang and Donaldson 2010).

Despite the changes outlined above, the continued existence of the TMP determines that the divide between the officialdom and commoners would persist. In some areas, this divide is intensifying. With the retreat of TMP, social services ranging from healthcare to education to housing, which used to be subsidized for urban residents, have been marketized. As a result, for many urban residents now working in the non-state sectors (PCMP and CMP), rising prices for these goods and services are now consuming an increasing portion of their income and becoming heavy burdens. In the housing market in particular, they have shifted from recipients of state transfer of surplus under the socialist TMP to subjects of extraction under the post-socialist CMP, paying monopoly rent to state and corporate actors that now control the privatized urban housing.

Thus, the access to state transfer of surplus under the TMP, in the form of subsidized housing and healthcare, job security, pension, and even the potential to collect 'informal incomes', became an even scarcer opportunity and greater privilege. This explains the great enthusiasm shown by young people in pursuing a career in state sectors. In recent years, a civil service job has become the most sought after in the job market. In 2010, over a million applicants participated in the nationwide qualifying examination for civil service jobs, competing for 16,000 openings, making it the most competitive examination in the country and showing the huge appeal that a place in the civil service still has to the young generations.

Those who are already in the civil service are also acutely aware of their privileges and are actively engaged in passing down such privileges to their children. In many local government agencies or state firms, the recruitment of new employees has become an intensely guarded process that is only open to insiders: children of the officialdom and those well-connected. Enriched by the privileges granted by state institutions and protected by the rampant abuse of official power, some civil servants' children have so antagonized the public with their reckless behaviours and condescending attitudes that they have been labelled the 'officials' second generation', or *guan erdai*, a group that is equally widely loathed as the *fu erdai*.

Conclusion

Many aspects of Chinese society are still in a constant flux; but the set of hierarchies that are taking root now in the social structure, as described above, are likely to be long-lasting features. Fundamental changes have taken place in areas ranging from property rights and corporate governance to market regulation to lay a stable institutional foundation for the operation of the three modes of production: tributary, petty-commodity, and capitalist. The balance between the three will shift; but, barring the unlikely event of regime change or economic collapse, these three modes of production and the socioeconomic hierarchies they generate will be here to stay.

There is probably little doubt that the CMP is going to grow even stronger, as foreign investment continues to pour in and domestic firms get bigger. The increasing clout of big capital and the growth of the CMP are squeezing the space for petty-commodity production. Unless the state steps in to curb the power of big capital, petty-commodity producers will face increasing competition in markets. Experiences from developed countries, however, show that petty-commodity production remains viable even in capitalist economies dominated by big firms. In China's case, the vast number of petty-commodity producers in rural areas provides an even stronger base for the persistence of the PCMP. So long as the collective land ownership in rural areas remains unchanged, which the central government has repeatedly asserted, rural petty-commodity producers will retain some protection against capital's encroachment on their land rights and continue their independent commodity production. Their rank may even grow as more subsistence farmers gain the skill, capital and market access to make the transition into commercial farming, a process that is currently unfolding in many areas of rural China (Zhang and Donaldson 2010).

The number of large SOEs probably will decline slightly, as the central government announced plans to further divest itself of some less profitable SOEs in competitive sectors. The large SOEs that are protected by state-imposed market monopolies and constitute the core of the state sector, however, will remain strong. The central government has made it clear that these national champions will be a pillar in the national economy. In fact, some scholars even worry that preferential treatments given to these state firms and persistent restrictions imposed on domestic private firms are tilting the market in the state firms' favour and could suppress the growth of the CMP (Huang 2008).

Just like the hybrid economy, the social structure of Chinese society will also be characterized by a hybridity of hierarchies. While the politically defined statuses of officials and commoners continue to bring sharply different life chances to groups possessing different statuses, this status divide is no longer the only dimension that differentiates people and creates different life chances. People who are excluded from the officialdom now can nevertheless gain economic wealth in markets through both the PCMP and CMP. Success in the market economy has already given rise to a growing class of economic elite.[3] Some of them may not enjoy as much social prestige as officials and may even be harassed and extorted by corrupt officials, but their economic wealth and the freedom they have to dispose of it, nevertheless, are still the envy of many, even members of the officialdom.

The urban–rural divide is increasingly sustained through the unequal division of labour and exchange relationships under a capitalist economy. The declining significance of political status and rising significance of economic conditions in determining rural–urban inequality can also change the structure of the rural–urban hierarchy. In rural areas, the strong institutional protection of small farmers' land rights and intrinsic barriers in agriculture against the penetration of capital provide stronger foundations for the survival and even growth of petty-commodity producers in agriculture. In the urban economy, in contrast, petty-commodity producers face increasing competition from big capital and declining profits in the production process. Proletarianized urban workers who are exposed to the brute forces of markets are in even worse condition. Compared to agricultural petty-commodity producers in rural areas, they may find that the social status they enjoy as urban residents, which used to put them in enviable positions in the status hierarchy under socialism, now provides few material comforts and is dwarfed by the economic disadvantages they confront in their low positions in the new class hierarchy.

Notes

1 Some rural residents worked for state factories as part time workers – they did manual labour and were kept out of the regular payroll. At the end of each year, they went back to their villages and bought work points from their production teams with cash they earned in city jobs, so that they would receive their grain rations. I am grateful to the editor for pointing this out.

2 In recent years, the state has started to open up these protected monopoly sectors to private firms. In 2005 and 2010, two rounds of liberalizing measures were implemented to ease and encourage the entry of private capital into these previously protected sectors. However, given the huge size and market dominance of state firms in these sectors, private firms' role will continue to be marginal.

3 In reality, however, people who rose to the economic elite through success in the CMP were more likely to have close ties with the officialdom. In a hybrid economy where the TMP remains powerful, ties with officials help private entrepreneurs to either keep the state's grabbing hand at bay from predatory extraction of their wealth, or gain access to monopoly rent protected by state power.

Bibliography

Bernstein, Thomas P. and Xiaobo Lu (2000) 'Taxation without representation: peasants, the central and the local states in reform China', *China Quarterly*, 163: 742–63.

Bian, Yanjie (1994) *Work and Inequality in Urban China*, Albany, NY: State University of New York Press.

Davis, Deborah and Feng Wang (2008) *Creating Wealth and Poverty in Postsocialist China*, Stanford, CA: Stanford University Press.

Gates, Hill (1996) *China's Motor: A Thousand Years of Petty Capitalism*, Ithaca, NY: Cornell University Press.

Ho, Ping-Ti (1964) *The Ladder of Success in Imperial China: Aspects of Social Mobility, 1368–1911*, New York: Science Editions.

Huang, Yasheng (2008) *Capitalism with Chinese Characteristics: Entrepreneurship and the State*, Cambridge: Cambridge University Press.

Khan, Azizur Rahman and Carl Riskin (1998) 'Income and inequality in China: composition, distribution and growth of household income, 1988–95', *China Quarterly*, 154: 221–53.

Logan, John R. (ed.) (2008) *Urban China in Transition*, Oxford: Blackwell Publishing.

Polanyi, Karl (1957) 'The economy as instituted process', pp. 243–70 in Karl Polanyi, Conrad M. Arensberg, and Harry W. Pearson (eds.), *Trade and Market in the Early Empires*, New York: Free Press.

Walder, Andrew G. and Litao Zhao (2006) 'Political office and household wealth: rural China in the Deng era', *China Quarterly*, 186: 357–76.

Wang, Feng (2007) *Boundaries and Categories: Rising Inequality in Post-Socialist Urban China*, Stanford, CA: Stanford University Press.

Watson, James L. (ed.) (1984) *Class and Social Stratification in Post-Revolution China*, Cambridge, MA: Harvard University Press.

Whyte, Martin King (2010) *Myth of the Social Volcano: Perceptions of Inequality and Distributive Injustice in Contemporary China*, Stanford, CA: Stanford University Press.

Whyte, Martin King (ed.) (2010) *One Country, Two Societies: Rural-Urban Inequality in Contemporary China*, Cambridge, MA: Harvard University Press.

Zang, Xiaowei (2000) *Children of the Cultural Revolution: Family Life and Political Behavior in Mao's China*, Boulder, CO: Westview Press.

Zhang, Qian Forrest and John A. Donaldson (2010) 'From peasants to farmers: peasant differentiation, labor regimes, and land-rights institutions in China's agrarian transition', *Politics & Society*, 38(4): 458–89.

Zhou, Xueguang (2004) *The State and Life Chances in Urban China: Redistribution and Stratification, 1949–1994*, Cambridge: Cambridge University Press.

Related novels and lighter reading

Chang, Leslie T. (2009) *Factory Girls: From Village to City in a Changing China*, New York: Spiegel & Grau.

He, Liyi (1993) *Mr. China's Son: A Villager's Life*, Boulder, CO: Westview Press.

Hong, Ying (2000) *Daughter of the River: An Autobiography*, New York: Grove Press.

Pomfret, John (2007) *Chinese Lessons: Five Classmates and the Story of the New China*, New York: Holt Paperbacks.
Yu, Hua (2010) *Brothers*, New York: Anchor.

Films

Cell Phone (2003 Feng Xiaogang)
Still Life (2006 Jia Zhangke)
The World (2004, Jia Zhangke)

9   Ethnic minorities

Colin Mackerras

The borders of the People's Republic of China (PRC) are mainly those established by the Qing Dynasty (1644–1911) and inherited by the Republic of China (ROC, 1912–49). The territory the Chinese sometimes call 'Outer Mongolia' belonged to Qing China, but is now an independent state called the Republic of Mongolia, although Inner Mongolia remains part of China. Potter (2011: 2) notes the importance of the 'frontier' in 'China's sense of itself' and its relations with its neighbours, as well as with the communities that live in the frontier areas, which include Tibet, Xinjiang and Inner Mongolia. There is a good deal of overlap between China's border regions and the 'ethnic areas' (*minzu diqu*), which are those places where there are significant ethnic minority populations.

What is an ethnic minority?

The term 'ethnic minority' is the usual English translation of the Chinese *shaoshu minzu*, which means literally 'minority nationality'. The word *minzu* is understood as a community of people with a shared history, territory, language, economic life and culture. First proposed by Stalin in 1913, this definition was adopted by the PRC in its early days and has survived substantially unchanged ever since. Chinese-language texts from the PRC still talk of the *shaoshu minzu*; those in English having changed to current usage from 'minority nationality' or 'national minority'.

The Chinese state recognizes 56 ethnic groups, the Han and 55 ethnic minorities. Everybody is registered as belonging to a particular ethnic group, the decision as to which one resting less with individuals than with the state. The process of reaching the number 56 has been complex, but broadly successful in the sense that Chinese people overwhelmingly accept their assigned ethnic classification. (See Mullaney 2011: especially 120–36.)

There are many ways of categorizing these minorities, including economic life in the pre-modern era, language, culture and religion. The one with the largest territory, though not the most populous, is the Tibetans, who live in the southwest in areas making up nearly a quarter of all China. Two of them formerly ruled the whole of China. The first was the Mongolians who ran the largest land empire in world history, including the Yuan dynasty in a united China from 1280 to 1368; the second the Manchus, whose ruling family were the emperors of the Qing Dynasty. A range of ethnic minorities lives in China's south to southwest, especially Yunnan, Guangxi and Guizhou. These include several with significant cultures and identities, such as the Zhuang, the Yi, the Miao and the Yao. Finally, a very important group is the Islamic minorities. There is a total of ten, but the two most noteworthy are the Hui and the Uyghurs. The Hui live all over China; they are ethnically and culturally Chinese, except for their Muslim faith. The Uyghurs are Turkic linguistically and culturally, with almost all of them living in Xinjiang, in the far northwest.

Some of the ethnic minorities are quite similar culturally to the Han, but others are very different indeed. Although there are many commonalities among them, they illustrate great diversity in terms of language, religion, the arts, architecture, diet and family practices. On the whole, China has managed this cultural diversity quite well and the great majority of the members of the ethnic minorities appear willing, even happy, to remain within the PRC. The overall trend since the middle of the twentieth century has been towards a better-integrated Chinese state. However, there have been occasions when factors such as political dissatisfaction, the fear of being culturally submerged, ethnic and other inequalities, and the fanning of discontent from outside or inside China have led to ethnic violence and animosities, including movements that have tried to separate particular ethnic areas from China. Among the minorities that have seen separatist movements, the two most notable are the Tibetans and the Uyghurs.

Population

Although the territory of the 55 ethnic minorities takes up about 65 per cent of China's total area, their population is small relative to the whole country. The 'ethnic areas' are actually much less thickly populated than those inhabited by the Han. They include the dry pastoral areas of Inner Mongolia, the Gobi and Taklamakan, among the largest deserts in the world, and the relatively infertile high-lying Tibet-Qinghai Plateau. This vast plateau is home to almost all China's Tibetans, as well as quite a few other people belonging to an ethnic minority.

There have been six censuses under the PRC, held in 1953, 1964, 1982, 1990, 2000 and 2010. In China the census includes ethnic breakdown and also gives aggregate figures for the ethnic minorities as a whole as well as their proportion in China's total population. The 1953 census showed the minorities at 34 million, or 5.89 per cent of the total population; that of 1982 put them at 66.4 million, or 6.62 per cent of the total, while the proportion in 1990 was 8.01 per cent of the total, which had by 2010 risen to 8.49 per cent or 13.79 million people. The most populous of the ethnic minorities is the Zhuang, who numbered just over 16 million in the 2000 census. Others

Figure 9.1 A trance medium (shaman) in the Tu village of Keshiman, which is in the far east of Qinghai Province, not far from the capital Xining. Taken by Colin Mackerras in October 2008.

with large populations (all according to the 2000 census) include the Manchus (10.68 million), the Hui (9.8 million), the Uyghurs (8.4 million), the Mongolians (5.8 million), and the Tibetans (5.4 million). The smallest in population was the Lhoba, who live in Tibet, and numbered just under 3,000.

The ethnic populations have been rising consistently under the PRC. More importantly, the proportion of the minorities within the total Chinese population has increased significantly since 1953, and especially between 1982 and 1990. There are a few reasons that are worthy of comment.

First, the policy of one-child-per-couple adopted in the late 1970s did not apply to the minorities. This did not mean that there were no rules or recommendations for the minorities, but they varied greatly from place to place and from one minority to the other. In general, sensitive ethnic minorities with relatively low and thinly spread populations were subject to more flexible and lenient rules than others. A good illustrative example is the Tibetans, a government statement of 1999 stating that Tibetan farmers and herdsmen in the Tibet Autonomous Region (TAR) may have as many children as they like. (See discussion, including relevant figures in Mackerras 2003: 134–41).

With the end of the Cultural Revolution, it became more socially accepted to belong to certain ethnic groups than had been the case before. Moreover, the government reinstituted and broadened its programme of affirmative action or 'preferential policies' (*youhui zhengce*) for the minorities. The result was that groups and individuals who had hidden their identity were happy to expose it, even with pride. Perhaps the best example is the Manchus, whose population in the 1982 census numbered 4.3 million but had more than doubled to 9.85 million in that of 1990. This extraordinary growth in just eight years was largely due to re-registration, meaning that the state allowed groups or individuals who had initially been called Han to change their registration to Manchu. Formerly, Manchus had felt a sense of shame, because their ethnic group had ruled China's last dynasty, the Qing, being in effect colonizers. But with the passage of time, and with new policies, such a history was no longer relevant, and there was no reason why Manchus could not share the privileges accorded other minorities.

The Han and the ethnic minorities

Given that the ethnic minorities make up less than 10 per cent of China's people, it follows that the Han are overwhelming in terms of the population, and in more or less all other respects. Indeed, with about 1.3 billion people, the Han are the world's most populous ethnic group. Given that the Han is so dominant and the ethnic group one normally associates with the Chinese, the question arises whether the ethnic minorities should be regarded as Chinese. Both the PRC and the ROC have been very clear that they are indeed Chinese, with the combination of the Han and the ethnic minorities making up 'the Chinese nation' (*Zhonghua minzu*).

Actually, this concept dates back only to the early twentieth century but has become important to various Chinese leaders since then. Among these, the main one was Sun Yat-sen (1866–1925), who Chinese of virtually all political persuasions honour as the founder of the ROC. Sun developed the 'three people's principles' (*sanminzhuyi*), which became the ROC's guiding ideology. The first of them is 'nationalism', a doctrine requiring the assimilation of the ethnic groups into a unified Chinese nation (*Zhonghua minzu*) based on the Han.

Sun recognized only five ethnic groups, the Han, Manchus, Mongolians, Tibetans and Hui, the last one including all Muslims, not just the Sinic ones. The PRC expanded the number and replaced the idea of assimilation with that of 'the unity of the nationalities' (*minzu tuanjie*). However, all PRC leaders have followed Sun in stressing Chinese unity. They have retained the notion of 'the Chinese nation' and, although it has received stronger emphasis at some times than at others, it has always remained acceptable in the PRC.

While the idea of a unified nation is a reasonable one that enjoys a great deal of support both inside and outside China, there could be a problem with the term *Zhonghua minzu*. This is the risk of 'essentializing the Han', a potentially racist notion signifying that the 'subordination of nationalities in China leads to the clear promotion of the Han to the vanguard of the peoples of the

People's Republic' (Gladney 2004: 59). In ancient times, the term *Huaxia* (the *Hua* being the same character as in *Zhonghua*) referred to China's majority ethnic group, so *Zhonghua* appears to give the focus to ethnicity as opposed to *Zhongguo* (the current Chinese term meaning China), which could be taken to emphasize place. The implication is that the use of *Zhonghua minzu*, instead of *Zhongguo minzu*, to represent the totality of the Chinese nation, could lead to a revival of assimilative thinking, if not in theory then at least in practice. The idea of the superiority of Han culture is extremely widespread in China, both among the Han themselves and even the minorities.

There will be more to say about how minority cultures fare in the context of Han-led modernization. However, here I think it fair to point out the rise of consciousness among some minorities, especially since the 1980s. Scholarly works have noted this rise of identity feelings among such peoples as the Hui (Gladney 1991), and the Zhuang and Yao of the south-western region of Guangxi and elsewhere (Kaup 2000; Litzinger 2000). Observers have given more attention to ethnic minorities like the Tibetans and Uyghurs, but that does not mean they are the only ones to have experienced a growing ethnic identity.

The ethnic minorities: policy and reality

The basic policy of the PRC towards the ethnic minorities allows them to exercise autonomy in their own areas, but absolutely forbids separatism. The PRC has set up five autonomous regions, which are equivalent in status to provinces, namely the Inner Mongolian Autonomous Region (set up 1947), the Xinjiang Uyghur Autonomous Region (1955), the Guangxi Zhuang Autonomous Region (1958), the Ningxia Hui Autonomous Region (1958), and the TAR (1965). There are also 30 autonomous prefectures and some 120 autonomous counties or units of equivalent status.

As defined in Chinese law, autonomy has a range of meanings. The head of government in the ethnic areas must belong to the ethnic group that exercises autonomy. The government tries to increase the number of minority members holding positions of influence or power or professional qualifications. Minorities are entitled to preserve the good aspects of their own cultures. There are preferential policies for minorities in a range of areas, such as employment in government positions, enrolment in higher education, and in matters of population control.

There are, however, severe restrictions on autonomy. The main one is that there is no requirement on the Chinese Communist Party (CCP) to select minority members for high positions in the minority areas. So, the government head of Xinjiang must be a Uyghur, but the party secretary need not be so. Moreover, it is well known that the CCP actually holds far more power everywhere in China than the government. Although members of ethnic minorities are encouraged to join the CCP, those of religiously dedicated ethnic groups, such as the Tibetans or the Muslim minorities, are generally reluctant and there is a sense among some CCP members that they are untrustworthy anyway. The result is that the proportions of such ethnic groups entering the CCP are fairly low.

The economy

Probably the highest of all Chinese government economic priorities in the ethnic areas is to promote development. This has been especially the case in the reform period and in general appears to have gathered momentum. Chinese authorities believe that raising the standard of living will persuade the ethnic minorities to wish to remain part of the PRC and promote their loyalty towards the state, as well as improve ethnic harmony and good relations among the various ethnic groups. Successive official reports and white papers have claimed, for the ethnic areas, continual rises in overall production and in consumption levels, improvements in infrastructure, housing and health delivery, and increases in tourism and outside investment.

In 2000 the government launched its Great Western Development Strategy. This aimed not only to push economic development in general but to reduce the economic gap between the prosperous coastal areas and the comparatively poor remainder of the country. Mainly focused on the western half of the country, the targeted regions include the great majority of the ethnic areas.

Successive visits to Tibet, Xinjiang, Inner Mongolia and various other ethnic areas have made me witness to gigantic improvements in living standards, both in the urban and rural areas. The capital of Xinjiang, Ürümqi, was a totally different world during my 2010 visit from when I first went there in 1982. It was much more modern, much cleaner, with generally far better housing, more prosperous markets and larger numbers of tall buildings. There could, however, be a cost in terms of cultural preservation, because modernization does not generally sit well with traditional cultures (see next section). Moreover, despite the overall growth, poverty remains a problem and inequalities, especially between Han and ethnic minorities, appear to have widened during the reform period.

One of the greatest gaps in China is between urban and rural, the former being considerably better off than the latter. On the whole the proportion of ethnic minorities living in the countryside is even higher than of the Han. There has been a rapid process of urbanization since the early 1980s, but on the whole it has affected the Han much more than the minorities. Historically, especially in south-western provinces like Guizhou and Yunnan, the Han have tended to take over the agricultural land in the plains, chasing the minorities into the mountains. The result is that the minority communities are mostly at a severe disadvantage in achieving economic parity with the Han.

The Chinese government's record in reducing absolute poverty is a good one by international standards. The number of Chinese living beneath the absolute poverty line has sunk greatly since the 1980s, one government figure putting the total number of rural poor nationally in 1990 at about 85 million, but only 42 million in 1998. Several major programmes have targeted ethnic areas and populations in poverty alleviation. These have succeeded in reducing absolute poverty among the ethnic minorities, but the rate remains much higher than in the population as a whole. On 30 March 2007, China's official Xinhua News Agency reported a vice-director of the government's State Ethnic Affairs Commission as stating that about 7 per cent of China's minority people were living in absolute poverty, as opposed to about 2.6 per cent of the total population. Translated into absolute figures, about 8.5 million members of ethnic minorities, out of a national total of about 34 million people, were afflicted by absolute poverty. Although it has since raised the line, the cited 2007 figures assumed a boundary of US$0.66 income per person per day, as opposed to the US$1 generally used internationally. As for the causes behind the persistent disparity, a major study of poverty and inequality among China's minorities puts them down not to cultural differences but to factors like locality, mountainous terrain, underdeveloped infrastructure, and low education levels (Bhalla and Qiu 2006: 168).

Some aspects of culture

This claim brings us to culture. The focus here is less anthropological than political, taking up the controversial issue of cultural survival among ethnic minorities in the PRC. The term culture is so broad that it becomes necessary to break it down. Here I discuss only two aspects: language and religion. Language is essential to the lives of all ethnic groups, and of crucial importance to cultural survival. Religion generally weighs more heavily with the ethnic minorities than with the Han, especially Tibetan Buddhism and Islam.

The languages of China's minorities belong to several different families, Sino-Tibetan and Altaic being best represented. The Hui are Chinese-speaking, but the other ethnic minorities have their own language, some of them two or more. Although they once ruled all China, the number of Manchus who still speak their own language is vanishingly small.

Minorities are entitled to use their own languages not only at home but in the public sphere, such as in government, law and education. In many parts of China where school-children belong to one ethnic minority, it has been common practice for teachers to use the local language in primary school as the medium of instruction, though the higher up the education system, the more Chinese tends to become the language for teaching. As the economy has grown, it has become more important for nation-building that all citizens be able to converse and be literate in Chinese. More and more parents want their children to know Chinese for one very simple reason: if they do not know Chinese, they are at a great disadvantage in finding good employment.

Figure 9.2 An old Uyghur man in the ancient village of Tuyuk, near Turpan,
         Xinjiang Uyghur Autonomous Region. Colin Mackerras in May 2007.

The implication is that Chinese has tended to become increasingly dominant
in the public sphere, resulting in the decline of ethnic languages. Among
several ethnic minorities, especially Tibetans and Uyghurs, this has been a
matter of enormous concern and resentment.

Chinese law guarantees freedom of religion. Although the Cultural Revolution saw great persecution against all religions and faiths, they have experienced powerful revivals since the 1980s. However, Chinese law bans the use
of religion to try and destabilize the state; and in politically sensitive regions
authorities are frequently so cautious in interpreting religious observation as
political opposition as to contravene freedom of religion. Moreover, the state
has control over senior clerical appointments and remains extremely suspi-
cious of any non-state-sponsored political activity on the part of religious
personnel. As we shall see later, Buddhism is interwoven with politics among
the Tibetans, and Islam among the Uyghurs, but on the whole religions and
faiths of various kinds flourish openly among the ethnic minorities. The inter-
connection between Islam and ethnicity is of particular interest. In China, *all*
Muslims belong to an ethnic minority, not to the Han. This is because anybody
who is Chinese culturally but also Muslim is automatically Hui, not Han.

Evidence from impressions gathered through extensive travelling in ethnic
areas of China over a long period suggests to me that religious practice and

thinking there are open and very much alive. It is likely that there is a higher proportion of the population in the clerical order among Tibetans than any other ethnic group in the world. Islam remains very strong, both politically and in social influence. Are these religions in gradual decline as modernization gathers momentum, just as has happened with Christianity in countries such as France or the United Kingdom? Possibly male urban Muslims pray less and pay less serious attention to religious duties than their fathers or grandfathers. Trends in the countryside are less clear, but possibly moving in a similar direction. The Tibetan Buddhism of the Mongolians is clearly weaker than it was, with urbanites not allocating it much attention. Particular ethnic religious traditions may die out over the coming decades. However, I doubt a more general death of religious faith and practice among the ethnic minorities. In particular, I do not foresee the day when Buddhism is no longer a social force among the Tibetans or Islam among the Uyghurs, Hui or a range of other ethnic groups in China.

Main problem areas

The ethnic minorities to have posed most difficulty for the Chinese state are the Tibetans and the Uyghurs. Both groups have strong religiously influenced

Figure 9.3 An Islamic graveyard beside the Golden Mosque, Yarkant, east of Kashgar, which is in the far southwest of Xinjiang. Taken by Colin Mackerras in October 2010.

Figure 9.4 Uyghur dancers performing just after a big Uyghur lunch, Turpan, taken by Colin Mackerras in April 2007.

cultures, Tibetan Buddhism in the former case, Turkic Sunni Islam in the latter. The Tibetans have an internationally admired leader, the Dalai Lama, whereas there is no figure of comparable stature representing the Uyghurs.

In 1950 the People's Liberation Army (PLA) moved into Tibet and on 23 May 1951, the Dalai Lama's representatives and the central Chinese government signed an agreement, under which Tibet was recognized as part of the PRC, but with the Tibetans enjoying autonomy. On 10 March 1959, a major uprising erupted against Chinese rule, the Dalai Lama escaping to India, where he set up the Tibetan government-in-exile (TGIE). The Chinese government undertook major reforms, the TAR's 1965 establishment being one of the results.

After a period of severe persecution of Tibetan religion and culture during the Cultural Revolution, the reform period saw a major revival, with attempts to strengthen autonomy and relieve the people of certain types of taxation. In 1985 the only non-Han ever to hold the position of CCP secretary in Tibet arrived in Lhasa. This was Wu Jinghua, who was Yi and thus a member of an ethnic minority. Though not a Tibetan, he encouraged policies of Tibetanization, renamed streets in Tibetan and attended religious functions himself, wearing Tibetan dress.

However, from 1987 to 1989 there were major disturbances in Tibet, especially Lhasa, with monk-led demonstrations calling for Tibetan independence.

The Chinese suppressed the demonstrations, and blamed the Dalai Lama and his American supporters for inciting them. In March 1989, the Chinese government declared martial law in Lhasa, two months earlier than the similar move to curb the student demonstrations in Beijing, and did not lift it until April 1990.

In 1995, there was major international controversy over the choice of the eleventh incarnation of the Banchen Lama, the most important figure in Tibet after the Dalai Lama, since the tenth had died in January 1989. Beijing and the Dalai Lama favoured different boys. Of course, the Chinese government won the day, holding a grand ceremony to enthrone its own choice as the Eleventh Banchen Lama, and blocked the Dalai Lama's from communication with visitors from outside China. Most Westerners interested in the issue had sided with the Dalai Lama in the argument and charged the PRC with imprisoning the child they had wanted as the Eleventh Banchen Lama.

Yet despite this controversy, the 1990s and the first years of the 2000s were relatively free of incident in Tibet or other Tibetan areas. There were no major demonstrations pushing independence, and no serious rioting. The Chinese government actively promoted economic development and allowed a considerable degree of religious and cultural freedom, provided nobody used this flexibility to seek independence or threaten China's stability.

The lack of an outside focus comparable to the Dalai Lama made Xinjiang simpler than Tibet for China in the period before 1990. The PLA easily took over Xinjiang in 1949. Demobilized Han troops were the basis of a peculiarly Xinjiang body, the Production and Construction Corps, which aimed to develop the region economically and secure its position within China. It also effected large-scale Han immigration into Xinjiang from the 1950s onward. The Cultural Revolution saw the same repression of religion and traditional culture as everywhere else in China, but the aftermath witnessed major restoration of the traditional faiths and cultures of Xinjiang's ethnic minorities, Islam reviving with special vigour.

Unlike in Tibet, the 1990s saw quite a few disturbances in Xinjiang. A major study on the Uyghurs lists all the 'organized protests and violent events in Xinjiang' from 1949 to 2005, about half taking place in the 1990s (Bovingdon 2010: 174–90). One factor of great significance was the decline and collapse of the Soviet Union. There was, for instance, serious ethnic conflict in the Tajikistan capital Dushanbe in February 1990, with the final Soviet disintegration at the end of the following year. It is likely that the Dushanbe conflict was one contributor to a two-day armed uprising in Baren Township, Southwestern Xinjiang, in April 1990. The uprising's leader, who appears to have espoused holy war Islamist ideology, was killed but the influence of the event persisted. Among a series of incidents in the 1990s, a particularly serious one was a riot in February 1997 in Guldja (Chinese: Yining) in the northwest, not far from the border with Kazakhstan. China, Russia, Kazakhstan, Kyrgyzstan and Tajikistan had begun annual meetings at presidential level in April 1996 in an attempt to counter Islamist and other destabilizing influences, and in June 2001 added Uzbekistan at a meeting that formed the Shanghai Cooperation Organization.

The September 11, 2001 incidents impacted on Xinjiang. China and the United States had common interests in attacking Islamist terrorism. In 2002, the United States accepted China's claim that a body it called the East Turkestan Islamic Movement was terrorist in nature, the United Nations following suit. The first few years of the twenty-first century saw China keeping a more watchful eye against separatism and extremism in Xinjiang, and there were in fact far fewer incidents than in the preceding years. At the same time, the Uyghur diasporic groups strengthened their organization and in 2004 united to form the World Uyghur Congress. Although it presented itself as entirely secular and condemned terrorism and violence, this body contains elements that advocate independence for Xinjiang, giving it the name East Turkestan.

Disturbances in 2008 and 2009

The relative calm that had obtained in the Tibetan areas since the 1990s was broken in March 2008. Protests by monks commemorating the 10 March 1959 uprising remained peaceful, but were followed by serious ethnic rioting on 14 March. For several weeks, disturbances flared all over the Tibetan areas, some of them violent. Estimates of casualties varied greatly depending on the source, with Chinese officials claiming 27 deaths and the TGIE 220.

These protests differed greatly from those of the late 1980s in several respects. Two stand out. One is that they took place all across the Tibetan areas, not just in the TAR, let alone only in Lhasa. Second, whereas the overwhelming majority of protests in the late 1980s were led by monks or nuns, with comparatively few laypeople involved, less than a quarter of those in 2008 were by monks or nuns, with 17 per cent being student protests and most being by mixed or lay groups, including farmers, workers and students (Barnett 2009: especially 11–13).

There were numerous causes for the disturbances, both internal and external. Among the former was a widespread feeling among Tibetans of marginalization in society, including a lack of appreciation for their culture, and a sense that they were not doing nearly as well from economic development as Han immigrants. The external causes are linked with the international dimension of the Tibetan disturbances, which we now briefly consider.

The Beijing Olympic Games were about to start on 8 August 2008. Because this was the first time they were held in China, they mattered greatly to the overwhelming majority of Chinese people. Human rights activists in the West declared their intention to use the occasion of the Olympic Games to turn the spotlight on China's human rights abuses, especially in Tibet. At the same time, various groups had declared their intention to lead a Tibetan People's Uprising. To this end, a march of monks began on 10 March in Delhi and, although the Indian police stopped it quite soon, it was among the factors giving the Chinese authorities grounds for putting the blame on the 'Dalai clique', meaning not only the Dalai Lama himself but also his many followers. The Olympic Torch proceeded from Olympia in Greece late in March to many world cities, becoming involved in anti-Chinese protests connected with the disturbances in the Tibetan areas, especially in a scuffle in Paris.

These Tibetan disturbances were followed by riots in July 2009 in Ürümqi. Initially sparked by reports that Han men had murdered two Uyghurs, falsely rumoured to have raped Chinese women, ethnic rioting flared on 5 July, attackers being mainly Uyghurs and victims Han and Hui. The Han counterattacked two days later. According to official reports, the riots cost the lives of 197 people, with about 1,600 injured, most of the victims being Han. The next month, there were attacks against ordinary people with syringes. In the event, these do not appear to have been infected, but syringe attacks of this kind cannot fail to spread rumours, fear and panic.

As with the Tibetan disturbances, there were internal and external causes of these riots. Of course the situation had changed over the sixteen months or so since March 2008. The Olympic Games were over, and the global financial crisis had weakened the world economy, including in China.

The disparities and sense of marginalization was a factor among the Uyghurs, as with the Tibetans, and levels of wealth, health and education were considerably lower among Uyghurs than Han. The proportion of Han in the Xinjiang population was considerably greater than in the Tibetan areas, let alone the TAR itself, and the resentment caused to the Uyghurs through seeing the Han do better from economic growth possibly even greater.

The Chinese authorities put the blame for the riots on the World Uyghur Congress, an anti-China international body set up in 2004, and its president, former businesswoman Rebiya Kadeer. I remain sceptical of the evidence I have seen for pinning all the responsibility on her. However, the World Uyghur Congress was probably happy at the embarrassment China suffered from the riots. Moreover, there is little doubt that Islamist forces outside Xinjiang try to influence what happens inside the autonomous region, with quite a few local Uyghurs happy to answer to them.

Both sets of disturbances created an impact on the Chinese leadership, inducing them to re-examine policies. In January and May 2010 there were high-level central meetings on the Tibetan areas and Xinjiang respectively. In both cases, the main panacea offered was enormous investments aimed at raising the standard of living, improving infrastructure and carrying out further modernization programmes in the hope that these would reduce discontent and increase the incentives of the Tibetans and Uyghurs to remain part of the PRC.

Despite general similarities, there were also some differences in approach. For instance, the communiqué following the meeting on the Tibetan areas included the phrase 'Chinese characteristics, Tibetan flavour' (*Zhongguo tese,*

Xizang tedian). This could potentially suggest more appreciation of Tibetan culture, especially as Premier Wen Jiabao's speech at the closing session made a laudatory reference to the 'material and intangible cultural heritage of Tibet'. However, there is no guarantee that the change in priority will be substantial.

In the case of the meeting on Xinjiang, the centre directed that billions of yuan should go towards strengthening Uyghurs' command of Chinese language. The idea is to teach the language not only taught as a major subject but as the medium of instruction from the earliest grades in all classes other than those teaching Uyghur language to Uyghur children. Just as before 2010, classes in Uyghur aim to ensure the maintenance of Uyghur literacy among Uyghur children.

Conclusion

In some ways, China's handling of ethnic problems has been successful, in other ways not. The country is probably better integrated than it used to be, with less likelihood of splitting up or separatist movements succeeding. Its people are much more prosperous, including its ethnic minorities, and their living standards higher. It appears on the path towards reasonably successful modernization. Minority traditions that harmed particular groups of people, especially women, are weaker now than they used to be. In most places, ethnicity is not a marker when it comes to relations among people.

On the other hand, there are respects in which success is much less obvious. In the Tibetan areas and Xinjiang, ethnic relations are still tense and have probably worsened over the decades since the Cultural Revolution. These poor relations and hostility to the state have erupted into violence on occasion, especially in 2008 in the Tibetan areas and 2009 in Xinjiang. Ethnic cultures and languages appear to have declined in strength as the country has modernized. Almost all minority languages are now quite weak in the public sphere, and the signs are that they will weaken still more in the coming decades.

Few countries in the world have been truly successful in handling ethnic issues. Complaints about racial and ethnic inequality and discrimination have loomed large in societies across the world. Considering its history, ethnic and territorial diversity, and the enormous problems it has faced, China would probably not come off too badly in a fair transnational comparison on the handling of ethnicity.

Bibliography

Barnett, Robert (2009) 'The Tibet protests of spring, 2008: conflict between the nation and the state', *China Perspectives*, 3: 6–23; reprinted in Colin Mackerras (ed.) (2011) *Ethnic Minorities in Modern China*, vol. 1.

Bhalla, A.S. and Shufang Qiu (2006) *Poverty and Inequality among Chinese Minorities*, London and New York: Routledge.

Bovingdon, Gardner (2010) *The Uyghurs, Strangers in Their Own Land*, New York: Columbia University Press.

Bray, David (2006) 'Building community: new strategies of governance in urban China', *Economy and Society*, 35(4): 530–49.

Bulag, Uradyn E. (2002) *The Mongols at China's Edge, History and the Politics of National Unity*, Lanham, MD: Rowman & Littlefield.

Gladney, Dru C. (1991) *Muslim Chinese, Ethnic Nationalism in the People's Republic*, Cambridge, MA and London: Council on East Asian Studies, Harvard University, distributed by Harvard University Press.

—— (1998) *Ethnic Identity in China, The Making of a Muslim Minority Nationality*, Fort Worth, TX: Harcourt Brace.

—— (2004) *Dislocating China, Reflections on Muslims, Minorities and Other Subaltern Subjects*, Chicago: The University of Chicago Press.

Goldstein, Melvyn C. (1989) *A History of Modern Tibet, 1913–1951, The Demise of the Lamaist State*, Berkeley, CA: University of California Press.

—— (1998) *Buddhism in Contemporary Tibet, Religious Revival and Cultural Identity*, Berkeley, Los Angeles and London: University of California Press.

—— (2007) *A History of Modern Tibet, Volume 2, The Calm Before the Storm, 1951–1955*, Berkeley, CA: University of California Press.

Harrell, Stevan (2001) *Ways of Being Ethnic in Southwest China*, Seattle, WA and London: University of Washington Press.

Kaup, Katherine Palmer (2000) *Creating the Zhuang: Ethnic Politics in China*, Boulder, CO and London: Lynne Rienner.

Litzinger, Ralph A. (2000) *Other Chinas, The Yao and the Politics of National Belonging*, Durham, NC and London: Duke University Press.

Mackerras, Colin (1994) *China's Minorities, Integration and Modernization in the Twentieth Century*, Hong Kong: Oxford University Press.

—— (2003) *China's Ethnic Minorities and Globalisation*, London and New York: RoutledgeCurzon.

—— (ed.) (2011) *Ethnic Minorities in Modern China, Critical Concepts in Asian Studies*, 4 vols., London and New York: Routledge.

Mullaney, Thomas S. (2011) *Coming to Terms with the Nation, Ethnic Classification in Modern China*, Berkeley, CA: University of California Press.

Potter, Pitman B. (2011) *Law, Policy, and Practice on China's Periphery, Selective Adaptation and Institutional Capacity*, London and New York: Routledge.

Schein, Louisa (2000) *Minority Rules: The Miao and the Feminine in China's Cultural Politics*, Durham, NC and London: Duke University Press.

Shakya, Tsering (1999) *The Dragon in the Land of Snows, A History of Modern Tibet Since 1947*, London: Pimlico Press.

Shih, Chih-yu (2002) *Negotiating Ethnicity in China, Citizenship as a Response to the State*, London and New York: Routledge.

Starr, S. Frederick (ed.) (2004) *Xinjiang, China's Muslim Borderland*, Armonk, NY: M.E. Sharpe.

Zang, Xiaowei (2007) *Ethnicity and Urban Life in China, A Comparative Study of Hui Muslims and Han Chinese*, London and New York: Routledge.

Related novels and autobiographies

Bstan-d'zin-rgya-mtsho, Dalai Lama XIV (1964) *The Autobiography of His Holiness the Dalai Lama of Tibet: My Land and My People*, London: Panther.

Goldstein, Melvyn C., with William R. Siebenschuh and Tashi Tsering (1997) *The Struggle for Modern Tibet: The Autobiography of Tashi Tsering*, Armonk, NY and London: M.E. Sharpe.

Gyatso Palden, with Tsering Shakya (1998) *The Autobiography of a Tibetan Monk*, New York: Grove Press.

He Liyi, with Claire Anne Chik (1993) *Mr. China's Son: A Villager's Life*, Boulder, CO: Westview Press.

Jiang Rong, trans. Howard Goldblatt (2008) *Wolf Totem*, London: Penguin.

10 Religious influence in China

Yunfeng Lu

Introduction

Is religion important in China? While some people think that China is one of the least religious societies in the world, others hold that religion has strong and pervasive influence in China. In the nineteenth century, the prevailing view among Western intellectuals was that Chinese were immune to religion. The Jesuits thought that Confucian rites which focused on remembrance of the ancestors were not a kind of worship, so that Confucianism was not 'religious' in nature; Buddhism was foreign; Daoism was superstitious; and in sum, China was a country without religion. But this view was challenged in the twentieth century. Some scholars argue that China is 'a religious state' (Lagerwey 2010). Historically, China has described itself as *Shenzhou* which literally means a 'continent of the spirits' since the Zhou dynasty (1046 BCE–256 BCE). Various religions have enjoyed explosive growth, and China is arguably experiencing a religious revolution. This chapter, beginning with an introduction to Chinese religious traditions, will centre on the transition of religion and state regulation since 1949.

Religion in pre-1949 China

When describing the religious landscape in traditional China, Erik Zurcher (1980) focuses on Buddhism, Daoism, Confucianism, and popular religion. Confucianism involved worship of ancestors and gods; Buddhism 'conquered' China and became an integral part of Chinese society; Daoism is a complex synthesis of Chinese cosmology, Daoist philosophy, and shamanistic practices.

China also has a long sectarian tradition. While its origin could be traced to *Taiping Tao* which emerged in the Han dynasty (200 BCE–220 CE) (Seiwert 2003), Chinese sectarian tradition became fully fledged in the Ming dynasty (1368–1644) and Qing dynasty (1644–1911) when hundreds of sects emerged. Most of those sects accepted the Eternal Venerable Mother myth, produced their own scriptures, emphasized personal salvation, and had a hierarchical structure headed by their respective Patriarchs (*zushi*). When the Chinese

Republic was founded in 1911, there was a veritable explosion of sectarian movements among which Yiguan Dao was well-known. While these sects were nearly uprooted in mainland China by the Chinese Communist Party (CCP) after 1949, some of them survived in Taiwan and Hong Kong which were beyond the control of the CCP (Lu 2008). Since the 1980s, some sects have begun to spread and thrive in the mainland again (Dean 1998).

Popular religion is widely practised by Chinese people. It is not 'a religion' with theologies, organizations and theists peculiar to itself; rather, it is a synthesis of the following elements: the popular religious practices, including pilgrimage (*Jinxiang*), fortune telling (*Suanming*), spirit possession (*shenling futi*), geomantic omen (*kan fengshui*), merit accumulation (*Ji gonde*), etc.; the worship of the three classes of supernatural beings: gods, ghosts and ancestors (Jordan 1972); annual religious rituals and communal religious activities (e.g. temple fairs) associated with these supernatural beings (C.K. Yang 1961); and territorial-cults organizations which manage the communal rituals and activities (Sangren 1987).

Followers of popular religion do not engage in religious congregations; they put the primary and explicit consideration to a deity's reputation for efficacy (*lingyan*). They usually ask for divine help from a god when personal crises or desires emerge. If the god satisfies their wish, they reward the god with incense, foods, images, new temples, or spectacular plays. If the god fails to perform miracles, however, they do not feel obliged to make offerings to the god and they usually turn to another deity who is believed to be more responsive. Folk temples may have many deities from different religious traditions, with one main deity. Usually there are no clergies residing at the temples.

When the deity was supposed to be efficacious, the temple might expand its influence by means of 'efficacy division' (*Fenling*), which refers to 'the practice by which new temples are chartered by the division of incense representing a god's efficacy from a source temple' (Sangren 2000: 99). The branch temples normally continued to retain a relationship with the source temple by means of pilgrimage. To increase the efficaciousness of gods, the branch temples made a yearly pilgrimage to the mother temple, usually at the 'birthday' of the god they worship. All branch temples could return to the founding temple but were treated on an equal basis. Thus, extensive pilgrimage networks existed in traditional China: the source temple occupied the precedent status of the incense-division network, and various competitive branch temples shared the efficaciousness of the gods and made pilgrimages to the founding temple (Sangren 2000).

In past centuries, both Buddhism and Daoism extended influences to the grass-roots by developing their own complex pilgrimage networks which were headed by the various pilgrimage centres where the source temples are located. Four famous 'Buddhist mountains' (*fojiao mingshan*) are important Buddhist pilgrimage centres, each of which is associated with a particular bodhisattva (*pusa*).[1] Daoism also had its own pilgrimage centres. Equally important as the four famous Buddhist mountains are the 'five famous Daoist mountains' (*wuyue*). Daoism also adopts some gods who emerged as popular religious deities, such as Huang Daxian (Lang and Ragvald 1993). The original place of the god tends to become a new centre for pilgrimages.

Along with these pilgrimage centres, there existed 'territorial-cult organizations' (Sangren 1987: 75) at the grass-roots level, which were in charge of the local patron gods' temples, pilgrimages and various rituals. These ritual associations were loosely and temporarily organized. When the rituals were over, these associations were disbanded or performed secular functions, such as managing irrigation issues, etc. (Dean 1998).

In sum, although there were distinctive religions in traditional China, the main religious suppliers were various folk temples spotted across the country. These were so syncretic that people could not tell whether they belonged to Buddhism, Confucianism or Daoism. There might be many deities from various religions in these temples, although there would be a main deity. These temples formed complex pilgrimage networks which focused on the supposed efficacy of deities. In this sense, in traditional China, religion exerted its influence 'not through formal organization and bureaucratic discipline, but through informal institutions such as the pilgrimages of wandering monks and lay devotees' (Sangren 1987: 123).

Religion in communist China: 1949–79

When the CCP came to power in 1949, it employed strict regulation on religion although the Chinese constitution permits people to enjoy the freedom to believe or not believe in religion. According to orthodox Marxist theory, religion is the people's opium; when socialism is established, religion is supposed to wither away. Against this background, atheism became the official policy. Popular religion was defined as 'feudal superstition' unworthy of recognition as religion and became a subject of repression and destruction. Traditional sects were labelled 'reactionary organizations'; most sectarian leaders were sentenced to death while key followers were put in jail. Confucianism was regarded as the relic of feudalism and was not permitted to be a kind of religion; Confucius became a target of criticism and stigma.

The Chinese government only permits the existence of five religions: Buddhism, Daoism, Islam, Protestantism and Catholicism. These religions were strictly regulated. Foreign Christian missionaries were regarded as 'evil partners' (*bangxiong*) of Western imperialism and thus were expelled from China. The state selected a few dependable religious leaders to organize new religious associations. After tremendous efforts, the Chinese Buddhist association and the Chinese Islamic association were founded in 1953, which were followed by the Three-Selfs (self-administration, self-support and self-propagation) Patriotic Committee of Protestantism in 1954, the Chinese Daoist association in 1957, and finally the Chinese Catholic association in 1958. These associations became the Party's tools for regulating religion.

In addition, the Party forbade religion from entering into public areas such as cultural, educational and charitable; most hospitals, schools and colleges run by religious groups were confiscated.

The suppression of religions became harsher during the Cultural Revolution period. All religions were forbidden to exist; 'patriotic' religious associations mentioned above were dismissed; there were no public religious activities; temples and churches were destroyed or used for other purposes; traditional festivals for the gods were stopped; statues of gods and religious artefacts were destroyed; religious scriptures and sculptures were smashed; many monks were forced to get married and have children. The CCP was attempting to eliminate religions.

When all traditional religions were repressed, the worship of Chairman Mao Zedong became popular. In a sense, it was the main channel for people to satisfy their religious need at the time. Mao Zedong was glorified as 'the Red Sun' (*Hong taiyang*) and 'the great saviour of the people' (*renmin de dajiuxing*), a living god. Mao's portrait could be found in each household in the country. Before Mao's portrait, people would 'ask for guidance from Mao in the morning and report to Mao in the evening' (*Zaoqingshi wan huibao*), singing revolutionary songs, dancing, confessing and making revolutionary vows (Zuo 1991). Mao's portrait was so sacred that it was a crime to make Mao's portrait unclean. The 'red treasure book' (*hong baoshu*) of Mao's words was revered. When people wanted to express themselves, they had to begin with the words of Chairman Mao. Jin gangshan and Yanan, where Chairman Mao had once lived, became sacred places attracting hundreds of thousands of pilgrimages each year. Anything related to Mao became sacred. 'In 1968, Chairman Mao received some mongo from African friends as gifts. He gave this mongo to workers. But there was not much mongo, so the Party produced some fake mongo. When people got Chairman Mao's mongo, they were extremely excited, and kept sniffing the mongo' (Zhou 2010). The worship of Chairman Mao became an alternative to religions which had hundreds of millions of devotees during the Cultural Revolution (Yang 2005).

After the Great Cultural Revolution ended in 1976, Mao worship gradually diminished and the 'eliminated' religions appeared again. In fact, religions were never eliminated. For example, Wenzhou claimed to be the first so-called 'area without religion' (*Wu zongjiaoqu*) in China in the 1950s. Before that, the government sent a work team (*gongzuozu*) to Pingyang county, Wenzhou. The task was to eliminate religion, especially Protestantism. To achieve this purpose, the work team first regulated six Protestant denominations, forcing each denomination to hold religious activities together in one church. Next, the work group combined these denominations into one organization and required them to worship in the Western Church. Finally, the Western Church was used for other purposes, selling newspapers in the day and becoming a cinema at night. In May 1959, the government claimed that Wenzhou had become the first 'area without religion'. While people could not find any religion in public, underground religious activities never ceased even during the Cultural Revolution. From 1971 to 1980, according to Lin's estimate (Lin, unpublished manuscript), Protestantism in Pingyang county had recruited more than 100,000 believers, 600 missionaries, and around 400 congregations. There were around 140 congregations, 14,000 Christians and more than 300 missionaries in central Wenzhou.

Religious policy in contemporary China

The Cultural Revolution ended with Mao's death in 1976. Two years later, Deng Xiaoping began a series of economic and social reforms. In March 1982, the CCP issued a document titled 'The Basic Viewpoint and Policy on the Religious Affairs during the Socialist Period of Our Country'. This document has exerted much influence on the following three decades' religious policy. Considering that religions in China have five natures – long-term nature, mass nature, complex nature, international nature and ethnic nature – the document proposed to end the policy of religious suppression and recognized Buddhism, Daoism, Islam and Protestantism and Catholicism. These religions were controlled by government-sanctioned 'patriotic' associations; they must hold activities within state-defined limits and activities outside these limits would be repressed. Following Document Number 19, the newly revised PRC Constitution of 1982 reaffirms freedom of religion.

But China's religious policy is still restrictive. Mr. Ye Xiaowen, the former Director-General of the State Administration on Religious Affairs, once wrote that:

> We cannot use administrative forces to distinguish religion, but it is not to say that we agree to develop religion. It is even worse to employ administrative forces to strengthen religion. No matter how difficult the task is, we hope to reduce religions' influence step by step through direct or indirect ways.
>
> (Ye 2007: 136)

To achieve this goal, the government has issued circulars, enacted ordinances, and installed administrative orders. In 1991, the CCP Document No. 6 increased the number of cadres in religious affairs bureaus. In 1994, the State Council published two ordinances, requiring that all religious groups must be registered to be legal, and prohibiting foreigners in China from proselytizing to Chinese. In 1995, the State Council issued a circular labelling several groups 'evil cults'.[2] In the 1990s, the rise of *Falun gong* posed challenges to the Party. To cope with the challenge, the Standing Committee of the National People's Congress passed a 'legislative resolution banning heretical cults' in October 1999. Many of the Qigong organizations and underground religious groups, together with *Falun gong*, were suppressed. In 2005, new 'religious affairs regulations' were issued, serving as the national guide-line for religious administration. Yet religions have revived quickly in China despite these policies.

Religious influence in China

How many religious believers are there in China? According to the government, there are around 100 million religious followers, a figure which has not changed in the past six decades. Yet a study done in 2005 shows that there are more than 300 million people affiliated to a religion.[3] Horizon survey, a Chinese public opinion polling firm, conducted three representative surveys in 2005, 2006 and 2007 respectively. Based on these surveys, Grim (2008) has estimated the number of Chinese religious believers (Table 10.1). Perhaps the figures are inaccurate, but they are helpful in understanding the religious landscape of contemporary China. As the table shows, around 16 per cent of Chinese have some kinds of religious affiliation. Since there are 1.3 billion people in China, it can be estimated that there are more than 200 million believers in the country.

Popular religion

Table 10.1 also shows that more than 80 per cent of the Chinese people are not affiliated to any religious group. But this does not necessarily mean that they are atheists. A sample investigation of Taiwan shows that 87 per cent of Taiwanese who claim to have no religious belief actually believe or worship gods; only 6.3 per cent of the sampled population have no religious belief and do not believe in or worship gods (Zhang and Lin 1992: 102). The 2005 Pew poll also found that approximately three-in-five Chinese believe in the possible existence of supernatural phenomena, religious figures or supernatural beings that are often associated with Chinese folk religion. Grim (2008) thus suggests that 'popular religious beliefs may be more widespread than is suggested by religious affiliation alone'.

As mentioned above, popular religion was stigmatized as 'feudal super-stition'. Publicity campaigns were conducted to discourage people from engaging in folk religious practice such as worship, fortune telling and pil-grimages. Some practitioners of folk religion, such as fortune-tellers and spirit mediums, were arrested and prosecuted. Today, local popular religion gains some sort of legitimacy. The government has recognized some popular reli-gious beliefs, such as the Mazu belief, as a means of uniting overseas Chinese. Because the Mazu belief is very popular in Taiwan, and because it could be a medium of 'Culture building the stage, the united front playing' (*Wenhuadatai, tongzhanchangxi*), it has received official permission to exist.

Other popular religious beliefs have gained their legal status under the name of 'intangible cultural heritage' (*Feiwuzhi wenhua yichan*). The Baoji Temple Fairs in Shanxi Province and the Lucheng Temple Fairs were listed in the

Table 10.1 Chinese religious affilitation (in %)

	2007	2006	2005
Total religious believers	14	18	16
Buddhist	12	16	11
Christian	2	1	4
Protestant	*1*	*1*	*2*
Catholic	*1*	*<1*	*2*
Muslim	<1	1	1
Taoist	<1	<1	<1
Other	–	<	1
None	81	77	77
Refused or DK	5	5	8
Total respondents	4,104	2,180	2,191
Sampling error	±1.6	±2.3	±2.3

Question wording: What is your religious faith?

Note: The differences in the three estimates may be due to sampling error and the cities sampled rather than significant shifts in religious adherence among years.

Source for 2007 is Horizon survey reported by C100; source for 2006 and 2005 is Horizon survey reported by the Pew Global Attitudes Project.

Source: Grim 2008

first batch of the National Intangible Cultural Heritage in 2005. In the second batch of the National Intangible Cultural Heritage, ten temple fairs and seven local popular religious beliefs were listed in the name of 'popular beliefs and traditions' in 2008. Some spirit mediums and fortune-tellers have become the inheritors of national cultural heritage, targets for protection rather than suppression (Wu 2009). Folk religious beliefs have come bubbling to the surface in China.

Buddhism

Buddhism is the most influential institutional religion in contemporary China. In 1997, the State Council issued the White Book of Religion – *Freedom of Religious Belief in China*, which shows that there were 200,000 Buddhist monks and nuns out of 300,000 ministers of religion in China, i.e. the number of Buddhist priests was twice the sum of all other religious clergies. Table 10.1 shows that the majority of self-claimed religious believers regard themselves as the followers of Buddhism although they might not have had any conversion ceremony or have comprehensive understanding of Buddhist scriptures. Clearly, Buddhism has a widespread and pervasive influence in China.

Buddhism has undergone a revival in contemporary China. First, more and more intellectual elites have converted to Buddhism. In 2010, a news report on Mr Liu Zhiyu's conversion to Buddhism attracted widespread attention from Chinese society. Liu was an undergraduate student of Bejing University and a former winner of International Mathematical Olympiad Gold Medal. He won a full scholarship from the Massachusetts Institute of Technology in 2010, but he finally rejected the offer and converted to Buddhism. The case of Liu Zhiyu is not an isolated one. More and more elite intellectuals have devoted themselves to Buddhism; and this will have profound influence on the development of Buddhism in China.

Second, compared with Christian and traditional sects, Buddhists did not carry out aggressive missionary work. But since the 1990s, Buddhism has begun to reach out in an effort to recruit more followers. The Bailin Temple held the first Zen Summer Camp in 1993 and has held the seventeenth Zen Summer Camp now. The camps are aimed at training young lay Buddhists, providing them with an opportunity to experience Buddhist lifestyles, understand the three treasures (*Sanbao*), and strengthen their faith (Yang and Wei 2005). 'The participants are mainly from the Buddhist intelligentsia, which is good for discovery and training of talented people to prepare for the future development of Buddhism.'[4]

Finally, Buddhism has been developing fast in urban areas in the past decades. China has experienced rapid social changes since 1978 and many rural people have migrated to cities. Those new migrants have lost their original social networks, and their traditional moral order and social norms have faced great challenges. Urban life is full of uncertainty, disorder and loneliness, which is characterized as 'anomie' by sociologists. Religion plays the role of a bridge in social life, bringing 'order, stability and hopes' (Miller and Yamamori 2007: 23), and helping people to adapt to the strange environments of cities. When I interviewed Beijing businessmen from Wenzhou, I found that more than 80 per cent of them regarded themselves as Buddhist followers. They donated money to temples and held Buddhist congregations (*Fahui*). They rarely read Buddhist scriptures because they were poorly educated. At the same time, more and more Buddhists at universities have begun to organize 'study groups of Buddhism' (*xuefo xiaozu*). The Buddhist expansion in cities will no doubt influence the future of Chinese Buddhism.

'Qigong fever' and Falun gong

In the 1980s, the most visible religious revival was Protestantism's growth in rural areas and the rise of Qigong in urban areas. Qigong is a cultivation system focusing on meditation, physical movements, and breathing exercises. Qigong was once tightly associated with various religious traditions. When religion was repressed after 1949, Qigong became an independent medical technique and many hospitals offered Qigong services. In the 1970s, Qigong began to return to the public sphere and many patients began to practise Qigong in parks. In the late 1970s, many intellectuals, including China's leading scientist Qian Xueseng, became interested in 'paranormal abilities' (*Teyi gongneng*) and 'body science' (*Rentikexue*). Qigong, labelled a body science, attained legitimacy in the 1980s and early 1990s. Against this background,

'Qigong fever' (*qigong re*) swept China (Palmer 2007). Chen (1995: 347) estimated that there were 60–200 million Qigong practitioners in the mid-1980s, including many CCP cadres and intellectuals. By 1986, there were over 2,000 national Qigong organizations (Ownby 2003: 233–4), and more emerged in the following decade. These organizations were usually led by a charismatic leader called 'master', actively recruiting practitioners, publishing related books, selling Qigong DVDs and tapes and practising Qigong publicly. Qigong had become a business.

Qigong movements became a hotbed of new religions among which *Falun gong* is the most famous. Its leader, Li Hongzhi, was born into an ordinary family in Jilin Province in the 1951. When Qigong fever was under way in the 1980s, Li got involved in several kinds of Qigong. The experience helped him to establish *Falun gong* in 1992. From May 1992 to September 1994, *Falun gong* focused on treating diseases. After Li Hongzhi published *Zhuan Falun* (Turning the Law Wheel) in 1994, *Falun gong* was transformed from a Qigong organization to a new religion (Lu 2005). In 1996, Li formally changed his organization's name from *Falun gong* to *Falun Dafa* (the Great Way of the Law Wheel). With *Zhuan Falun* as its core scripture, *Falun Dafa* presents a theological system centring on salvation; Li was deified as the saviour of the world. *Falun gong* also formed a complex organizational structure headed by Li Hongzhi. In the late 1990s, *Falun gong* developed so quickly that it was arguably the largest Qigong group in China, and Li claimed that there were more than 100 million *Falun gong* practitioners worldwide.

Some scientists who criticized Qigong as pseudoscience began to denounce *Falun gong* in the late 1990s, and this led to *Falun gong* practitioners' discontent. From 1996 to 1999, there were more than 300 *Falun gong* protests against the media, forcing the media to clarify 'erroneous' information (Ownby 2005: 208). The protest finally developed into the 'April 25 Incident'. On April 25, 1999, an estimated 10,000 to 30,000 *Falun gong* practitioners assembled at Zhongnanhai, the heart of Beijing and the symbol of political power in China (Lum 2001), and the sit-in protest continued for thirteen hours. The government was stunned and outraged by the protest. Three months later, the Chinese government outlawed *Falun gong* as an 'evil cult', mobilizing its entire bureaucratic machinery to crack down on *Falun gong*. *Falun gong* was uprooted in China and Li Hongzhi fled to the United States, where he has kept fighting for *Falun gong*.

Protestantism

Protestantism has enjoyed explosive growth in the past decades. When the CCP seized power in 1949, there were around 0.7 million Protestant Christians. Despite decades of government suppression, Protestant Christians have multiplied into 4.5 million in 1988, 12 million in 1997 and 23 million in 2009 (Jin and Qiu 2010). These figures are official estimates, while some scholars estimate that there are more than 50 million Protestant Christians.

The rise of Protestantism in China will change the face of global Christianity (Jenkins 2002). As Bays (2003: 488) argues, 'on any given Sunday, there are almost certainly more Protestants in Church in China than in all of Europe'.

Many factors have contributed to the growth of Protestantism, among which its missionary efforts must be mentioned. While all religions experienced repression, Protestantism is more successful than any other religion in recruiting believers. The success can be partly attributed to its missionary efforts. Even under the harsh suppression during the Cultural Revolution, Protestant missionaries kept converting people. As mentioned above, Wenzhou was the first so-called 'area without religion' in 1959, but at the end of 1970s, the number of Protestant Christians multiplied. Suppression cannot prevent the growth of religion; rather, it has some unintended consequences which ironically have led to religious revival (Lu 2004). Protestantism's missionary efforts first paid off in rural China in the 1980s. Many peasants, especially the old, the sick, the poor, the illiterate and women, were converted to Protestantism (Hunter and Chan 1993).

The development of Christianity in cities has been notable in the past decade. Generally, there are three kinds of Christian groups in the urban areas. 'The first kind is "boss Christians" (*Laoban jidutu*), including businessmen, entrepreneurs, managers, member of the Board, and shareholding employers. The second kind is intellectual elite Christians, including professors, graduate students, postgraduate students, doctors and lawyers' (Chen 2005: 73). In addition, migrant worker churches have emerged in urban areas. Many migrant workers who were originally Christians found that it was hard for them to be socially integrated into the two kinds of churches described above. Therefore specific churches for migrant workers have emerged (Huang 2007).

The growth of Protestantism in China has caught much attention. Aikman (2003) predicts that one third of the Chinese will become Christians in 2030, turning China into the biggest Christian country in the world. However, the future of Christianity in China is uncertain. There was a golden period for the increase of Christians in Taiwan in the 1950s, but soon growth slowed down and then stagnated. Will Protestantism conquer China, as Buddhism did in history?

Catholicism

Catholicism entered China several centuries ago. Yet the development of Catholicism is not as successful as that of Protestantism. In 1949, there were 3,000,000 Catholics, representing 1 per cent of the whole population in China. In 2009, with regard to the total population of Chinese Catholics, 'there are three versions: 5.6 million (underground churches not included), 8 million, and 12 million (underground churches included) respectively' (M. Wang 2009: 96). In any case, 'the increase in the Catholic population – has roughly matched China's general population increase since the establishment of the PRC' (Madsen 2003: 407).

PRC-Vatican relations have exerted much influence on the development of Chinese Catholicism. The relations have been full of ups and downs since 1949. From 1949 to 1955, the Vatican exercised its religious authority, appointing eighteen Chinese bishops. Since then PRC-Vatican relations became difficult for twenty years because of the Vatican's strong anti-communist policy as well as the CCP's anti-religious policy. After the Chinese Patriotic Catholic Association was established in 1958, some Catholic churches refused to join and became underground churches. In the early 1980s, the PRC and the Vatican started to talk to each other. But until now, the PRC has not established diplomatic relationships with the Vatican (M. Wang 2009). Although Vatican City is a small state with less than 2,000 people, it is the headquarters of some 1.1 billion Catholics all over the world. In a sense, it is an international religious organization. It is important for China to maintain effective communication channels with the Vatican.

Daoism

As the only state-recognized native institutional religion, Daoism has also revived in China, but it is still weak. First, Daoism lacks an 'eminent Daoist' (*Gaodao*) (Li 2008), not only in mainland China but also in Hong Kong, Macau and Taiwan. In comparison, there are 'eminent monks' such as Monk Shengyan and Monk Xingyun. There are reports of intellectuals' conversions to Buddhism or Protestantism, but there are few elite Chinese converts to Daoism.

Second, Daoism lacks a strong organization and influential Daoist temples. In mainland China the best-known Buddhist temples are the Bolin Temple and the Longquan Temple. By comparison, contemporary Daoist temples are not very influential due to the lack of an 'eminent Daoist' leader. Besides, Daoism 'is not united internally, which makes weak Daoism more ineffective. Compared with the scale of other religions, it is obvious that Daoism is not competitive'(Li 2008: 112).

Finally, the history Daoism and folk beliefs were closely connected to each other. For example, the Mazu belief used to belong to folk beliefs, but eventually it was integrated into Daoism. However, in contemporary China, Daoism is 'relatively conservative, not open-minded, lacks inclusiveness, self-closed in a certain degree and fails to perform the function of integrating folk beliefs and folk religions sufficiently' (Li 2008: 114–15).

Islam

Islam entered China more than 1,000 years ago. Like other religious traditions, it has revived since the 1980s and the population of Muslims has increased steadily. Because the main groups that believe in Islam are from ten minority nationalities including Hui, Uyghur, and Kazak, and because the population of these minority nationalities is 20 million, the Chinese Islamic Association estimates that there were 22 million Muslims in 2009.

In recent years, Islam has begun to expand from western China to eastern China and from rural areas to cities. Take Shenzhen for example. There were few Muslims there before 1978, but there were about 50,000 to 100,000 Muslims and more than 1,000 Muslim restaurants in Shenzhen in 2009. There were no Muslims in Yiwu, Zhejiang. With the development of trade between China and the Middle East, a large number of Arabic interpreters are needed. As a result, around 10,000 Muslims have moved from western provinces to Yiwu, and an Islamic community has come into being in Yiwu (Y. Wang 2009: 78). The Islamic revival is part of a general growth of religion throughout China.

Conclusion

The religious economy model (Stark and Finke 2000) holds that religious demand remains relatively unchanged while religious suppliers changed dramatically. This viewpoint is helpful for us in understanding religious change in the past six decades in China. Mao worship was on the rise when all traditional religions were banned during the Cultural Revolution. The decline of this political religion was accompanied by the religious revival in the 1980s, especially the expansion of Protestantism in rural areas and the growth of Qigong organizations in cities. When Qigong organizations were prohibited in the late 1990s, Buddhism and Protestantism occupied the market niche and developed quickly in cities. Also, many new religions emerged in urban areas.

When discussing the religious revival in contemporary China, Madsen (2003: 469) argues that this revival can be 'attributed to factors like the collapse of Marxist ideology, increased social mobility, decreased government capacities for repression, and renewed communication with the outside world'. In addition to these factors, this chapter shows that religious demands play an important role in this general revival. State regulation can exert much influence on the fate of specific religions (e.g. the Qigong movement), yet it fails to reduce religious demand. Where there is religious demand, there are religious suppliers.

Notes

1   Pu-tuo Shan, in the eastern province of Zhejiang, is related with Guan-yin *pusa* who represents mercy; Wu-tai shan, in the northern of Shanxi, is associated with Wen-shu *pusa* representing wisdom; O-mei Shan, located in the western province of Shichuan, is linked with Pu-xian *pusa* who represents happiness; and Jiu-hua Shan, in the central province of Anhui, is associated with Dizhang *pusa* who represents filial piety.
2   They are the Shouters (huhanpai), Full-scope Church (Quanfanweijiaohui), New Testament Church (XinyueJiaohui), Eastern Lightening (Dongfang shandian), Society of Disciples (Mentuhui), Spirit Church (Linglingjiao), Guanyinfamen, the Established King Church (Beiliwang), Family of Love (Ai de Jiating), Dami mission (DamiXuanjiaohui), and the Lord God sect (zhushenjiao).

3 Please refer to http://news.sina.com.cn/s/2007-04-04/162312696051.shtml.
4 Please refer to http://www.bailinsi.net/06xly/xly.htm.

Bibliography

Aikman, David (2003) *Jesus in Beijing: How Christianity is Transforming China and Changing the Global Balance of Power*, Washington, DC: Regnery.

Bays, Daniel H. (2003) 'Chinese Protestant Christianity today', *The China Quarterly*, 174: 488–504.

Chen, Cunfu (2005) *Zhuanxinqi de zhongg jidujia – zejiang jidujiao gean yanjiu*, Dongfang Chubanshe.

Chen, Nancy N. (1995) 'Urban spaces and experiences of Qigong', pp. 247–61 in Deborah S. Davis, Richard Kraus, Barry Naughton and Elizabeth J. Perry (eds), *Urban Spaces in Contemporary China*, New York: Cambridge University Press.

Dean, Kenneth (1998) *Lord of the Three in One: The Spread of a Cult in Southeast China*, Princeton, NJ: Princeton University Press.

Grim, Brian (2008) 'Religion in China on the eve of the 2008 Beijing Olympics', available at http://pewresearch.org/pubs/827/china-religion-olympics, accessed on February 6, 2011.

Huang, Jianbo (2007) 'Chengshihua jincheng zhong de zhongguo jidujiao', in Yu Guoliang (ed.), *Chaihui le zhongjian geduan de qiang*, Beijing: Zongjiao wenhua chubanshe.

Hunter, Alan and Kim-Kwong Chan (1993) *Protestantism in Contemporary China*, Cambridge: Cambridge University Press.

Jenkins, Philip (2002) *The Next Christendom: The Coming of Global Christianity*, New York: Oxford University Press.

Jin, Ze and Qiu, Yonghui (2010) 'Zhongguo jidujiao ruhu wenjuan diaocha baogao', in Jin Ze and Qiu Yonghu (eds), *Zongjiao lanpishu:zhongguo zongjiao baogao (2010)*, Shehui kexue wenxian chubanshe.

Jordan, David K. (1972) *Gods, Ghosts, and Ancestors: the Folk Religion of a Taiwanese Village*, Berkeley, CA: University of California Press.

Lagerwey, John (2010) *China: A Religious State*, Hong Kong: Hong Kong University Press.

Lang, Graeme and Lars Ragvald (1993) *The Rise of a Refugee God: Hong Kong's Wong Tai Sin*, Hong Kong: Oxford University Press.

Li, Gang (2008) 'Xinshengtai, xinwenti, xintiaozhan xia daojiao wenhua de juese gongneng', in Jin ze and Qiu Yonghui (eds), *zongjiao lanpishu:zhongguo zongjiao baogao*, Beijing: Shehui kexue wenxian chubanshe.

Lin, Naimu. *Lin Naimu huiyilu* (温州教会历史), available at http://www.360doc.com/content/11/0122/16/4133105_88313137.shtml, accessed on February 16, 2011.

Lu, Yunfeng (2004) 'The unintended consequences of religious suppression', Paper presented at Third Annual Conference on Religion, Economics and Culture, Kansas City.

—— (2005) 'Entrepreneurial logics and the evolution of *Falun Gong*', *Journal for the Scientific Study of Religion*, 44(2): 173–85.

—— (2008) *The Transformation of Yiguan Dao in Taiwan: Adapting to a Changing Religious Economy*, Lanham, MD: Lexington Books.

Lum, Thomas (2001) 'China and "Falun Gong"', *CRS Report for Congress*, Congressional Research Service, Library of Congress.

Madsen, Richard (2003) 'Catholic Revival during the Reform Era', *The China Quarterly*, 174: 468–87.

Miller, Donald and Tetsunao Yamamori (2007) *Global Pentecostalism: The Face of Christian Social Engagement*, Berkeley, CA: University of California Press.

Ownby, David (2003) 'A history for Falun Gong: popular religion and the Chinese state since the Ming Dynasty', *Nova Religion*, 6(2): 223–43.

—— (2005) 'The Falun Gong: a new religious movement in post-Mao China', pp. 195–214 in James R. Lewis and Jesper Aagaard Petersen (eds), *Controversial New Religions*, New York: Oxford University Press.

Palmer, David A. (2007) *Qigong Fever: Body, Science, and Utopia in China*, New York: Columbia University Press.

Sangren, P. Steven (1987) *History and Magical Power in a Chinese Community*, Stanford, CA: Stanford University Press.

—— (2000) *Chinese Sociologics: An Anthropological Account of the Role of Alienation in Social Reproduction*, London, NJ: Athlone.

Seiwert, Hubert Michael (2003) *Popular Religious Movements and Heterodox Sects in Chinese History*, Leiden and Boston: Brill.

Stark, Rodney, and Roger Finke (2000) *Acts of Faith: Explaining the Human Side of Religion*, Berkeley, CA: University of California Press.

Wang, Meixiu (2009) 'Zhongguo tianzhujiao guancha', in Jin Ze and Qiu Yonghui (eds), *Zongjiao lanpishu: zhongguo zongjiao baogao*, Beijing: Shehui kexue wenxian chubanshe.

Wang, Yujie (2009) '2008 nian zhongguo yisilanjiao gaikuang ji dui musilin liudong wenti de fenxi', in Jin Ze and Qiu Yonghui (eds), *Zongjiao lanpishu:zhongguo zongjiao baogao*, Shehui kexue wenxian chubanshe.

Wu, Zhen (2009), 'Cong fengjianmixin dao feiwuzhi wenhua yichan', in Jin Ze and Qiu Yonghui (eds), *Zongjiao lanpishu:zhongguo zongjiao baogao*, Shehui kexue wenxian chubanshe.

Yang, Fenggang (2006) 'The red, black, and gray markets of religion in China', *Sociological Quarterly*, 47(1): 93–122.

Yang, Fenggang and Dedong Wei (2005) 'The Bailin Buddhist Temple: thriving under Communism', pp. 63–86 in Fenggang Yang and Joseph Tamney (eds), *State, Market, and Religions in Chinese Societies*, Leiden and Boston: Brill Academic Publishers.

Ye, Xiaowen (2007) *Zongjiao wenti zenmokan zenmoban*, Beijing: Religious Culture Press.

Zhang, Maogui and Benxuan Lin (1992) 'The social imaginations of religion: a research problem for sociology of knowledge', *Bulletin of the Institute of Ethnology Academia Sinica*, 74: 95–123.

Zhang Weiqing, and Qiao Gong (1999) *Falun Gong Chuangshiren Li Hongzhi Pingzhuan*, Carle Place: Mirror Books.

Zhou, Hualei (2010) 'You "shen" de zhongguoren' (有"神"的中国人), 《中国新闻周刊》 总482期, 2010年32期, 第43页? (*Zhongguo xinwen zhoukan*), 32: p. 43, available at http://www.chinesefolklore.org.cn/web/index.php?NewsID=8260, accessed on February 16, 2011.

Zuo, Jiping (1991) 'Political religion: the case of the Cultural Revolution in China', *Sociological Analysis*, 52(1): 99–110.

Zurcher, Erik (1980) 'Buddhist influence on early Taoism', *T'oung Pao*, 66: 84–147.

Related novels and autobiographies

Brother Yun (2009) *The Heavenly Man: The Remarkable True Story of Chinese Christian Brother Yun*, Peabody, MA: Hendrickson Publishers.

Culp, Lance K. *Falun Gong Stories: A Journey to Enlightenment*, Golden Lotus Press, available at http://www.clearwisdom.net/emh/download/publications/enlightenment_whole_web.pdf, accessed on February 16, 2011.

Wesley, Luke (2006) *Stories from China*, Milton Keynes: Authentic.

11 Transformation of work in post-1978 China

Yi-min Lin

With one fifth of the human population on earth, China has the world's largest workforce, which totalled 780 million in 2009 (NBSa 2010: 117). Some 38 per cent of these working people were farmers or undertook related economic activities, where the family constitutes the primary organizing unit. The bulk – some 62 per cent – of the workforce was employed in various non-farm sectors. Public institutions and organizations, including various government agencies and political establishments, only accounted for about 15 per cent of the workforce in these sectors, whereas domestic private enterprises, self-employment, and foreign-invested companies constituted the sources for 85 per cent of the non-farm jobs.

The economy that employs China's enormous workforce has been undergoing fundamental transformations since 1978. Perhaps the most remarkable change is the decline and fading of state socialism and the rise of capitalism as the basic mode of economic organization. This transformation has taken place thanks to three mutually reinforcing developments: marketization, internationalization, and privatization. It has also been accompanied by accelerating processes of industrialization, urbanization, and demographic transition, as well as profound technological advancements, breakthroughs, and diffusion. Along the way, the organization of work has been redefined and restructured, with far-reaching implications for the economy and society.

This chapter highlights some important aspects of the remaking of the Chinese workplace, focusing primarily on non-farm economic organizations. It begins with an overview of the pre-reform system in urban and rural China. That will be followed by a brief account of the major areas and processes of economic institutional change since 1978. The ensuing sections discuss the ramifications of such change for economic organizations

The organization of work in the Mao era

When the Chinese Communist Party (CCP) came to power in 1949, China was a predominantly agrarian economy, where the rural sector absorbed some 92 per cent of the workforce (NBSb 1987: 5) and the family was the basic unit of both social and economic organization. Within the short span of 10 years, the government eliminated private ownership and established a totally state-owned and controlled economy. The organization of work in that economy was significantly influenced by the development strategies of the CCP. In view of China's economic underdevelopment, CCP leaders regarded industrialization as a top priority. Yet they faced severe resource constraints. During and after the Korean War (1950–3), Western countries cut off their economic ties with China. While Soviet aid during the early to mid-1950s played a vital role in broadening China's industrial base, it quickly diminished towards the end of the decade when the relationship between the two countries deteriorated. With limited domestic supply, CCP leaders decided to concentrate the allocation of resources in what they considered to be the strategically most important sectors for the country's long-term development, namely, producer goods industries.

An important implication of such a strategy is that the absorption of the rural work-age population into the urban workforce could not grow at very fast rate due to the capital intensive nature of producer goods industries. From 1958 to 1978 the share of the rural sector in the total workforce only went down slightly from 80 to 77 per cent, whereas the share of the industrial sector in total gross domestic product (GDP) rose from 32 to 44 per cent (NBSb 1987: 5; NBSa/b 1998: 56). To facilitate the official strategy of development the government created a pecking order of resource allocation biased towards urban industries, and stratified economic organizations according to that order. Under the central planning system, there were three basic types of economic organization: state-owned enterprises controlled by national, provincial, and city/county authorities; urban collective enterprises controlled by sub-provincial authorities; and people's communes under the purview of county governments. State-owned enterprises and urban collective enterprises were the main carriers of non-farm economic activities. The level of direct supervising authority over an enterprise signified the importance that the government attached to it. With the same level of direct government control capital goods producers tended to enjoy higher priority in resource allocation than their peers producing consumer goods or providing services. People's communes were at the bottom of the system by both criteria.

To squeeze out more resources for capital intensive industrial development and to limit the demand for consumer goods and services, wages were maintained at very low and stagnant levels; the supply of essential daily necessities was rationed through a rationing coupon system; and for urban employees and their families the provision of basic social services, such as housing, health care, and old age support, was internalized or administered at the level of each formal organization, known as the *danwei* or work unit, whereas rural citizens had only minimal health care benefits under a cooperative medicine system. Closely coupled with such an employment practice was a household registration (*hukou*) system (Cheng and Selden 1994). It classified citizens into urban and rural categories with spatially fixed residential status, and strictly restricted inter-category change, extra-locale employment, and even inter-locale travel such that the allocation of human resources and their means of living could be centrally planned and extra-plan provision and distribution of consumer goods and services (including transportation services) for working people and their families could be minimized.

What resulted from the implementation of these measures was a socialist economy, where the working people had job security as well as the most essential in-kind provisions for themselves and their families. But there was no freedom of choice regarding employment and mobility. The standard of living was low and stagnant. And, ironically, there existed systematic inequalities among employees of different types of organizations and especially between urban and rural sectors (Solinger 1999). That was due to the trickle-down effects of the government's stratified resource allocation policy: more resourceful organizations provided relatively better pay and fringe benefits for their employees than less resourceful ones, and urban citizens also benefited from the overall better physical and social infrastructure of cities, where industrial activities were concentrated.

Acceleration of industrialization, however, was not the only imperative that shaped the way work was organized. CCP Chairman Mao Zedong (1893–1976) believed that a socialist society could not be built without true believers of socialism and that the workplace was not only the venue for producing goods and services but should serve the function of transforming the mind and behaviour of citizens and mobilizing them to participate in political campaigns and events orchestrated by central leaders. In accordance with this view, a CCP cell, often known as a party branch (in work units of small size and low rank) or committee (in work units of large size and high rank) and led by a party secretary, was installed in each and every formal organization as the centre of decision making and behavioural control.

A major mechanism of behavioural control by the CCP is the so-called personnel dossier system. Under that system a biographical file was maintained for the vast majority of citizens, including all adults as well as students. Not accessible by the person concerned and typically kept by the personnel office and (in the case of CCP members) the CCP cell of his or her work unit, it contained cumulative information about his or her family background, school records, work history, professional qualifications, results of periodic behavioural assessments by pertinent authorities, and the person's own political confessions and manifestations. The information was used in decisions about work assignment, transfer, and promotion or demotion. It also had ramifications for the family members of the person concerned, as cross referencing was a common practice in important decisions.

There was, however, no consensus among CCP leaders on the strategies to control and drive employees for the implementation of the party-state's many-sided agendas. Mao was against extensive use of material incentives to motivate work efforts, which was nevertheless emphasized by some other leaders within the CCP. During the Cultural Revolution (1966–76) when Maoist radicalism prevailed, the party-state relied heavily on political incentives and tactics to shape workplace behaviour. According to Walder (1986), the typical urban work unit featured three intertwined mechanisms of behaviour control: institutionalization of urban citizens' total dependence on state-allocated jobs and related benefits, extensive use by management of politically particularistic incentives and divisive tactics to foster loyalty and compliance, and alignment of informal social relations and networks with the formal organizational agendas defined by the party-state.

In rural areas the commune organization provided a similar tool of party-state control. Encompassing and administering the area of several traditional villages, each commune contained a dozen or so production brigades. Each brigade contained several production teams. Each team contained dozens of households and functioned as the basic unit of daily work organization and accounting. The CCP dominated decision-making at all three levels. Production was collectively carried out, and agricultural wages were determined using a work point system that emphasized presence at work and physical faculty rather than actual work efforts and outcome. The distribution of grain for consumption was egalitarian and based on household size; and in most farming communities each family was allotted a small plot of public land to grow supplementary food items for self consumption. Despite collectivization of farmland, housing remained private in the countryside. Although formal kinship organizations were abolished, kinship relations persisted in rural communities; so did the social networks, differentiations, and divisions anchored in such relations. The paucity of resources allocated to the rural sector also limited the incentives and abilities of rural officials to carry out party-state policies as forcefully as in urban work units.

Highlights of post-Mao transformations

The first major change in the post-Mao economic reforms was the decollectivization of agriculture during 1979–83. It replaced the commune system with a family farming arrangement based on publicly owned land contracted out by local authorities (for a fee) to individual households. Along with this change was the increase of freedom for farmers to make economic decisions, including those concerning the deployment of human resources. An important consequence of decollectivization of agriculture was the diversification of rural economic activities into industry, construction, transportation, and services. From 1978 to 2008 the share of entities undertaking such activities in rural GDP increased from 17 to 72 per cent and their share in the rural workforce rose from 9 to 33 per cent (Gao 2009: 99; Gan 2003: 5, 7; NBSa 2010: 38, 117). The predecessors of these entities were the non-farm work units under the people's commune system, known as commune and brigade enterprises. During the mid-1980s they were renamed township and village enterprises (TVEs) in that their property rights were transferred to township and village authorities that replaced the communes and brigades and subsequently played a much more active role in promoting the expansion of non-farm economic activities. In the meantime, these collective enterprises were joined by increasing numbers of private non-farm entities. Initially organized as self-employment establishments, these private entities gradually grew and eventually overtook TVEs in the 1990s as the leading force in the transformation and development of the rural economy. Unlike public enterprises in the urban sector, employees of TVEs and rural private enterprises have only earned a wage income reflecting labour market conditions, and they have not been provided with housing and other essential social service benefits.

In addition to family farming and employment in the fast growing local non-farm enterprises, rural working people have gradually gained a third occupational choice: migration to other locales, especially major urban centres of industry and commerce, for work. This first took place during the process of decollectivization, which set free the rural workforce from the commune system. The initial push factor of migration was economic hardship and shortage of income-earning opportunities in many rural communities. Underdevelopment of the service sector in urban areas under central planning and, more importantly, the rising demand for cheap labour in manufacturing as a result of the inflow of foreign capital in the coastal region provided the main pulling force for such migration. In view of the economic benefits brought about by rural-urban migration, many local governments in the destination locales bent centrally imposed restrictions and tolerated the presence of migrant workers who had no permanent local resident status. In 1988 the central government lifted the ban on temporary economic migration and thus opened the gate for free rural-urban flow of workforce. The number of migrants has since steadily increased, now totalling some 200 million.

When a migrant resides in a locale away from his or her place of origin for more than six months, he or she is classified as a local resident in official statistics. But this resident status does not confer on the migrant the same rights as those enjoyed by permanent local residents (Solinger 1999). They are second-class citizens in that they are excluded from the provision of local public goods and services, such as education for children, health care subsidies, low income housing, subsistence allowance for unemployment, and other social welfare benefits administered by the local government. They are not eligible for permanent jobs in local government or government-funded establishments, and their applications for business licenses may face more stringent scrutiny than those from permanent local residents.

Foreign-invested entities have been the major employers of migrants. In 1979 the Chinese government reopened the door for foreign trade and investment, especially foreign direct investment that involves direct ownership and management by foreign investors of the entities where the investment is made. Initially most foreign-invested entities were joint ventures with controlling stakes held by their local partners, which typically were public enterprises. Since the mid-1990s, however, wholly foreign-owned ventures, joint ventures dominated by foreign investors, and joint ventures with domestic private owners have become increasingly important. There are also many Chinese firms that undertake processing or assembly work for foreign companies through various subcontracting arrangements, where *de facto* control oftentimes lies in the hands of foreign company representatives and quality control personnel. As a result, foreign influence has increased in the organization of work.

With the deepening of the reform process initially led by the rural and foreign economic sectors, traditional public enterprises in urban areas have also experienced important changes. The early theme of these changes was marketization. Starting from the mid-1980s, state-owned enterprises (SOEs) and urban collective enterprises shifted the focus of their operations from fulfilling government-imposed output plans to profit making. They were granted increasing freedom to make decisions in response to market conditions on both the input and the output side. Over time, micro-management and protection by the government decreased and competition intensified for the vast majority of them. Along with TVEs in rural areas, these marketized public enterprises in the urban sector showed some improvement in economic performance during the late 1980s and early 1990s. But the financial health of both groups of public enterprises subsequently deteriorated, mainly due to the growth of internal and external governance problems. The ballooning of their losses and financial liabilities left the government with no choice but to close down or privatize most of them while only retaining for restructuring a small number of very large enterprises in strategically important sectors, such as tobacco, banking, telecommunications, energy, rail transportation, public utilities, and defence. The tipping point came in 1997, when the central government announced the new policy of 'hanging onto the big ones and letting go of small ones'. Massive privatization followed and resulted in the layoff of large numbers of former employees of these enterprises, especially in urban areas.

Before the massive lay-off of public sector employees in the late 1990s, the government had started a series of reforms to shift the provision of essential social services away from government-controlled organizations. Starting from 1986 urban public enterprises adopted employment contracts for all new employees, which marked the beginning of the end of the life-time employment system implemented under central planning. Into the 1990s experiments were carried out to restructure the ways pensions, health care, unemployment benefits, and housing were provided in the public sector. The essence of these reforms was to establish specialized funds for the provision of these benefits, which would be based on contributions from employers and employees, with the government serving as the backup. The reform was started in the public sector but extended in the late 1990s to all formal economic organizations in urban areas, covering both employees with permanent urban resident status and migrant workers. Since then contributions to pensions, health care and unemployment funds have become mandatory for urban employers and employees, though many problems remain, such as inadequate contributions, barriers to inter-locale transfer of benefits, poor quality of service, and lack of coverage of the rural sector.

The decline of public enterprises has been accompanied by the rise of the private sector, which has now absorbed the vast majority of the employees laid off by public enterprises and become the main provider of jobs for new entrants into the workforce. The resurgence of private economic activities started in the late 1970s, when the government relaxed restrictions on self-employment in rural and urban areas. But the government limited the size of private economic entities to no more than seven people. That limit was lifted in 1988, though private enterprises continued to face discrimination and restrictions. It was not until 1992 that the political climate started to change. In the mid- to late 1990s the government gradually relaxed the restrictions on the private sector so as to address the two policy imperatives that public enterprises failed to address: employment and revenue. In 1998 a constitutional amendment was made to formally recognize the private sector as an 'important integral part' of China's 'socialist market economy'. Since 2001 the CCP has even welcomed and indeed encouraged private business people to become party members. In 2007 the National People's Congress enacted the *Property Law*, which proclaims equal protection to public and private property rights. As a result of these changes in the institutional environment, the private sector has steadily grown and become the leading producer of economic output and main provider of employment in China.

Organizational implications of economic institutional change

The economic institutional change highlighted above has had far-reaching implications for the organization of work. The once all-encompassing, CCP-dominated work unit system has faded into history. In the meantime, tension and conflict have grown, partly as a result of the adoption of exploitative, proto-capitalist labour practices in some parts of the economy. Yet such practices also face increasing constraints as further changes unfold in the evolving political and economic environment of work organization.

Decline of direct party-state control of work organization

The deepening of economic reforms has shaken loose the foundation of state socialist economic organization. The rise of family farms, non-farm self-employment, domestic private enterprises, and foreign-invested companies has crowded up the economic space that used to be dominated by public ownership. Gone with its dominance are the various behavioural control instruments that the CCP relied upon. The vast majority of working people no longer depend on jobs directly allocated by the government. Beginning from the late 1980s the bureaucratic allocation of essential daily supplies gradually gave way to rising markets of consumer goods and services. While the household registration system has yet to be abolished, it has been delinked from employment right and related benefits. As the public sector shrinks, the personnel dossier system has also lost its grip on most working people, and the CCP is unable to maintain its presence and dominance in private business organizations. Even in the remaining public enterprises, the CCP has retreated from many aspects of daily decision making, as the focal agenda has shifted from bureaucratic and political imperatives to profit making.

With direct bureaucratic and political control in decline, work-age citizens have gradually expanded their choice sets. Occupational and spatial mobility has significantly increased. Along the way, labour markets have developed and spread throughout the economy. The relationship between employers and employees has increasingly become a contractual arrangement, both outside and within the shrinking public sector. Human capital has become an important factor in influencing the direction and destination of workforce movement, the level of remuneration and benefits, as well as the resultant inequalities among working people.

Tension and conflict

China's transition from state socialism to capitalism has been accompanied by increasing contentiousness in industrial relations. Labour disputes have been on the rise, and so have been various other forms of complaint, protest, and resistance against employers, the government, or both (Lee 2007; O'Leary 1998; Pun 2005). Three developments have been identified as the main contributing factors. The first one is the growth of economic insecurity in terms of employment, health care, housing, old age support, and education of children. Such insecurity is perhaps most strongly felt by SOE employees who used to have the highest degree of security but have seen rapid dissipation of such security with the deepening of reforms. Under the Maoist system, they were more 'privileged' in terms of income, benefits, and status than employees in urban collective enterprises and people's communes. But the decline of bureaucratic allocation of jobs and related benefits, the onslaught of competition, and the deteriorating performance of public enterprises during the 1980s and 1990s led to a steady worsening of their economic situation. The most difficult time came during the mid- to late 1990s, when massive layoffs took place in the public sector.

The most vulnerable workers were those who joined the workforce after the start of urban economic reforms. When the downsizing of SOEs began, they were employed on contract terms and did not have the kind of employment protection, housing, and retirement benefits that older workers had. Already middle aged and with poor education and limited skills, they were ill-equipped to compete on the job market. Making matters worse was the fact that many of their employers had failed to contribute to the newly established pension, health care and unemployment funds due to poor financial performance. Unlike migrant workers from rural areas who in the event of unemployment in cities can return to their home villages to survive on the farmland that their families have leased out from local authorities, these urban workers had nowhere to turn upon losing their existing jobs. It is not surprising that many of them felt betrayed by the state and were among the most determined protesters against the government during the restructuring of SOEs around the turn of the century.

A second contributing factor to labour insurgence has to do with perceptions of injustice, especially in regard to systematically created and maintained inequalities and failures of government officials to enforce formal rules to protect the basic rights of working people. The treatment of migrant workers as second-class citizens in cities has been a major issue that spawns resentment and protest. A widespread practice adopted by urban employers is not to make legally required contributions on behalf of migrant workers to local pension, health care, and unemployment funds, resulting in the exclusion of these workers from pertinent benefits. This is often unaddressed by local authorities since they depend on business organizations for revenues and employment of permanent local residents and tend to have cosy relationships with them. The tolerance of such practice has become a major trigger for collective protests by migrant workers seeking to gain equal rights (Lee 2007).

A third source of growing tension and conflict in the workplace is poor and sometimes inhumane treatment of workers by their employers, especially those in the private sector and some foreign-funded enterprises. Long work hours, poor working conditions, exposure to work-related hazards, verbal and physical assault or abuse, arbitrary imposition of punishment, unreasonable firing, under-compensation, pay delays, and even wage non-payment, are some of the common problems that are present in work organizations where labour relations experience serious disharmony. When such treatment becomes unbearable to the workers, resistance, protest, or even more drastic reactions (such as strikes) may result.

Governance of the new workplace

With the state socialist system of work organization fading into history, new patterns of authority relations have emerged. But what exactly they are remains an issue awaiting close examination. Considerable media and analytic attention has focused on one particular type of internal organization – the so-called 'sweatshop' labour practice – in the new economy. As discussed above, it has been, among other things, a major source of tension and conflict.

A sweatshop may be defined as a workplace where authority is arbitrarily used without substantive legal and/or contractual safeguard for the basic rights of employees and where coercion and intimidation are the main form of behavioural control (Lin 2006). It is a proto-capitalist practice that tends to be prevalent under conditions of poor state protection of labour, underdevelopment of labour market, concentration of economic activities in low tech and self-contained labour processes, weak social pressures, and disorganization of collective action on the part of workers. There are numerous accounts of widespread use of this practice in certain parts (e.g. labour-intensive industrial enterprises funded by foreign or domestic private capital) of the economy (Chan 2001; Lee 1997; O'Leary 1998; Pun 2005), especially during the early years of reform. But the conditions conducive to its adoption and sustenance may have been weakening due to the growth of constraints.

To curb the erosion of its political legitimacy and fend off criticisms about its pro-capital approach to economic development, the government has been trying to reinstitute labour laws and regulations and improve their implementation. Further integration of China into the global economic system has also increased international pressure on the government to do more in terms of both labour-related legislation and enforcement. After much internal debate, for example, the National People's Congress enacted the *Labour Contract Law* in 2008. It represents an overhaul of the inadequate *Labour Law* enacted in 1996 and contains a number of clauses that define labour rights more clearly, impose more limits on grey areas of compliance, and make it more difficult and costly for employers to unilaterally terminate employment contracts. Although it remains unclear how closely the new law has been forced, it does set more limiting boundary conditions for employers' labour practice and provide a clearer benchmark for workers to gauge and struggle for their legal rights.

In the meantime, labour markets have become more developed. A key facilitating factor for this development is the accessibility of information about alternative jobs. In the early years of reform poor abilities of many workers to access and evaluate such information in a clear and timely fashion made them easy prey to exploitative employers. This has dramatically changed since the late 1990s, when the telecommunication revolution began in China. The cost of owning a mobile communication device has sharply decreased in both absolute and relative (to income) terms, making it affordable to ordinary working people and thereby greatly expanding their choice sets. Such diffusion has been coupled and reinforced with the rise and spread of the Internet and the broadening of information dissemination through further extension of the reach of conventional mass media, especially television. Clearer contrast and comparison between different workplace practices enable workers to vote with their feet more effectively, making it difficult for exploitative employers to maintain their old ways of labour control.

The sectoral distribution of work organizations has experienced structural change too. While industry has remained China's largest economic sector and home to many sweatshops, in terms of both output and employment it is the tertiary sector (services) that has seen the fastest growth in the reform era, with its share in the total workforce rising from 12 to 34 per cent during 1978–2009 (NBSa 2010: 120). The frequent interactions between front-line service providers and customers (whose business holds a key to profitability) make it counter-productive and even self-defeating to subject these employees to extensively abusive treatment, hence limiting the use of sweatshop practice. The upgrading of technology in many industrial processes poses another constraint, as the functionality of some technologies imposes more stringent requirements for the quality of the work environment (e.g. in terms of temperature and dust control, ventilation, storage and handling of hazardous materials) and concentration of attention among workers, and as the use of expensive equipment runs the risk of heavy financial losses resulting from damage rendered deliberately or carelessly by disgruntled workers.

Social pressures on abusive labour practice have also increased over time. While media organizations are still subject to official censorship, they have gained greater freedom and faced intensifying competition in reporting, including social reporting. Negative publicity creates a deterrence effect on employers, especially with the expansion and multiplication of the channels of mass communication. The composition of foreign investment has changed too. In the early years of reform, small and medium enterprises from neighbouring economies in Asia, which tended to be more reliant on cost cutting through sweatshop-type practices, led the inflow of foreign capital. Since the early 1990s, the role of multinational corporations, especially those from Western countries, has greatly increased. The domestic and international pressures for them to fulfil corporate social responsibility outside their home economies have forced many of them not only to pay closer attention to and demonstrate better compliance with local labour regulations than their forerunners, but to require their local transaction partners to do the same. Coupled with the development of labour markets, their regulatory compliance may thus have had a ripple effect on the foreign sector as a whole and beyond.

There have been changes in the organization of collective action among workers as well. With better education, higher expectations and stronger networking skills than their parents, workers from the post-1980 cohorts tend to be more active in pooling efforts to fight for their rights and interests. Mass diffusion of information technology has enabled many workers to mobilize and organize collective action more effectively, and to share and coordinate strategies to struggle against abusive employers in ways that were not possible before. An example of the growing role of information technology in this regard can be found in the outbreak and spread of large-scale strikes at Honda and Toyota plants in multiple locations in 2010 (Barboza and Bradsher 2010). Improved channels of communication also connect more effectively collective labour actions in China with international labour movements and the foreign media, though official restrictions and surveillance remain a significant limiting factor.

There are likely spatial variations in the intensity of the constraints highlighted above. Systematic empirical investigation is needed to ascertain this and to explore whether stronger constraints indeed have led to a decline of sweatshops. Even if one finds significant affirming evidence, however, it does not necessarily imply effective solutions to the wide-ranging labour problems in China's new economy. Nor does revealing what accounts for the rise and fall of sweatshops in itself offer a clear view of other coevolving patterns of authority relations and where and why their presence tends to be weak or strong. Further research is necessary to address these issues. What the foregoing discussion of the constraints on sweatshops suggests is that such research needs to consider, among other things, the roles of technology, globalization, and in particular the historical legacies from the era of state socialism. An issue among such legacies that has received prominent analytic attention but needs to be further investigated is the possible impact from changes in gender relations.

China's reform era has seen the continuation of a development that started after the 1949 revolution, i.e. the erosion of male centrality in the family and to a lesser extent in society despite remaining gender gaps. Among the contributing factors are the gender egalitarian policies of the CCP since the enactment of the *Marriage Law* in 1950 (which abolished, among other things, patrimonial ownership of family assets), active workforce participation by women (and resultant growth of economic independence), the rising age of marriage for women (partly as a result of the marriage deferral policy in the 1970s), improvement in female educational attainment, active involvement of women in family businesses and migration since the start of economic reforms, and the one-child policy under which significant numbers of urban singletons are female (Lin 2010). The implications of greater presence of women in the workforce and even in business decision making are yet to be more fully explored, though. Some ethnographic studies have documented 'gendered practices' of labour control that are tailored or adapted to the social and physiological characteristics of women in factories hiring large numbers of female workers, as well as unique ways or strategies of resistance and protest among female workers (Lee 1997; Jacka 2006; Pun 2005). While these accounts are very revealing, further efforts are needed to produce more systematic evidence concerning their findings, to broaden the focus of analysis from unidirectional (female-centred) 'gendered' behavioural control measures and responses to those that are male-centred or gender-neutral, and to explore the causes and consequences of all three types of practices and responses in different organizational contexts.

Summary

Within less than a decade after 1949, the communist government eliminated private ownership of economic resources and monopolized the allocation and employment of the country's workforce. In the ensuing twenty years, the organization of work was carried out through a system that combined economic, political, and social control of behaviour under a unitary authority structure of the party-state. Despite variations among different strata, across space and over time, the system featured a considerable degree of structural uniformity in terms of the basic mechanisms of governance.

Such uniformity has become increasingly unsustainable in the post-Mao era, when the rise of markets, economic internationalization, and privatization have all eroded the foundation of bureaucratic job allocation and work organization. In the process of such change, however, labour relations have become more contentious. While this is symptomatic of early capitalist development, the underlying driving forces are more complex than those in the direct transition from agrarian to capitalist systems in the West and the developing world, as the re-emergence of capitalism in China has taken place on the institutional remains of state socialism and in an era of profound technological revolution and globalization. Understanding such historical context helps illuminate the forces that condition the rise, decline, and longevity of proto-capitalist labour practices as epitomized in the ideal-typical 'sweatshop'. Questions remain, though, as to what other patterns of work organization have emerged in parallel or tandem, and what the causes and consequences are of these patterns.

Bibliography

Barboza, David and Keith Bradsher (2010) 'In China, labor movement enabled by technology', *New York Times*, June 16, available at http://www.nytimes.com/2010/06/17/business/global/17strike.html, accessed on January 22, 2011.

Chan, Anita (2001) *China's Workers under Assault*, Armonk, NY: M.E. Sharpe.

Cheng, Tiejun and Mark Selden (1994) 'The origin and social consequences of China's *hukou* system', *The China Quarterly*, 139: 644–65.

Gan, Shiming (ed.) (2003) *Zhongguo xiangzhen qiye tongji ziliao 1978–2002* (Statistics of China's Township Enterprises, 1978–2003), Beijing: Zhongguo nongye chubanshe.

Gao, Hongbin (ed.) (2009) *Zhongguo xiangzhen qiye ji nongchanpin jiagongye nianjian* (Yearbook of China's Township Enterprises and Agricultural Product Processing), Beijing: Zhongguo nongye chubanshe.

Jacka, Tamara (2006) *Rural Women in Urban China: Gender, Migration, and Social Change*, Armonk, NY: M.E. Sharpe.

Lee, Ching Kwan (1997) *Gender and the South China Miracle*, Berkeley, CA: University of California Press.

—— (2007) *Against the Law: Labor Protests in China's Rustbelt and Sunbelt*, Berkeley, CA: University of California Press.

Lin, Yi-min (2006) 'The sweatshop and beyond: authority relations in domestic private enterprises', pp. 82–96 in Anne Tsui, Yanjie Bian, and Leonard Cheng (eds), *China's Domestic Private Firms*, Armonk, NY: M.E. Sharpe.

—— (2010) 'Post-revolution transformations and the re-emergence of capitalism in China', pp 78–99 in Cindy Chu (ed.), *Chinese Capitalisms*, New York: Palgrave-Macmillan.

National Bureau of Statistics a (NBSa) (Various years) *China Statistical Yearbook*, Beijing: Zhongguo tongji chubanshe.

National Bureau of Statistics b (NBSb) (1987) *Zhongguo laodong gongzi tongji ziliao, 1949–1985* (China Labor and Wage Statistics, 1949–1985), Beijing: Zhongguo tongji chubanshe.

O'Leary, Greg (ed.) (1998) *Adjusting to Capitalism: Chinese Workers and the State*, Armonk, NY: M.E. Sharpe.

Pun, Ngai (2005) *Made in China: Women Factory Workers in a Global Workplace*, Durham, NC: Duke University Press.

Solinger, Dorothy J. (1999) *Contesting Citizenship: Peasant Migrants, the State, and the Logic of the Market*, Berkeley, CA: University of California Press.

Walder, Andrew G. (1986) *Communist Neo-traditionalism: Work and Authority in Chinese Industry*, Berkeley, CA: University of California Press.

12 Mass media in China

Xiaoling Zhang

The economic reform in China since 1978 has brought a radically changed communication landscape shaped by an unprecedented growth in the number of newspapers, TV stations, satellite channels and Internet expansion. It has become more pluralized, commercialized, and liberalized. Changes in China's media sphere during this period are not the result of a single event, but the consequence of a number of overlapping and interrelated factors and forces, including commercialization, the new global and regional structure and environment, pluralization which partly (but not exclusively) results from commercialization, China's multifaceted interactions with the outside world, and the advancement of new information and communication technologies (ICT). More importantly, all these changes are happening in the context of the Chinese Communist Party (CCP) wanting to manage the whole process and to stay ahead of the unwanted consequences of the reform. These overlapping and interrelated factors and forces constitute the backdrop of the transformation of mass media, although the backdrop itself is in continuous flux. This chapter starts with a brief review of the history of China's communist communication, which serves to provide the context within which the country's media reform and the fast-moving social transitions in the reform era have been occurring. It then introduces the transformation of mass media as a result of accelerated commodification, globalization, rapid advancement of media technologies, and intensified ideological and social struggles. This chapter serves to improve our understanding of the continuities and changes in China's mass media after the economic reform. It finishes with challenges both the Party-state and the media industry face in furthering the development of mass media in China.

Mass media in Mao's era

China's philosophy of media was derived from Marxist theory whose central theme is that media and communication are an ideological state apparatus, and that their first and foremost function is to reflect the regime's point of view on ideological issues. As a party that came to power as much through the power of the pen as through the barrel of the gun, the Chinese Communist

Party (CCP) leaders knew all too well the importance of ideological domination and the use of mass media as part of the Party's ideological apparatus for social mobilization.

Mass media in the CCP history before 1978 could be divided into three periods. The first period began in 1921 when the CCP was founded, and ended in 1949 when the CCP under the leadership of Mao Zedong founded the People's Republic of China (PRC). The CCP leaders from the start had been highly sensitive and attentive to the political role of the media, which played an important role in communicating to the Chinese people the ideas and values that the CCP believed to be crucial to their revolutionary objectives. Many newspapers and periodicals were developed to make ideological preparations for the founding of the new China by promoting Marxism and the views of the CCP (Chang 1989: 13). During the Japanese War and the Civil War in the 1930s and 1940s, the CCP developed its own journalistic institutions, successfully organizing and mobilizing the people. With increasingly rich experience of using the media to promulgate the CCP's guidelines and arousing people's political awareness, the CCP gradually developed its own theory of the media that emphasized the Party principle with three components: that the media must accept the CCP's guiding ideology as its own; that they must propagate the CCP's programmes, policies, and directives; and that they must accept the CCP's leadership and stick to the CCP's organizational policies and the press policies (Zhao 1998: 19).

The second period ran from 1949 to 1965. After it took power in 1949, the CCP quickly took over the entire mass media. By the early 1950s all private newspapers, radio stations, and publishers had been taken over by the state. The mass media system was thus integrated fully into the CCP-led government and became focused on contributing to system maintenance by teaching the attitudes, values, aspirations, and behaviours the nation's leaders considered desirable (e.g. Schramm 1973; Chu 1983). Since the media system was largely built on the Soviet model, the media were considered the vehicle for social and political control. It must be run by the CCP and become the CCP's 'loyal eyes, ears, and tongue' (Chang 1989: 163). Because of its important role, media in the early years of the PRC grew rapidly.

In the late 1950s came the Great Leap Forward, during which the CCP's Chairman Mao Zedong hoped to rapidly develop China's agricultural and industrial sectors. The media played a notorious role during this period: it exaggerated production figures and concealed famines and crop failures. Ironically, those who invented this news-fabricating machine started to believe in the reports themselves. Famine and disaster followed as a result of miscalculation and blind pursuit of industrialization. During the last few years of this period, emerging in the top leadership was a view that a general cleansing and a restoration of the revolutionary spirit were essential (Starck and Xu 1988). The reawakening was the Cultural Revolution, which started the third period of the media industry in Mao's era.

Mass media during the Cultural Revolution from 1966 to 1976 were characterized by complete control of the CCP, single-minded expressions of opinion, politicization to the extreme and personal cultism of Mao Zedong (Ibid.). The *People's Daily*, for instance, was under direct control of the CCP's top leadership. It was used against Mao's enemies, and copied verbatim by every other newspaper in the country. By the end of the Cultural Revolution, the media had lost much of their credibility (Fang, Chen and Zhang 1982).

When Mao died in 1976, the media he left had served as the propagandist, agitator and organizer. They were taken as part of the ideology and super-structure of China's socialist economy, designated to define the objectives and philosophy of the CCP and the government. The media were also regarded as weapons in class struggles against the CCP's enemies (White 1990; Chu 1994). The media had generally focused on the communication of goals rather than reality (Chu 1986). The flow of information was decidedly top-down, and emphasis was placed on constructing a mass-media and telecommunications system that could relay orders hierarchically from Beijing to every corner of the country, and from the state to society. The mass media were used, to the greatest possible extent, by the CCP to create a 'total institution' and to impose ideological hegemony on society (Lee 1990).

Mass media since the economic reform – changes and continuities

The CCP launched the economic reform in 1978, which, pragmatic as it seems, was necessary to salvage the CCP from the brink of losing its legitimacy after the Cultural Revolution. The Chinese economy has since then grown dramatically, which has in turn brought an unprecedented proliferation of media outlets and diversification of media sources, thus changing the communication landscape in China for ever.

Marketization of the media industry has also given rise to globalization. In contrast to the Maoist period when China was economically autarkic and culturally sealed off from the outside world, China has increased its interaction with the world. The period from 1980 to the late 1990s is characterized by China as a recipient of influence from global media companies. Because of the proliferation of media outlets, there was a severe shortage of domestic content provision. As a result, China Central Television (CCTV) alone imported 30 per cent of its programmes from abroad, and one quarter of the TV dramas throughout the nation were imports. As China's economic growth remains strong, every major international media player wants a foothold in the Chinese market. In the past decade, however, another trend seems to have set in: as it grows more confident, China has been building up its international networks to air its views, in an effort to break the Anglo-American monopoly, enhance China's international influence, and showcase its rise as a great power in a non-threatening and non-confrontational manner.

Marketization has also stimulated other important changes to the field of mass media such as the rapid development of technological advances, including television and recorded movies in the 1980s, and the Internet from 1994. For example, the number of Internet users in China has been growing at an exponential rate. Within less than twenty years, the number of users has expanded almost 150 times from a mere 2.1 million in 1998 to 384 million by the end of 2009.[1] Numerous netizens, the urban youth in particular, prefer to express opinions, exchange ideas and share information with their peers on the Internet.

More refined and sophisticated management from the Party-state

In spite of the reform they have launched, the CCP leaders have inherited from Mao a clear understanding of the importance of mass media in dominating society. It is therefore not surprising that as the CCP struggles to manage all aspects of the reform since 1978, it has invested high stakes in mass media, accelerating and strengthening its efforts to occupy the 'commanding heights' (Zhao 2008: 101) including strengthening structure to enhance regulating capacities.

The institutional communication system extends from Beijing to the lower administrative levels and can be largely divided into two broad categories, namely government agencies and CCP organizations. For both categories, there is the horizontal sector coordinating system and the vertical four-tier (national, provincial, prefectural and county) linkage. At the horizontal government level, the key government organizations under the State Council enforcing laws related to information flow within, into, and from China include those shown in Table 12.1, each responsible for the regulations of certain sectors in the media industry. Each media sector at different tiers is owned, regulated and operated by the corresponding level of government.

Table 12.1 State organs responsible for regulating and monitoring the mass media

State Council				
State Administration of Radio, Film and TV (SARFT)	*General Administration of Press and Publication (GAPP)*	*Ministry of Culture*	*Ministry of Information Industry (MII)*	*State Council's Information Office (SCIO)*
Radio, TV, films, animation (including those on the Internet)	Newspapers and magazine publications	Art, entertainment	Telecommunications, wireless service, broadband	Online media, internet

However, all these government agencies are subject to the directives of the Central Department of Propaganda (DOP), which reports directly to the Standing Committee of the Political Bureau of the Central Committee of the CCP, the most powerful decision-making body in China. It answers for the information and cultural networks of institutions, and coordinates with different government agencies to make sure content remains consistent with Party doctrine. Parallel to the state media institutions, the DOP also has the four-tier local units. Thus activities in the lower-level media organizations are circumscribed by the local DOPs, answerable to the Central DOP in Beijing.

The development of mass media in China after 1978 can be divided into three stages known as marketization, conglomeration and capitalization, each reflecting the Party-state's efforts at maintaining control of the reform process and dealing proactively with unintended consequences.

Marketization

The first period started in the late 1970s when Deng launched sweeping reforms covering the country's economy, politics, ideology, culture, and mass media. Three critical policies marked this period. The first one was in 1978 when the government issued a policy removing the rein on media advertising. Before 1978, the government owned, controlled and financed all media outlets. In 1978, the financially stressed state started to progressively withdraw direct subsidies from media organizations, particularly those at local levels. This policy marked the beginning of the whole process of marketization. Since then advertising has become an increasingly important source of income for all kinds of media.

The central government began another important policy in 1983, which stated that the media system henceforward would have four levels: central, provincial and autonomous regions, prefectural cities and county-level cities. It allowed governments at different levels to establish, finance and operate their own media outlets. The primary purpose of this policy was to improve the effectiveness of the media as a medium for the dissemination of Party-state policy initiatives and as its 'eyes and ears'. It also resulted in the four-tier media structure.

In late 1992, another policy was issued as part of a concerted plan to dislodge inefficient state enterprises. It required all newspapers to be financially independent by 1994 except a few major CCP organs such as the *People's Daily*. The state acknowledged the economic significance of non-political coverage and no longer required afternoon and evening publications, news digests, culture and lifestyle papers and trade journals to carry ideological propaganda (Lee 1994: 12).

These three policies resulted in an unprecedented proliferation of media outlets. At the beginning of the reform period, China only had a handful of media. In the 1980s newspaper titles multiplied at great speed, with one new title published every one and a half days (Chang 1989: ix). At the same time, general and specialist papers also increased their page numbers. TV stations increased rapidly from 47 in 1982 to 366 in 1987 (Zhu 2009: 203). By the end of the 1980s, China had developed a rather elaborate media network.

Although the crackdown on the pro-democracy movement in 1989 suppressed discourses on political liberalization and re-imposed tight political control on the media, market forces gained momentum again after Deng Xiaoping gave his personal approval to more aggressive economic reform in 1992. Media organizations, like much of the rest of China, responded to the opportunity by embracing the market economy in an unreserved way. As a result the Chinese media expanded enormously in the 1990s.

The proliferation of media outlets also led to the diversification of media products. In sharp contrast to the pre-1978 media landscape that had been dominated by a few newspapers and journals published by the central government, a network of central, provincial and municipal 'People's Radio Stations' and TV stations which had carried more or less the same ideologically charged reports and commentaries about national and international events, a myriad of new types of newspapers, journals, magazines, radio and TV programmes/ channels burst onto the media scene. They varied widely in content and style, catering to different interests such as the economy, sports, health, culture, and environment, and served specific groups of people, such as business people, legal professionals, youths, retired people, and women. In addition, the Internet since 1994 introduced to the Chinese public even greater varieties of information and entertainment. By the end of the twentieth century the communication system in China included all the modern advanced media.

An accompanying change with marketization was a redefinition of the political role of the media. The CCP, while retaining ultimate control over politically sensitive information, wanted the media to play a major role in the promotion of a market economy, consumerism, and the nationalistic project of building a 'wealthy and powerful' nation. The media aired people's desires and grievances in an effort to act as the channels with which the CCP has reinvented and reconnected itself with the public.

While marketization of the media launched by the Party-state led to the transformation of the whole media landscape, it also brought about unintended consequences. Take the press for example. First of all, marketization gave rise to an unprecedented expanding array of media outlets, which posed a threat to the dominant position of the central and provincial CCP organs both in terms of number and overall circulation. For one thing, CCP organs had mandatory propaganda topics to cover, and had to reach CCP functionaries at the village level, while market-oriented mass appeal papers were less bound by a requirement of this kind. They targeted urban consumers, which rendered them far more attractive advertisement vehicles.

Second, commercialization transformed political restrictions into economic assets, thus weakening the Party-state's control of the media content. For example, in book publishing, only officially approved publishers had the right to grant the licence to publish a book. These licences became valuable commodities that could be bought and sold; similarly no newspapers were to be set up as independent businesses – all must be assigned an official rank and must be registered under a recognized institutional publisher or sponsor. Obviously the financial interests of media organizations and the government and CCP organizations that owned them were often best served by collaborating with anyone who could provide marketable content and effective distribution. Not all these sponsoring institutions or individuals were keen on the communist ideology of the products.

Third, the four-tiered media structure led to the rapid growth of local media. In the broadcasting sector, for instance, TV stations mushroomed, especially at the county level, which increased dramatically from hardly any in 1980 to 60 in 1985, and then to 1,262 in 2001, accounting for nearly 80 per cent of the total number of TV stations in China (Yuan 2004). These television stations created tensions between local and central interests: the state insists on local stations transmitting CCTV's National News at 7:00pm as a 'political task' – after all, it was the Party-state's main means of broadcasting its propaganda and ideology to the vast regions and diverse ethnic groups of the country. However, local stations, while relaying the national news as a political mission, created more channels with a commercial interest, thus attracting audiences away from CCTV with 'soft' news and various entertainment programmes.

Conglomeration

The second stage from the mid-1990s to 2002 saw the Party-state not only deepen the market logic but also determined to maintain control of the commercialized media industry. From the mid-1990s the government started to curb the proliferation of media outlets by tightening the issuing of licensing. In the second half of 1995, it stopped issuing new licences completely. In 1996 the state decided to encourage the formation of media groups, which were believed to be ideal organizational forms for optimal integration between control and business by matching enterprising media outlets with its own regulating organs. Only those centrally approved media papers that met a series of operational criteria could take other papers. The first media group in China – *Guangzhou Daily Group* – was established that year. By July 1998, China had officially set up six national and regional press groups.

Today, there are altogether 40 press groups in China, a blend of media outlets and government regulators. However, media conglomerates have not been as successful commercially as the CCP and the state policy-makers would have wished. The commercial failure is largely due to the fact that they were more for the maximization of ideological control over media for political stability than for the maximization of profits. This means although they were financially independent and were expected to rationalize production and take advantage of economies of scale, the groups were not officially incorporated as independent businesses, nor were they registered with the government's industry and trade bureau. Rather, they were affiliated with the DOPs at different levels, and their publishers and editors-in-chief were appointed by and accountable to their affiliated CCP committees.

Capitalization

The third stage saw a new reform programme for the Chinese culture sector. In July 2003, the government started to substantively differentiate the concept of public cultural institutions from commercial cultural enterprises and attribute to each clear-cut missions, different means and ends of development. There are many reasons for this move. First, in line with the state's policy adjustment towards a more balanced development and social harmony, cultural development in this way entails equalizing cultural opportunities for all fragments of society. Second, it re-conceptualizes culture as a commercial industry, thus making culture including the media a new site of economic growth and a strategic site for the development of both economic power and cultural or 'soft' power in a competitive global context. Finally, this concept effectively displaces media reform as a key component of political reform within the broad agenda of cultural system reform, making media reform part of China's economic reforms.

Following this new policy, different organizations in the media sector were to separate into two sub-sectors: the public service sector and the commercial sector. All of the mainstream state-owned media entities like the CCP organs, be they press groups, broadcasting groups or publishers, are public service units. They provide political information including news and current affairs. Other entities such as advertising, printing, distribution and transmission are open to non-state investment and ownership. This move shows the state's determination to maintain control over the political information, but at the same time to allow the commercial sector to flourish. This move also authorizes state capital to monopolize media heavyweights, but to exit gradually from medium and small ones through asset sales and transfers, mergers, and bankruptcy.

However, to ensure that these medium or small media companies keep their 'socialist' nature, they are not fully left to private capital, domestic or foreign. A further distinction is thus made between the editorial and business operations of these organizations: for the operational sectors, they may be split off from the editorial sectors and restructured into shareholding or limited commercial companies, which can open up the service-related value chains such as printing and publishing, retail, information transmission and distribution to investment from non-media state-owned enterprises.[2] Although these domestic investors from non-media sectors are shareholders, they are barred from intervening in content delivery and asset management of the company. The same holds true for foreign investors whose sphere of influence is for the time being contained within the publishing sector only. The editorial sectors, on the other hand, must remain state-monopolized and no overseas and private investment would be allowed. The government takes full responsibility for their functioning. Similarly, although the production of TV programmes and the distribution of publications can absorb overseas and private resources, the state must be the dominant shareholder in order to stay in the dominant position. With state capital no less than 51 per cent and its control of the final editorial rights, the dominant owner in this state-private partnership is obvious.

Social and political implications

Marketization

Scholars and observers are divided in their assessment of the political and social impact of marketization. Many hold the view that marketization has turned media organizations into self-interested economic entities, which in turn has motivated the media to challenge CCP control. The logic is simple. Severance of state subsidies to the media would unleash media practitioners' energy to meet intense market competition. To satisfy the preference of an ever more demanding public and compete with one another to win sizable market shares, different media outlets would have to distribute content that attracts the media publics advertisers want. Therefore while the headlines may still be dominated by CCP content, a substantial portion of the content would focus on social problems that used to be taboo subjects such as poverty, unemployment, crime and corruption. Mundane issues that used to be unworthy of news reporting such as traffic congestion, family relationships, consumer information, and entertainment programmes of various shades as well as celebrity gossip which used to be viewed as a manifestation of unhealthy bourgeois taste and sentiment now appear daily. Those who believe in the liberating force of the market hold that the regime is far less able than before to wield financial leverage over the media, which have increasingly become self-supporting through advertising revenues and circulation.

Not everybody subscribes to this view. Some scholars have regarded marketization as a double-edged sword. It may give media organizations incentives to challenge CCP control in order to pursue commercial profits, but it can also lead to the reorientation of the content provided by the media on the one hand, and self-censorship on the other. Some even believe that marketization has actually helped the government reach the public faster and in greater numbers as the media try to deliver the largest number of media publics to advertisers. The media are believed to have not only gone from mass propaganda to mass entertainment but have also continued to operate within the orbit of the Party-state as they are still owned by or affiliated to CCP and government organs who have given them enough interest to stay within the Party-line. They argue that although there are exceptions, by and large, media marketization has contributed to the entrenchment of state control in the media.

Globalization

Many observers have taken globalization as a strong force that would inevitably increase pressures for political reform in China. First, Beijing's domination of the circulation of political information is eroding as it cannot prevent broadcasters such as the VOA and the BBC from entering the country's communications networks. Second, transnational satellite television such as the Chinese language services of CNN has significantly expanded its reach in China. Third, the government cannot easily block the borderless Internet transmissions. Competition from outside mainland China also impels domestic media organizations to improve their attractiveness to the public by providing content that is more diversified and critical.

China's membership of the WTO has added another force for further liberalization of the media market. Under the WTO agreement, China agreed to allow foreign investment in its advertising market, the participation of foreign companies in the printing and packaging of publications and in the retail and wholesale of books, magazines, and newspapers. China also agreed to import a growing number of foreign films each year. The introduction of transnational capital into the previously state monopolized media sector will help establish a more financially rational and professionally constructive media system.

As China opens up to the world, freer policies, albeit *ad hoc*, such as the Regulations on Reporting Activities in China by Foreign Journalists during the Beijing Olympic Games and the Preparatory Period, give foreign journalists wider freedom to conduct their work in China. The large numbers of foreign journalists who have enjoyed the freer policy and the foreign-invested and foreign-owned advertising companies along with their clients will have an impact on Chinese media and media publics.

Again, not all observers share this view. Many have aired concerns over the considerable degree of ideological convergence between global capitalism and 'socialism with Chinese characteristics'. China has adopted a pragmatic, partial opening-up policy, aiming at absorbing Western capital and know-how, and very few Western capitalists can resist the temptation of the Chinese media market's huge potential. This mutual need paves the foundation of corporatism. These observers also point out that in the final negotiations over China's entry into the WTO, the Chinese government only committed itself to opening up certain sectors of its audio-visual market to foreign investment, but the broadcasting market was excluded (Dudek and Xu 2002). Neither do China's WTO agreements bind it to content liberalization. The partial opening of the media sector should therefore be considered an initiative from China to absorb capital and advanced technology. In addition, Beijing has applied some carefully planned devices to ensure control of foreign content such as rigorous censorship prior to distribution.

With China's rise as not only an economic power but also a political power in recent years, some observers have started to notice China's influence on the rest of the world, especially China's soft power. China has greatly increased its investment in building its international communication capacity. Organizations such as CCTV, Xinhua News Agency and *People's Daily* could reportedly receive up to RMB 15 billion respectively for ambitious schemes geared towards enhancing China's international influence (Lam 2009).

Advances in new media technology

From the very beginning Internet technology is believed to have overcome authoritarian restrictions on the flow of information and posed an insurmountable threat to the regime. Indeed in the face of a mounting number of netizens having easier access to alternative sources of information, the Party-state would have to adjust and refine its institutions and methods of governance to remain in the dominant position. Being interactive and reciprocal in its nature of communication, the Internet is also believed to be able to constrain negative consequences resulting from the old format of one-way communication between the state and society. It is even believed that new media such as the 'blogosphere' make the debate over state control or interference irrelevant as bloggers find other ways to get their news and information.

Indeed, the Internet in China has become an important forum for public opinion. When major events occur, very intensive and extensive discussions suddenly emerge on websites, placing high political pressure on the authorities, and pushing the latter to change existing policy practices. For example, China's Ministry of Industry and Information Technology announced that all computers produced or sold in China would have to be installed with some filtering software (known as Green Dam) from 1 July 2009. The purported intent of the Green Dam software was to filter violence and pornographic content on the Internet. Critics, however, slammed the move as a means for the government to keep tabs on Internet users who visit politically sensitive websites. In the face of intense public opposition, much of it online, the authorities have postponed the installation of this controversial software.[3]

Of course, opposing views are strong. They argue that the Internet is not a force that by itself alone can topple or even change the current Chinese regime. There is only minimal evidence that dissidents have been able to make effective use of the Internet. Neither is there evidence that any dissident group is using the Internet to mount a credible threat. Furthermore, similar to incidents of social protest such as riots and demonstrations that happen in the real world, protests on the Internet typically have no leaders or political objectives, characterized by un-institutionalized and chaotic patterns of political participation. The institutionalization of government transparency and citizen participation lag far behind government efforts to strengthen and refine methods of control and governance. Indeed the establishment and growth of the political control regime has led to various pessimistic conclusions regarding the impact of the Internet on political changes in China: since 2003, the Ministry of Public Security has led the operation of the so called 'Golden Shield Project', more commonly known as the Great Firewall of China, with 30,000 employees screening out information sent from specific Internet addresses. It seems that China has experienced phenomenal Internet growth without the government losing much control. Although the countervailing strategies of Internet users are outstanding in China, the regulators appear to have had the upper hand so far.

Some also argue that in the long-run, the Internet may hasten the process of democratization in China by exposing users to alternative ideas and views. Yet, the democratizing effect of the Internet should not be exaggerated given the dominant role the CCP plays in Chinese politics, and the fact that there are still many in China who have no access to the Internet. Though the penetration rate is rising continuously, compared with developed countries, China's Internet penetration rate is still low: as of December 2009, China's Internet penetration rate was 28.9 per cent.

Most importantly, Chinese leaders have not treated the Internet as an evil monster but rather as an engine for economic and social growth, and have therefore adopted a proactive policy to develop the Internet. 'The authoritarian state is hardly obsolete in the era of the Internet' (Kalathil and Boas 2003), because the state plays a crucial role in charting the development of the Internet and in conditioning the ways it is used by societal, economic, and political actors.

To summarize, opinions differ on the implications of the changes in the Chinese media, but nobody disagrees that China's economic reform and opening up have resulted in pluralization within the media. Chinese citizens are much less dependent on official sources for information as they had to be before 1978. Even if the diversity is not directly political, it reduces the direct influence of the state over the private spheres of social life greatly. Chinese citizens no longer need consume the offerings of the central media outlets, and the messages the central Party-state seeks to impart. The symbolic environment that is created and managed by the Party-state alone is changed forever.

However, the widely different views also indicate that the link between changes in Chinese media and political reform is complex. Take the Internet for an example. On the one hand, the Internet may well have an enormous impact on how and what information circulates through Chinese society and may eventually require profound adjustments in the way the state regulates information and legitimates itself, and yet on the other the balance of evidence and opinion indicates that no new technology will create an ideal public sphere. A study of online activism in China shows neither the triumph of total control on the part of the Internet-control regime nor of resistance from Internet users and activists (Yang 2009: 62). It shows that technology matters but so do institutional and individual interests.

Conclusion: control, autonomy and credibility

The development of the media at different stages shows that as the CCP introduces reform to the media sector, gradualism has been the key which enables the CCP and the political system to evolve and to adapt to new political and social realities. So far, the CCP has stayed in control of the reform. However, over the long run, a nation's media can influence popular attitudes only to the extent that the media are believed and trusted. Therefore both the CCP and the media face the intertwined dilemma of control, autonomy and credibility in furthering the development of the media industry.

As the media have undergone dramatic changes since 1978, instead of playing the traditional instrumental role only, they are now also expected to perform multi-faceted functions: to create an environment favourable for political and social stability, to construct a good image of the Party-state, to harness popular support for the government, to compete with transnational media corporations for the global flow of information, and to be commercially successful in a very crowded marketplace. These expectations of the media from the Party-state, sometimes conflicting but always interrelated, cannot be fulfilled unless China's media become more autonomous from the state. The authorities in China know the need for press freedom but are worried about opening the door to the type of freedom that could lead to the regime's downfall. The nature of the political system in China decides that complete media autonomy from the state is highly unlikely to materialize in China in the near future: such autonomy would require the removal of the CCP's authority to supervise the media. Moreover, constitutional guarantees of press freedom and individual political expression and a thoroughgoing overhaul of the government-controlled judiciary would be required for a genuinely independent media sector to emerge in China. And yet, without autonomy, the Chinese media will continue to lack credibility, and popular trust of the media would not rise. How to balance control, autonomy and credibility is therefore a dilemma both the Party-state and the media in China have to face in the foreseeable future.

Notes

1 See http://www.cnnic.cn/uploadfiles/pdf/2010/3/15/142705.pdf, accessed on July 18, 2010.
2 'Chinese News Media Will Not Accept Foreign and Private Investment', *News Front* (2002): 2, at http://peopledaily.com.cn/GB/paper79/5498/566029.html, accessed July 20, 2010.
3 'China Postpones Mandatory Installation of Controversial Filtering Software', *Xinhuawang*, June 30, 2009 at http://news.xinhuanet.com/english/2009–06/30/content_11628335.htm, accessed on July 8, 2009.

Bibliography

Chang, Won Ho (1989) *Mass Media in China*, Ames, IA: Iowa State University Press.

Chu, Leonard (1983) 'Press criticism and self-criticism in communist China: an analysis of its ideology, structure, and operation', *Gazette*, 31(1): 47–61.

—— (1986) 'Mass communication theory: the Chinese perspective', *Media Asia*, 13(1): 14–19.

—— (1994) 'Continuity and change in China's media reform', *Journal of Communication*, 44(3): 4–21.

Dudek, Mitch and Xu, Lucy Lan (2002) 'Market access report: media and publishing', *China Law & Practice*, Issue: May, available at http://www.chinalawandpractice. com/Article/1693674/Channel/7576/Market-Access-Report-Media-and-Publishing. html, accessed on June 25, 2010.

Fang, Hanqi, Chen, Yeshao, and Zhang, Zihua (1982) *A Brief History of Chinese Journalism*, Beijing: People's University Press.

Kalathil, Shanthi and Boas, Taylor (2003) 'China's new media sector: keeping the state in', *The Pacific Review*, 16(4): 489–501.

Lam, Willy (2009) 'Chinese state media goes global: a great leap outward for Chinese soft power?' *China Brief*, 9(2) available at http://www.jamestown.org/single/? no_cache=1&tx_ttnews%5Btt_news%5D = 34387, accessed on March 18, 2010.

Lee, Chin-Chuan (1990) 'Mass media: of China, about China', pp. 3–29 in Chin-Chuan Lee (ed.), *Voices of China: The Interplay of Politics and Journalism*, New York: The Guildford Press.

—— (1994) 'Ambiguities and contradictions: issues in China's changing political communication', pp. 3–20 in Chin-Chuan Lee (ed.), *China's Media, Media's China*, Boulder, CO: Westview Press.

Schramm, Wilbur (1973) *Men, Messages, and Media: A Look at Human Communication*, New York: Harper and Row.

Starck, Kenneth and Xu, Yu (1988) 'Loud thunder, small raindrops: the reform movement and the press in China', *International Communication Gazette*, 42(3): 143–59.

White, Lynn (1990) 'All the news: structure and politics in Shanghai's reform media', pp. 88–110 in Chin-Chuan Lee (ed.), *Voices of China: The Interplay of Politics and Journalism*, New York: The Guildford Press.

Yang, Guobin (2009) *The Power of the Internet in China*, New York: Columbia University Press.

Yuan, Yan (2004) 'Dilemma and the way out for county-level TV stations during the reform era', *Journalism University*, 80(2): 56–62.

Zhao, Yuezhi (1998) *Media, Market, and Democracy in China: Between the Party Line and the Bottom Line*, Urbana and Chicago, IL: University of Illinois Press.

—— (2008) *Communication in China*, Lanham, MD: Rowman and Littlefield Publishers.

Zhu, Hong (2009) 'Experiences from the 30 years of reform in TV industry', pp. 203–7 in Baoguo Cui (ed.), *Blue Book of China's Media*, Beijing: China Social Sciences Academic Press.

13 Government and changing state-society relations

Xiaowei Zang

This chapter provides a brief history of the Chinese Communist Party (CCP) before 1949, the socialist transformation of China in the Mao era of 1949–76, and the post-1978 market reforms. It then examines the system of government, describing its institutional components, the principles by which they operate, and the way in which the CCP controls the government. Next, it discusses the changing state-society relations in the People's Republic of China (PRC) since 1978. While there has been continuity in major government institutions and the persistence of one-party rule in China, there have been significant political changes in the post-1978 era due to the receding role of the state in society, the imperatives of market reforms, and the open-door policy. This chapter shows some recent political developments and the move towards a stronger 'society' in China.

A brief history of the CCP and the PRC

The Qing dynasty, which had governed China since 1644, was overthrown in the Revolution of 1911 and replaced by the Republic of China in 1912. Regime change did not bring about peace and prosperity as the country soon fell prey to the political ambitions of warlords. It was not until the late 1920s when Generalissimo Chiang Kai-shek (1887–1975) temporarily unified China. Yet peace did not last long as the Japanese Army started to invade China in 1931. A brutal and protracted war between China and Japan broke out in 1937 and did not end till 1945 when the Japanese government surrendered to the Allied Forces of which China was a member. The end of the Sino-Japanese war was followed by a large-scale civil war in which Generalissimo Chiang and his Nationalist government fought with the CCP for the right to rule China (Bailey 2001).

The CCP was established in 1921 and was supported by the USSR in its struggle to remove imperialism, feudalism, and crony capitalism and build a socialist country in China. Mao Zedong moved to the centre of decision-making in the CCP in 1935, established his leadership of the party in the early 1940s, and led the CCP's victory over Generalissimo Chiang and his Nationalist government with the founding of the PRC in 1949 (Bailey 2001;

Karl 2010). The 1949 communist revolution was genuinely welcomed by the vast majority of Chinese people, as it promised to end the poverty and humiliation that Chinese people had suffered for almost a century. The CCP enjoyed widespread support and was able to carry out mass campaigns in the next three decades (see Chapter 2 for a discussion of the reforms the CCP carried out in the 1950s and 1960s).

In the 1950s, the PRC was allied with and received massive aid from the USSR. The PRC followed the 'Soviet model' as its development strategy in which economic life was governed by a powerful bureaucracy. Market transactions were replaced by central planning in the form of a series of 'Five Year Plans'. Production and investments were prioritized over consumption. Heavy industry was promoted at the expense of light industry and subsidized by surplus squeezed from rural areas. Natural and production resources were nationalized, and much emphasis was placed on the role of technology and science in development (Bernstein and Li 2010; Lowenthall 1970; Wilber 1969).

Maoism sought to replace the Soviet model as the dominant development strategy after the relations between the PRC and the URRS fell apart in the late 1950s. Maoism was similar to the Soviet model in that as the state controlled natural resources, production prevailed over consumption, and the divide between urban and rural areas was maintained. Maoism deviated from the Soviet model in its emphasis on mass mobilization through revolutionary struggle and politics in command. Mao had a bias against expertise and bureaucracy and had a strong belief in mass initiatives. He launched the Great Leap Forward campaign in 1958 so that the industrial outputs from China would surpass the UK in ten years and the USA in twenty or thirty years. Mao wanted to substitute capital and technology with sheer hard labour from workers and peasants, which led to the disastrous famines between 1959 and 1962 (Chan 2001; Dikötter 2010; Li and Yang 2005). The failure of the Great Leap Forward emasculated Mao's position in the CCP (Shih 1994). Liu Shaoqi replaced Mao as the Chairman of the PRC in 1959. He worked with Deng Xiaoping and other leaders to rescue the Chinese economy with pragmatic policies and experiment with limited economic liberalization. By 1963 the Chinese economy started to grow again, which bolstered Liu's prestige among the CCP apparatus at Mao's expense. Mao started the Cultural Revolution in 1966 to reclaim his power and re-assert the supremacy of Maoism in China. He launched a surprise attack and defeated his political rivals in the CCP. However, the triumph of Maoism during the heyday of the Cultural Revolution triggered its ultimate demise. This was partly because endless political mobilization and violence created massive political chaos and undermined economic life. The most horrifying aspects of the Cultural Revolution were the torture and killing of innocent people. Many CCP leaders indifferent to Maoism such as Deng Xiaoping were dismissed from office and subjected to violent struggle (MacFarquhar and Schoenhals 2006; Karl 2010).

The Cultural Revolution ended with the death of Mao Zedong in 1976. At that time, the Chinese economy was on the brink of collapse. The CCP was on the way to losing its mandate to govern given the colossal economic losses and immense suffering during the Cultural Revolution (Ding 1994). Deng Xiaoping came back to power in 1978 to restore the CCP's legitimacy by reforming the Chinese economy. Economic growth was to be achieved through measures such as expanding rural incentives, improving state enterprises' profitability, reducing central planning, encouraging foreign investment, etc. These measures have enhanced China's economic competitiveness and integrated the country into the global economic system. As a result, the post-1978 era has seen healthy economic development in China. China overtook Germany to become the world's largest exporter in 2009 and surpassed Japan as the world's second-largest economy in the first half of 2010. Its economy was ninety times larger than it was when market reforms were launched in 1978, and there have been substantial gains in poverty reduction in China.

Post-1978 market reforms have also generated undesirable outcomes such as rampant corruption, growing inequality, and environmental degradation. The 'new three mountains on people's back' were the cost of education, housing, and health care. There are other social and political issues. Part of the reasons for social problems and malaise is slow political liberalization. Deng and his successors have insisted on 'building socialism with Chinese characteristics', namely market liberalization must be implemented under political dictatorship, which can unhesitatingly resort to force to defend one-party rule. Deng suppressed the demands for democratization by student demonstrators in Beijing in 1989. Liu Xiaobo, the winner of the 2010 Nobel Peace Prize, was tried on suspicion of 'inciting subversion of state power' and sentenced to eleven years' imprisonment in December 2009. The CCP has resisted the calls for democratic reforms and has continued one-party rule in China. The government institutions, to be discussed below, have remained largely unchanged since 1978.

Government institutions

The organizational structure of the PRC follows the Western-style division between the legislature, administration, and judicial system. However, the division is arranged in such a way that it goes along with one party rule in China as discussed below. The real power is in the hands of the CCP, which is led by its General Secretary and Politburo (currently twenty-four members) of the Central Committee. The Central Committee has about 300 members, is in theory the highest authority within the CCP, and nominally appoints the Politburo. In reality, the Politburo is self-perpetuating and appoints the Central Committee. As discussed below, the members of the Politburo simultaneously hold leading positions within the government and the armed forces of the PRC and are in charge of personnel appointments in central and local governments and CCP branches. Local CCP leaders similarly monopolize political, legal, financial, and personnel power in their jurisdictions.

Notwithstanding, according to the PRC Constitution, the primary organ of state power is the National People's Congress (NPC). It has over 3,000 members, elected for five-year terms. The current chairperson of the NPC is Wu Bangguo (吴邦国), who is concurrently a member of the Standing Committee of the CCP's Politburo. NPC deputies are elected by the people's congresses of China's twenty-three provinces, five autonomous regions, four municipalities directly under the Central Government, the special administrative regions of Hong Kong and Macau, and the armed forces. Provincial people's congress deputies are elected by prefectural people's congresses. Prefectural people's congress deputies are elected by the deputies to people's congresses of counties, cities, municipal districts, and townships, who are elected directly by their constituencies for five-year terms. It is possible for an individual to campaign for and be elected to these levels of people's congresses, and this has happened occasionally. But it is practically impossible for a person to be elected to provincial or national people's congresses. In fact, the membership of each level of the people's congresses is determined by CCP leaders. Unsurprisingly, election campaigning is rare. Candidates do not make house calls, distribute leaflets, or publicize their platforms to their constituencies. Chinese citizens are simply not familiar with terms such as electoral participation, campaign budgets, and campaign offices. Popular participation in politics is actively and publicly banned. No political party can be formed without the approval by the local government. A career in politics goes nowhere unless one joins the CCP.

The NPC and each of the local people's congresses meet once each year. The standing committee of the NPC and each of the local people's congresses exercise legislative authority in its jurisdiction when the full congress is not in session. In theory, a local people's congress has the constitutional authority to recall the heads and deputy heads of government at the provincial level and below. In reality, the local people's congresses are not independent of control by the local CCP organs. The chairpersons of local people's congresses are always local CCP leaders and the vast majority of the deputies are CCP members. For example, the current chairperson of the Hubei Provincial People's Congress is Li Hongzhong (李鸿忠), who is concurrently the secretary of the CCP Hubei Provincial Committee. Similarly, the current chairperson of the Fujian Provincial People's Congress is Lu Zhangong (卢展工), who is concurrently the secretary of the CCP Fujian Provincial Committee.

The candidate for the chair of a local people's congress is chosen by higher-level CCP leaders before the people's congress session and is often the only candidate for the post. The CCP also handpicks a minority of people's congress deputies who are from ethnic minorities, women, minor political parties, or intellectuals. These individuals are selected because they are politically reliable and have some influence in society. They serve the CCP's argument that the essence of people's democracy is the representation of different social groups in the people's congress rather than procedural justice (i.e. how deputies are elected). For this reason the CCP has from time to time promoted the rhetoric that women share equal social worth with men so there must be an increase in women's presentation in the people's congress (female representation in the NPC deputies has been around 20 per cent). Nevertheless, the majority of the deputies are men at or near retirement age since the people's congresses have become a *de facto* heaven for retired government officials and CCP cadres rather than an elected legislature.

Also in theory, the NPC is the legislative branch of government and passes laws and appoints the President of the PRC. While deputies have the right to send their proposals to the people's congress organizing committee, only those that are supported by the CCP can pass the legislation and be enacted as laws later. Similarly, only the candidate nominated by the CCP can become the President of the PRC. The President is the head of the state and the office was created by the 1982 Constitution. The current President is Hu Jintao (胡锦涛), who has held office since 2003. Mr Hu has been the General Secretary of the CCP since 2002.

The President of the PRC nominates the President of the Supreme People's Court and the Procurators-General of the Supreme People's Procuratorate for approval by the NPC. The term for each office is five years. The Supreme People's Court and the Supreme People's Procuratorate represent the judicial branch of government in China. The nominations have never been turned down by the NPC, and all the candidates for these posts are top CCP leaders. The current President of the Supreme People's Court is Wang Shengjun (王胜俊). He has been concurrently the Secretary General of the CCP's Central Political and Legislative Committee since 1998. The current Procurators-General of the Supreme People's Procuratorate is Cao Jianming (曹建明), a regular member of the seventeenth Central Committee of the CCP.

The President of the PRC also nominates the State Council, which is the executive branch of government in China. The State Council is led by the Premier, vice premiers, state councillors (protocol equal of vice premiers but with narrower portfolios), and ministers and heads of State Council commissions. The term of each office is five years. The current Premier is Wen Jiabao (温家宝), who has held this office since 2003. Most top leaders are men in their late fifties. The State Council maintains an interlocking membership with the top levels of the CCP. For example, Mr Wen is a member of the Standing Committee of the Politburo of the CCP. There is also an interlocking membership among the executive, judicial, and legislative organs of government at the provincial, prefectural, city, and township levels. The leaders of local governments are always CCP members as well as the judges and procurators.

The State Council oversees twenty-two provincial governments and their counterparts in the five autonomous regions, four municipalities directly under the central government, and two special administrative regions (Hong Kong and Macau). The provincial-level governments (except those in Hong Kong and Macau) oversee local governments at the prefectural, city/county, township, and village levels. Each provincial-level government, prefectural government, city/county government, and township government is staffed and overseen by a parallel group of local CCP leaders. For example, the provincial governor is often a deputy secretary of the provincial CCP committee, and sometimes is himself or herself the secretary of the provincial CCP committee. Similarly, a county magistrate is often a deputy secretary of the county CCP committee and sometimes is himself or herself the secretary of the county CCP committee. Not surprisingly, virtually all positions of significant power in the government structure are occupied by members of the CCP and are appointed by the CCP. It is however interesting to note that the PRC has enacted the 1998 Organic Law of the Village Committees, promoting elections for village leader in selected rural areas. Elections now reportedly occur in about 650,000 villages across China (Chapter 6).

Government officials at the township level and above are not subject to elections. They are recruited and promoted if they are politically reliable, have connections with the powerful, and have the right credentials. The majority of them are university graduates. This pattern of recruitment was first established in the early 1980s and has persisted into the twenty-first century (Zang 2004). The recruitment policy and the centralization of power ensure that dissent in the government bureaucracy is rare, and if dissent happens it leads to resignation or outright dismissal. In reality, there is a very low turnover of officials in both the State Council and local governments (Zang 2005).

Major changes in political life

Although government institutions have remained largely unchanged since 1978, there have been significant political transformation and changes in state-society relations in China. In the pre-1978 era, the CCP created the socioeconomic dependence of individuals on the state with its control over daily necessities, housing, and the job market (Walder 1986). The CCP also ruled with political pressure on individuals, surveillance, and political campaigns and mass mobilization (Bennett 1976; Bernstein 1991). It effectively penetrated Chinese society, leaving few buffers between individuals and the state. It was so powerful that it was able to weaken family ties and turned personal relations into 'comradeship' for the attainment of communism in China (Gold 1985). The PRC was not simply a totalitarian state, but it was also a mobilization regime. Both the Great Leap Forward campaign and the Cultural Revolution demonstrated how successful the state was in political mobilization. The success was the combined outcomes of organization, political indoctrination, and popular support for the CCP and the evidence of the dominance of the state over society. Mao's China can be viewed as a homogeneous, monotonous, and atomized society where individuals depended on the state and absolute obedience to authority was the norm.

Gone is the Maoist system of control in the post-1978 era. While some scholars argue that China has apparently moved slowly at best in political democratization (Yang 2006), there has been a consensus on the magnitude of political changes in that country. Because of the openness to the outside world, economic growth, and labour market diversification, post-1978 Chinese society has become increasingly heterogeneous. With the transition from central planning to a market economy in the post-1978 era, Chinese people are increasingly empowered to make their own economic decisions and pursue their life goals. As the CCP has removed itself as the key economic decision maker and with the development of labour markets, the CCP has lost its absolute control over society due to the reduced dependence of citizens on the state for livelihood, the reduced capacity of the state to collect information about individual behaviour and thoughts, and the reduced ability of the state to reward politically desirable behaviour and punish politically undesirable behaviour (Guthrie 2006). Major social developments include volunteering, citizen participation in local governance, ethnic unrests (Chapter 9), religious revival (Chapter 10), the emergence of interest groups such as autonomous homeowner associations (Chapter 6), and articulations of individual interests and demands in YouTube, blogs and Twitter feeds (Chapter 12). The post-1978 developments have reshaped political and social discourse and challenged the CCP to innovate in order to maintain one-party rule in China.

The retreat of the state

These dramatic developments have taken place thanks to the combined forces of the receding role of the state in society after 1978, market reforms, and China's open door policy. First, as noted, Deng started market reforms to rebuild the legitimacy of the CCP and one-party rule in China. Deng realized that the state did not have the resources to govern every aspect of social life in China, and that the perpetuation of one-party rule must be based on domestic political stability, which required sustained economic development. The CCP had no choice but to focus on economic growth and promised to cope with other social and political issues later (Yang 2006; Zheng 2010).

As a result, the CCP has changed itself from a revolutionary party to a governing party in the post-1978 era. A revolutionary party fights for total power and aggressively seeks to remodel society with the indoctrination of communist ideology, whereas a governing party is largely a defensive actor, whose main interest is to legitimize and maintain its rule over society for as long as possible. Unlike a revolutionary party, a governing party acknowledges its limited capacity to govern and does not have the ambition to conquer every corner of social space. As noted, the Cultural Revolution undermined the legitimacy of communist ideology in China (Ding 1994). Thus, like leaders in some governing parties in East Asia, Deng and his successors have chosen to legitimize one-party rule with economic growth, which relies on the growth of a market economy. This in turn requires the retreat of the state from the daily management of the economy. Once the CCP has retreated from its deep penetration into the Chinese economy, it has inadvertently opened up social space for the growth and articulation of autonomous interests and collective action in China.

The imperatives of market reforms

Second, the imperatives of market reforms, which aim at competitiveness, efficiency, and profitability, have further weakened the CCP's grip on Chinese society. To achieve these goals, the CCP has shifted the responsibility for provision of jobs, public health, pensions, education, care of the elderly, etc. from the state to ordinary citizens and laid off a large group of workers in money-losing state enterprises. The state has emerged from the reforms stronger in terms of its fiscal capacity, yet there have been consequences. Reforms have re-configured Chinese society. In the pre-1978 era, Mao promoted economic egalitarianism in an effort to eliminate the three great differences – between worker and peasant, between city and countryside, and between cerebral and manual labour. China had become one of the most equal societies in the world in the 1970s. In 1978, China's Gini Coefficient was 0.22, one of the most equal ever recorded (Adelmen and Sunding 1987). After thirty years, China became one of the most unequal countries in the world when its Gini Coefficient reached 0.475 in 2007. Although many people have improved their living standards, reform programmes have generated widespread suffering and life disruption, affecting many social groups. While the CCP has awkwardly identified capitalists, entrepreneurs and the other types of the 'new rich' as its new-found allies, many of its former supporters such as farmers and workers have lost their faith in the regime (Yang 2006; Zheng 2010). The CCP has recognized these social issues and has adopted policies to improve its capacity to govern. Its policy package has included measures to improve social security and health-care, the effort to build an 'eco-friendly society', the initiative to build a 'socialist harmonious society', and the recent campaign to 'build a socialist new countryside' in China.

Yet these measures and campaigns are far from adequate. Market reforms have sharpened disparities between urban and rural areas, among the professions, and between the coast and interior regions although the CCP has still spouted a socialist rhetoric. These developments have accentuated the sense of unfairness and sharpened social cleavages in society as demonstrated in the widespread 'hatred of the wealth' in China (Zang 2008). Inequality has generated widespread discontent and anger among the poor, the weak, and the dispossessed, which have been unequivocally directed towards the state for its failure to safeguard social justice. The CCP's support base has been reduced significantly since the winners of market reforms are the minority of the population, which has led to the decline in the state's governing capacity. It has become increasingly difficult for the CCP to direct citizens towards the path it wants them to take.

Equally important, not all the winners of market reforms are staunch supporters of the CCP. Market reforms have resulted in the decentralization of economic power from the state to private sectors. The market economy has created a myriad of new private interests that are independent of and in competition with the state's interests. Challenging forms of political competition have emerged as divergent interests and the disconnected elements of society seek political justice and coalesce into a viable opposition. Finally, while the state has forced citizens to be financially self-reliant, it has inadvertently made them socially independent, thereby producing potential agents of resistance and other forms of collective action. The post-1978 era has therefore witnessed repeated worker and farmer demonstrations against the loss of jobs and social displacement. Everyday resistance occurs in diverse and innumerable ways including cynicism, conversion to cult religions, underground political movements, blog discussions, etc. (Lewis and Xue 2003).

The open-door policy

Third, another key aspect of post-1978 reforms is to open China to the rest of the world. Deng and his successors hoped that the open-door policy would upgrade the Chinese economy since it would attract foreign investment, technology, and management skills from the West. They understood that Western values and norms would also enter China but felt confident that they would be able to contain these undesirable exports from the West. Unlike some other reform policies such as price reforms, state enterprise reforms, and housing reforms in the 1980s and early 1990s (Zang 1995, 1999), the open door policy has not met strong resistance and has been implemented consistently since 1978. This is partly because the open-door policy has not infringed the interests of the dense networks of collusive and cartelistic organizations that made up the Chinese socialist economy. In fact, these narrow interest groups have been the first beneficiary of the open-door policy given their strategic position in the Chinese economy and political system. This partly explains why conservative leaders suspended most reform policies right after the 1989 Tiananmen Square incident to protect socialism, yet they left the open-door policy alone. 'The Tiananmen event in 1989 did not interrupt the process; instead, it unexpectedly became a powerful motivation for the Chinese leadership to open the country's door even wider to the outside world.' China has become one of the world's most favoured destinations for foreign investments. Driven by large-scale foreign investments, the PRC had become the world's foremost manufacturing base and largest export economy (Zheng 2010: 800, 804).

While Deng and his successors have correctly calculated the economic benefits of the open-door policy, they have seriously underestimated its social and political implications on Chinese society. 'Openness produces distributive conflict among different social groups and regions. Some groups and regions have benefited more than others with some becoming winners and others losers.' More importantly, openness has been a major driving force behind China's rapid transformation. At the domestic level, openness creates an institutional environment in which different existing factors reorganize themselves, thus providing new dynamics for change. At the international level, openness links China and the world together, and the interplay between China and the world produces an external dynamism for China's internal changes (Zheng 2010: 800, 804).

More concretely, openness has generated the heterogeneous social landscape in China and engendered daunting governance challenges to the CCP. Openness has provided Chinese people with vital information about, and role models of, good governance. Information is power. The Internet and the rapid development of YouTube, blogs and Twitter have increased citizen access to information at the expense of the state's capacity to restrict the freedom of information. In 1994, China was connected to NSFNET (the Internet). By 2010, the number of Internet users in China reached 457 million (http://www. 2space.net/news/article/330882–1295426409/). The CCP has expressed a strong desire to restrict web freedom following the successful democratic revolutions in the Middle East (Buckley 2011; Lococo 2011); it remains to be seen how effectively it can achieve its goal.

Increased exchanges and interaction between China and the rest of the world have exposed Chinese people to what democracy is and how democracy works, thereby increasing their cultural capacity in their effort to reconstruct state-society relations. For example, good governance has been conceptualized and promoted in Western democracies. It has gained increasing popularity in the public discourse on government and social development among Internet users and citizen activists in China. In particular, they have used concepts such as transparency, accountability, and social justice in their struggle for political change in China. Since they understand well that they cannot openly ask for democracy and will not get it even if they ask for it, they have demanded good governance. This has created a challenge to the CCP since its mission is to promote social progress, economic growth, good government, and equality, which are more or less consistent with good governance. Netizens and citizen activists have exploited this consistency to challenge one-party rule. While the CCP has emphasized economic growth and political stability to promote good governance, netizens and citizen activists have emphasized transparency, accountability, and social justice to promote good governance, and have used these concepts to justify their moral high ground vis-à-vis the state. They have questioned government politics, evaluated the performance of government officials, and criticized officials who fail to meet the standards of good governance. The demand for transparency, accountability, and social justice has empowered Internet users and citizen activists at the expense of the state power and made it increasingly difficult for government officials to be autocratic and conduct government business in an arbitrary and unaccountable way. Mobilizing public opinion, netizens and citizen activists forced the court to change the 2009 verdict on the Deng Yujiao case that occurred in Badong County, Hubei province and the 2010 verdict on the Shi Jianfeng case in Pingdingshan in Henan province. Transparency, fairness, the incompetence of judges and unaccountable behaviour were used to mobilize mass protests.

Another example is the rapid growth of non-governmental (NGOs) in China. Learning from abroad, the government has fostered NGOs to mobilize societal resources to supplement its spending on welfare and to take over some of its burden of service provision. The government requires that NGOs must be registered with the government and must have a sponsoring government agency before registration can be requested. The sponsoring government agency is in charge of overseeing the activities of the NGOs. There were about 100 national social organizations in China before 1978. By 2005, there were nearly 315,000 registered NGOs. Yet there is a large number of both foreign and domestic NGOs without legal status in China. The total number of NGOs would have been around 8.8 million by 2003 if non-registered NGOs were included (Zheng 2010). These NGOs were not registered because they had engaged in activities that were not approved or endorsed by the government. The government's attitude towards them is one of 'no recognition, no banning, and no intervention' as long as they do not harm state security and social stability. Such hidden rules provide not only an implicit political and social framework for such NGOs to operate, but also exert influence on their modes of operation and the direction of their future development (Deng 2010). Nevertheless, many unregistered NGOs have refused to limit themselves to the provision of social welfare. They have represented a major aspect of political activism in society and worked on areas such as labour rights, civic rights, environmental protection, action against HIV/AIDS, etc. The fact that this large group of non-registered NGOs has existed and done things not endorsed by the CCP shows the growing strength of society vis-à-vis the state in China.

Conclusions

This chapter reviews political development since 1949 and discusses the changing state-society relations in the PRC. While there has been continuity in major government institutions and the persistence of one-party rule in China, there have been political changes in the post-1978 era due to the receding role of the state in society, the imperatives of market reforms, and the open door policy. Some scholars have complained bitterly about the slow process of political liberalization in China. This chapter shows the considerable extent of democratic reforms in China – after all, democratization implies 'the shift of political power from the state to social forces' (Zheng 2010: 804). One-party rule may persist into the foreseeable future, yet it will become increasingly difficult for the CCP to exercise dictatorship in both social and political life in the face of a growing and increasingly assertive society.

This chapter concludes this book and provides important contextual material for readers to reflect on their understanding of various aspects of contemporary Chinese society discussed in Chapters 2–12, such as ideas of continuity and transformation in work and the mass media, aspects of family planning, divorce, and gender, the impact of government policy on ethnic relations and religion, and the notion of relative hierarchy in China.

Bibliography

Adelman, Irma and David Sunding (1987) 'Economic policy and income distribution in China', *Journal of Comparative Economics*, 11(3): 444–61.

Bailey, Paul John (2001) *China in the Twentieth Century*, Oxford: Blackwell.

Bennett, Gordon A. (1976) *Yundong: Mass Campaigns in Chinese Communist Leadership*, Berkeley, CA: Center for Chinese Studies, University of California.

Bernstein, Thomas P. (1991) 'Chinese communism in the era of Mao Zedong, 1949–76', pp. 275–304 in Kenneth Lieberthal, Joyce Kallgren, Roderick MacFarquhar, and Frederic Wakeman (eds), *Perspectives on Modern China: Four Anniversaries*, Armonk, NY: M.E. Sharpe.

Bernstein, Thomas P. and Hua Yu Li (eds) (2010) *China Learns from the Soviet Union 1949–Present*, Lanham, MD: Lexington Books.

Buckley, Chris (2011) 'China president calls for more Internet oversight', February 19, available at http://www.reuters.com/article/2011/02/19/us-china-politics-internet-idUSTRE71I2Y720110219, accessed on February 20, 2011.

Chan, Alfred L. (2001) *Mao's Crusade: Politics and Policy Implementation in China's Great Leap Forward*, Oxford: Oxford University Press.

Deng, Guosheng (2010) 'The hidden rules governing China's unregistered NGOs: management and consequences', *China Review*, 10(1): 183–206.

Dikötter, Frank (2010) *Mao's Great Famine: The History of China's Most Devastating Catastrophe, 1958–62*, New York: Walker & Company.

Ding, Xueliang (1994) *The Decline of Communism in China: Legitimacy Crisis, 1977–1989*, Cambridge: Cambridge University Press.

Gold, Thomas B. (1985) 'After comradeship: personal relations in China since the Cultural Revolution', *The China Quarterly*, 104: 657–75.

Guthrie, Doug (2006) *China and Globalization: The Social, Economic and Political Transformation of Chinese Society*, London: Routledge.

Karl, Rebecca E. (2010) *Mao Zedong and China in the Twentieth-Century World: A Concise History*, Durham, NC: Duke University Press.

Lewis, John W. and Xue Litai (2003) 'Social change and political reform in China: meeting the challenge of success', *China Quarterly*, 176: 926–42.

Li, Wei, and Dennis Tao Yang (2005) 'The great leap forward: anatomy of a central planning disaster', *Journal of Political Economy*, 113(4): 840–77.

Lococo, Edmond (2011) 'China opposes use of web freedom as excuse to meddle', *Bloomberg News*, February 17, available at http://www.bloomberg.com/news/2011-02-17/china-opposes-use-of-web-freedom-as-excuse-to-meddle-update1-.html, accessed on February 20, 2011.

Lowenthall, Richard (1970) 'Development vs. utopia in communist policy', pp. 33–116 in Chalmers Johnson (ed.), *Change in Communist Systems*, Stanford, CA: Stanford University Press.

MacFarquhar, Roderick and Michael Schoenhals (2006) *Mao's Last Revolution*, Cambridge, MA: The Belknap Press/Harvard University Press.

Shih, Chih-Yu (1994) '*The Decline of a Moral Regime: China's Great Leap Forward in Retrospect*', *Comparative Political Studies*, 27(2): 272–306.

Walder, Andrew G. (1986) *Communist Neo-traditionalism: Work and Authority in Chinese Industry*, Berkeley, CA: University of California Press.

Wilber, Charles K. (1969) *The Soviet Model and Underdeveloped Countries*, Chapel Hill, NC: The University of North Carolina Press.

Yang, Dali (2006) 'Economic transformation and its political discontents in China', *Annual Review of Political Science*, 9: 143–64.

Zang, Xiaowei (1995) 'Industrial management systems and managerial ideologies in China: 1966–89', *Journal of Northeast Asian Studies*, 14(1): 80–104.

—— (1999) 'Urban housing reforms', pp. 53–80 in Xiaowei Zang (ed.), *Urban China since 1984*, New York: NOVA Science Publishers.

—— (2004) *Elite Dualism and Leadership Selection in China*, London/New York: Routledge.

—— (2005) 'Institutionalization and elite behavior in reform China', *Issues and Studies*, 41(1): 204–17.

—— (2008) 'Market reforms, the new rich, and status hierarchies in China', pp. 53–70 in David S.G. Goodman (ed.), *The New Rich in China*, London: Routledge.

Zheng, Yongnian (2010) 'Society must be defended: reform, openness, and social policy in China', *Journal of Contemporary China*, 19(67): 799–818.

Related biographies

Chang, Jung and Jon Halliday (2005) *Mao: The Unknown Story*, New York: Knopf.

Li, Zhisui (1996) *The Private Life of Chairman Mao*, New York: Arrow Books Ltd.

Chronology of the People's Republic of China

1949:	*October*: The foundation of the People's Republic of China.
1950:	*February*: China and the Soviet Union sign 'Sino-Soviet Treaty of Friendship, Alliance, and Mutual Assistance'.
1950:	*May*: New marriage law bans polygamy and arranged marriages.
1950:	*June*: Agrarian Reform Law: redistribution of land to poor peasants.
1950:	*October*: Chinese People's Volunteer Army entered Korean Peninsula to support their North Korean allies against the United States.
1950:	*November*: The People's Republic of China takes control of Tibet.
1951:	*September*: The Vatican City and China break off diplomatic relations with each other.
1953–7:	First Five Year Plan focusing on Soviet-style development of heavy industry.
1956–7:	'Hundred Flowers' campaign misleads intellectuals to complain about problems.
1957–8:	'Anti-Rightist' Campaign is used by Mao to eliminate critical intellectuals.
1958:	Farmland is collectivized and farmers are organized into People's Communes.
1958:	Beginning of the 'Great Leap Forward' campaign.
1959:	Sino-Soviet relations deteriorate dramatically.
1959–61:	'Great Leap Forward' triggers largest famine in human history with an estimated 14–30 million casualties.
1959:	*March*: Tibetan revolts against Chinese occupation suppressed with an 'iron fist'.
1960:	*July*: Khrushchev recalls Soviet advisors and technical experts in China.
1961–5:	Readjustment and recovery: 'Agriculture First' policy. Food situation improves.

1962:   Border dispute with India over areas in the Himalayas.

1962–72: In the 1960s China's population growth peaks. Between 1962 and 1972 some 300 million babies are born.

1962–72: High population growth (average of 26.7 million births per year) in the late 1960s increases pressure on natural resources.

1964:   *October*: Test of first nuclear bomb in China.

1965:   Tibet becomes an autonomous region.

1966–76: During the Cultural Revolution China's jurisdiction essentially ceases to operate.

1966–8:   Destruction of 'the four olds': old ideas, old culture, old customs, and old habits.

1966–76: During the Cultural Revolution, religious practice is condemned as feudalistic.

1967:   *June*: Test of first nuclear fusion device in China.

1969:   *March*: Clash with Soviet troops at Damanskii Island (Zhen Bao) on the Ussuri river (Wusuli Jiang).

1969:   *April*: Mao Zedong names Lin Biao as his heir.

1970:   *April*: First satellite launch ('Long March').

1971:   *July*: Henry Kissinger secretly visits China.

1971:   *September*: Lin Biao is killed in aeroplane crash while fleeing China.

1971:   *November*: The People's Republic replaces the Republic of China (Taiwan) in UN Security Council.

1972:   *February*: Visit of US President Richard Nixon to China. Normalization of relations between United States and China begins.

1976:   *January*: Death of Premier Zhou Enlai.

1976:   *July*: Massive earthquake (7.8 Richter scale) devastates the city of Tangshan (Hebei Province). At least 270,000 people die.

1976:   *September*: Chairman Mao Zedong dies at the age of 82.

1978:   *March*: The 1978 Constitution of the People's Republic of China guarantees freedom of religion with a number of restrictions.

1978–79: 'Democracy Wall' in Beijing with pro-democratic posters.

1978:   *June*: The State Council establishes a new 'Birth Planning Small Leading Group' to strengthen family planning.

1978:   *September*: e-mail link is established between Germany and China (CSNET protocol). First message from China: 20 September.

1979:   *January*: Diplomatic relations are established between the United States and China.

1979:   Introduction of the 'Household Responsibility System' in agriculture.

1979:   Introduction of China's strict 'one-child' family planning programme at provincial level. Introduced in 1980 at national level.

1979:   *February*: China invades Vietnam (for 29 days) after Vietnamese troops had ousted the pro-Beijing Pol-Pot regime in Cambodia.

1980:   *August*: First Special Economic Zones are established in Shenzhen.

1981:   *September*: Successful launch of three satellites (SJ-2, SJ-2A, SJ-2b) on one rocket into orbit.

1982:   China's population surpasses 1 billion people.

1982:   *December*: The Fifth National People's Congress adopts a new constitution for China.

1986:   *April*: The Sixth National People's Congress adopts new Civil Law.

1987:   Kentucky Fried Chicken (KFC) comes to China.

1987:   *January*: General Secretary of the CCP, Hu Yaobang, is forced to resign.

1988:   Excessive economic growth with rampant corruption and out-of-control inflation of 18.5 per cent.

1988:   *November*: TV series 'River Elegy' is criticized as 'wholesale Westernization' and banned.

1989:   *April*: Hu Yaobang dies.

1989:   *June*: Suppression of Tiananmen Square demonstrations with military power (official death toll: 200). Jiang Zemin replaces Zhao Ziyang as CCP General Secretary.

1989:   *June*: The European Council of Ministers agrees to an EU-wide arms embargo against China in Madrid.

1989:   *December*: Stock markets are opened in Shanghai and Shenzhen.

1991:   First McDonald's restaurant opens in Beijing.

1992:   Deng Xiaoping accelerates market reforms to establish a 'socialist market economy'.

1992:   Falun Gong religious movement was founded by Li Hongzhi from Changchun, Jilin province.

1994:   China connected to NSFNET (Internet).

1995:   Educational legislation stipulates 9 years of compulsory education.

1994:   *December*: Start of the 'Three Gorges Dam' project.

1997:   *February*: Death of Deng Xiaoping.

1997:   *July*: China obtains control over Hong Kong's sovereignty.

1998:   The Microsoft and Intel corporations establish high-tech research facilities in Beijing.

1998:   Worst flooding in years – 230 million people affected and 3,656 dead.

1998:   Zhu Rongji follows Li Peng as China's Premier.

1999:   The Falun Gong movement is declared illegal in China and a threat to national security.

1999:   Cooling of US-China relations after NATO bombs Chinese embassy in Belgrade.

2000:   Government consolidates Internet regulations for mainland China.

2000   *October*: The Vatican canonizes 120 'saints' that were 'martyred' in China.

2001:   Beijing wins bid for the 2008 Olympic Games.

2001:   *November*: After years of negotiations, China becomes a member of the World Trade Organization.

2002:   *September*: China's 700th KFC restaurant opened.

2002:   *November*: Hu Jintao replaces Jiang Zemin as head of the Communist Party.

2003:   *March*: Hu Jintao is elected President by National People's Congress.

2005:   *June*: China has at least 103 million Internet users, 45.6 million computer hosts, and 677,500 websites.

2005:   *October*: Two astronauts sent into space, circling Earth in the 'Shenzhou VI space capsule'.

2006:   *March*: The Chinese inaugural edition of *Rolling Stone* magazine sells out immediately.

2006:   *June*: China surpasses the United States in carbon dioxide emissions.

2007:   *December*: The number of Internet users in China reaches 210 million.

2007:   *to November 2008*: Yahoo! accused of having provided information that led to the imprisonment of civil rights activists in China.

2008:   *March*: The most violent ethnic protests in years erupt in Lhasa, Tibet.

2008:   *May*: An earthquake strikes Sichuan province: the death toll reaches 69,016, with more than 18,000 people missing.

2008:   *August*: China welcomes the world to the Beijing 2008 Olympic Games.

2008:   *November*: The government announces a $586 billion economic stimulus package.

2009:   *July*: Almost 200 people die and over 1,700 are injured in ethnic violence in Xinjiang.

2009:   *August*: China surpasses the United States as the world's largest producer of household garbage.

2009:   *November*: China is now the largest automobile market in the world.

2010:   *March*: Google stops its Chinese Internet search engine and re-routes mainland Chinese users to its Hong Kong site.

2010:   *October*: Jailed Chinese dissident Liu Xiaobo wins 2010 Nobel Peace Price.

2010:   *October*: Xi Jinping is appointed a vice chairman of the CCP's Central Military Commission.

Source: http://www.china-profile.com/history/hist_policy_1.htm, accessed on February 16, 2011

Index

Lightning Source UK Ltd.
Milton Keynes UK
UKOW040336150213

206313UK00004B/146/P